Make Up, Don't Break Up

Finding and Keeping Love
for Singles and Couples

by **DR. BONNIE EAKER WEIL**
with Toni Robino

Foreword by
Harville Hendrix, Ph.D., author of
Getting the Love You Want and *Keeping the Love You Find*

Adams Media Corporation
Avon, Massachusetts

Published by
Adams Media, an F+W Publications Company
57 Littlefield Street, Avon, MA 02322 U.S.A.
www.adamsmedia.com

ISBN: 1-58062-407-3

Printed in Canada

J I H G F E D

Library of Congress Cataloging-in-Publication Data

Eaker-Weil, Bonnie.
Make up, don't break up : rescue your relationship and rekindle your
romance / by Bonnie Eaker Weil, with Toni Robino
p.   cm.
Includes bibliographical references.
ISBN 1-58062-407-3 (pbk)
1. Love. 2. Man-woman relationships. 3. Interpersonal conflict. I. Title.
BF575.L8.E35   1999
306.7—dc21   99-36903
CIP

Except for the family and friends who have given permission to be mentioned in this book, names and identifying characteristics of individuals have been changed to protect their anonymity.

This publication is designed to provide accurate and authoritative information with regard to the subject matter covered. It is sold with the understanding that the publisher is not engaged in rendering legal, accounting, or other professional advice. If legal advice or other expert assistance is required, the services of a competent professional person should be sought.

—From a *Declaration of Principles* jointly adopted by a Committee of the
American Bar Association and a Committee of Publishers and Associations

Cover photo by The Image Bank/ADEO

This book is available at quantity discounts for bulk purchases.
For information, call 1-800-872-5627

Dedications

"Courage is not the towering oak that sees storms come and go, it is the fragile blossom that opens in the snow."

—ALICE MACKENZIE SWAIM

I dedicate this book:

To my loving parents, Hyman and Paula Eaker, who showed me *love really does conquer all*. It is because of your undying love for each other and for me that I am able to share with my patients and readers all of the skills they need to *Make Up, Don't Break Up*.

To my patients whose courage and belief in me, Smart Heart Skills, and yourselves propelled you to transform your relationships. You are the *torch carriers* of *Make Up, Don't Break Up*. It is your personal stories and triumphs that bring this book to life! Thank you for taking the journey with me and passing the torch. It will brighten the way . . .

To all of you in the dark: To those who are in the dark about love and relationships, take my hand and we'll find the light switch together. To all those who fell in love and want to stay in love; To all those who yearn for real and lasting love; To all those who want to make up, not break up . . . this book is for you.

To Jeff, *the most precious man in the world;* a real life prince, who encourages me to be the most I can be and supports me in reaching my highest and most inspired dreams. *For this I treasure you.* You have shown me:

> *"Love feels no burden, thinks nothing of trouble, attempts what is above its strength, pleads no excuse of impossibility . . . Though weary, it is not tired; though pressed, it is not straightened, though alarmed, it is not confounded; but like a lively flame and burning torch forces its way upwards and securely passes through all . . ."*
>
> —THOMAS À KEMPIS

Contents

PART ONE
What Makes a Relationship Last?
Wake Up, Don't Break Up

PART TWO
Smart Heart Skills
Shake Up to Make Up

Acknowledgments

"To be loved for what one is, is the greatest exception. The great majority love in another only what they lend him, their own selves, their version of him."
—GOETHE

To my talented wordsmith Toni Robino of With Flying Colours, without whose wisdom and dedication this book would not have been written. Your ability to understand my theories and concepts, meet pressing deadlines and keep a level head in the midst of some very chaotic circumstances, helped me to see the light at the end of the tunnel.

To my agent Katharine Sands of Sarah Jane Freymann Literary Agency, whose passionate commitment to this project helped bring my dream to fruition and cheered me on time and time again. I'll be forever grateful for your creative and cutting edge ideas.

To my mother-in-love, Helen Weil, whose undying dedication, belief in me, and creative ideas, including the name for this book, literally kept me going. You are one in a million!

To Ed Walters, of Adams Media, whose patience, cooperation and belief in me and this book, made it happen. Thank you for dodging the potholes and bending over backward *many times* to see this book through to the end. I am truly grateful to **Carrie Lewis, Nancy True, Will McNeill** and other staff who made this dream possible.

To all of the incredible friends, contributors, media and support staff who played a major role in making this book happen. There are no words to express the love and gratitude I feel for you. Thank you from the bottom of my heart!

Foreword

"You know quite well deep within you, that there is only a single magic, a simple power, a single salvation and that is called loving."
—HERMANN HESSE

That the institution of marriage is in a crisis is no longer news. For several decades the divorce rate for first marriages has fluctuated between 50 and 60 percent and the divorce rate for second marriages has been higher. The discussion about the impact of divorce on children has likewise fluctuated from benign to destructive. Given these factors, the institution of marriage itself has undergone massive changes in form from the traditional two-person heterosexual marriage to an advocacy of same-sex marriages. The discussion of the family also includes new forms that range from the two-parent family to the single-parent family, the blended family, to any persons who voluntarily live together. The ratio between these forms has changed so much that blended and single-parent families now outnumber the never-divorced families. For the first time in history, most children will grow up without constant access to their biological parents.

The date for this trend for divorce, the resulting debilitation of the traditional household, and the redefinition of the family has been associated with the end of the second World War. The disruption was triggered by divorces of marriages that were hastily formed prior to the long absences and later by the tensions created by "war brides" learning to speak English.

While divorce has always been frowned upon in our culture, this phenomenon led to a weakening of the taboo of divorce. Many couples in unhappy marriages followed the trend of changing partners instead of changing their relationships, and this led to the situation we have today.

While marital therapy began in the nineteenth century, its status grew in response to this situation. Early forms of marital therapy were based on the model of individual psychotherapy. Generally, couples were seen separately by separate therapists with the assumption that marital conflict was solely a function of conflicts caused by intra-psychic problems. Other therapists experimented with consultations between the separate therapists. Some tried four-way therapy with both partners and both therapists in the same room. The model that finally emerged was conjoint therapy with both partners and one therapist.

However, whatever the model or method, marital therapy rated low on the effectiveness scale, with success rates reaching only about 30 percent.

Several factors contributed to this dismal figure. The major factor was the application of the model of individual psychotherapy to marital conflict. Therapists with an analytic perspective saw the conflict between partners as a recapitulation of the relationship between the child and her parents. They analyzed personal impulses and defenses and sought to evoke insight into unconscious conflict with the assumption that with the resolution of the intra-psychic struggles of each partner, their relationship would improve. Therapists from a behavioral perspective attempted to teach partners relationship skills and help them positively reinforce effective behaviors with no reference to their interior worlds. In contrast to both of these, some therapists did "marriage counseling" with the aim of helping the couple rationally solve their relationship problems.

The other major factor was the neutrality of the therapist regarding the outcome of the therapy process. Following the value system of individual therapy, therapists tended to help partners in an intimate relationship decide whether staying in or leaving a relationship was in the interest of their personal well-being. Little interest was displayed in the dynamics of the relationship itself, or in the contribution of the parties to interpersonal conflict, thus including therapy among the many factors that led to the breakup of marriages.

In the past decade, we have seen a radical paradigm shift in marital therapy in which the relationship has become the client.

While maintaining an awareness of the contribution of family and personal history and internal dynamics to marital conflict, this new perspective mainly focuses on analyzing and modifying the interaction of the partners with each other in the service of restoring and maintaining connection. The inter-subjective has achieved status with the intra-psychic. *This new breed of therapists tend to believe that connectional rupture is the cause,* not the consequence of, relational conflict, and *that the restoration of connection should be the goal of marital therapy.* While assisting couples in understanding how their family of origin contributed to their own emotional wounding, and how their unmet emotional needs negatively impact their intimate relationship, they use the process of acquiring such understanding as the means of internal and interpersonal healing. The therapy process by which they assist couples to achieve deep levels of understanding is a therapeutic intervention called "dialogue," which is complemented by teaching effective relationship skills. Dialogue enables couples to *reconnect* and skills training assists them in maintaining connection. In addition, these therapists tend to have a positive bias toward marriage and an optimistic view of each couple's potential to maintain and improve their relationship.

Dr. Bonnie Eaker Weil is among this new breed of cutting-edge therapists. In this book, *Make Up, Don't Break Up,* she overtly states her bias in favor of marriage, the potential of almost all couples to "make up" and claims a 98 percent success rate for couples who persist in her process. She is definitely not neutral and she does not shy away from giving specific guidance and teaching relationship skills while including help in understanding the past and how it influences the present relationship.

She begins her message to singles and couples by challenging them to "wake up" to the fact that getting rid of their partner does not help them get rid of the problems. ***Using the creative theme of "connecting, disconnecting, and reconnecting," she then urges them to learn tools to navigate this three-part process.*** In the process she provides them with the tools for learning about their family of origin and their character defenses of "pursuing and distancing," and gives information on the wounds that led to these two defenses and provides clear guidance on how to heal those childhood wounds. She downplays the differences between men and women, seeing both in search of intimate connection by different behaviors. Outlining the stages of marriage, she shows how to navigate the inevitable changes that come at each stage. Her book is replete with specific instructions and examples. Her faith in couples is evident in the chapters on surviving adultery. She introduces the creative idea that "disconnection" can be in the service of restored connection for all couples. *Throughout she displays her vulnerability by using her own life and marriage and the marriage of her parents, as well as many other couples in her practice, as examples of the relationship potential that resides in each couple, if they will wake up and grow up.*

Dr. Eaker Weil has achieved an excellent synthesis of marital theory and practice. She has presented her effective process with such straightforward and simple language, extensive details, and enthusiasm that all singles and couples who read this book cannot help but be inspired to "make up." This is among the most helpful, complete, and positive manuals for saving a relationship that I have seen.

HARVILLE HENDRIX, PH.D.
Author of Bestsellers *Getting the Love You Want* and
Keeping the Love You Find and
co-author of *Giving the Love That Heals*

Preface

"As a therapist, you can only take your patients as far as you've gone yourself."
—THOMAS F. FOGARTY, M.D.

This book is for everyone who has dreamed of falling in love—and staying in love; for singles and couples who are in love, and for married and single couples who are not.

It is for all those who yearn for connection, intimacy, passion, and healing; for everyone who wants to make up, not break up.

It is for the frightened child in all of us who wants and needs to love and be loved.

Ever since I was a little girl, I've had a deep desire to help people. It has been my passion and my calling for as long as I can remember. I often sat with my grandmother Sarah while she watched the afternoon soap operas, and I wondered why the people on television had so many problems and so much turmoil in their lives. The single people couldn't meet the right mates, or if they did, they couldn't keep the relationship going. The married couples were either fighting without resolving their conflicts, being unfaithful to each other, or simply bored with their "polite" but unfulfilling relationships. When I was seven years old, I remember saying to my grandmother, "Grandma, I want to help these people."

That early decision paved the way for my calling in life to become a family therapist. When I earned my degree I learned that as a therapist *I can only take my patients as far as I have gone myself.* That was a wake-up call for me. I realized if I was going to help singles meet, connect, and develop lasting relationships, and show married couples how to stay together, I was going to have to master those skills myself. At that time I had been divorced for more than eight years and although I was dating, it seemed the road to love was filled with potholes and obstacles of every kind. I finally accepted and came to terms with the fact that I needed to "go back home" to my family of origin and continue to resolve the issues I had with my mother and father. I began the process of healing my own wounds and learning new skills that I am now convinced are *essential* for every stage of a relationship.

This is such an exciting book for me to share with you because it teaches you the same "Smart Heart Skills" that I personally tested and my parents, patients, and I use to stay in love! *Both my own success and the triumphs of my patients demonstrate how well these tools work.* I've been happily married to Jeff for more than ten years now and our relationship becomes more fulfilling and satisfying as time goes on. I also taught Smart Heart Skills to my parents, who now have a more gratifying and love-filled relationship than they ever had before. I was so inspired to write this book because I wanted people to see how easy and fun relationships *can be,* once you get the hang of it. *I did it, and so can you!*

The name for "Smart Heart Skills" comes from my childhood. Each week my family gathered together for what we called "Smart Heart Sundays." This was a chance for us to air some of our grievances and discuss how we could each change our behavior a little to accommodate each other. We always kept these discussions *light* and incorporated short skits and humor so we wouldn't hurt each other's feelings. It was a chance for us all to connect with each other, but at that time we didn't have the conflict resolution skills to take care of some of our issues. When the discussion got too heavy, my father *was notorious for walking out of the room and saying "Case closed."* As a child, this behavior was very upsetting to me and my mom. It was "incomplete," and the "little therapist" inside of me intuitively knew there was another step that could be taken to reach resolution; I just didn't know what it was. Now I smile when I remember those moments because I understand Dad was simply doing the best he could do! (You'll find out why this is true for most men later in the book.)

As I reflect back, it's clear that my entire life has led up to this book. My entire family divorced, except for my parents, and the question of how couples could make up and stay together has been dancing through my mind and heart through all of these years. I saw my favorite aunt and uncle divorce and I saw how unhappy they both were afterwards. I have also seen thousands of patients who were divorced and more lonely than ever before. I became convinced that breaking up is not the answer. I wanted to find the "missing link," and when I merged my life experiences, background, training, and professional experience, "Smart Heart" was born!

I knew from my parents that respect and courage are vital ingredients for love to grow. *I also learned that love is fragile, like a flower. My parents taught me that love is the most powerful force in existence;* when we treat love like a flower and nurture it by using our heads *and* our hearts, it blossoms and fills our lives with beautiful fragrance.

Today, I teach Smart Heart Skills and Dialogue to singles and couples around the world in seminars, workshops, therapy, and phone sessions and I have had the opportunity to share some of my insights on many talk shows. I have also been sharing these skills through many magazine and newspaper articles, and the response has been so overwhelming that I was inspired to put this all in *Make Up, Don't Break Up* so everyone can have access to this truly life-changing information.

Although more than 60 percent of today's marriages end in divorce, **98 percent of the couples who learn and use Smart Heart Skills and Dialogue make up, instead of break up.** They learn that men and women are not that different, and they discover there's a big difference between "giving their partner space," and "distancing." They also learn how to enrich their marriages and find the connection and fulfillment they only dreamed of in the past. Many of these couples have experienced the gamut of problems and challenges, including adultery, and yet they choose to stay together and create lasting "Smart Heart Love."

My private practice also supports singles who would love to connect with someone they can marry. Many of these men and women have a history of difficult times. They have had trouble meeting people, getting past the third date, and successfully making their way to the altar. But *98 percent of my single patients who learn how to connect, disconnect, and reconnect with potential mates marry someone they love, usually within a year or two of using these tools.* **These skills are so effective that I guarantee you'll see a change in your relationships, and in yourself, within seven days of putting Smart Heart Skills and Dialogue into practice.**

Most people want love. We become more complete, more fully human through a loving, intimate relationship. I want you to know you can find the love you want without playing manipulative games, if you just stop running away at the very moment when you should stay, stand your ground, and work "smarter." Men and women are not that different—as the thousands of patients who have taken this journey with me were relieved and thrilled to find out! All they needed were these ground-breaking skills and dialogue to bridge the distance between them and close the gap with respect, understanding, and love.

It's truly a pleasure to share these "treasures" with you. May they provide *you* with the bridge you need to grow "smarter" in love!

Dr. Bonnie Eaker Weil

part one

What Makes a Relationship Last?
Wake Up, Don't Break Up

"Genuine love is volitional rather than emotional. The person who truly loves, does so because of a decision to love. This person has made a commitment to be loving, whether or not the loving feeling is present."

☙ M. SCOTT PECK

~ 1 ~

Challenges to a Lasting Relationship

"Of all the misconceptions about love, the most powerful and pervasive is the belief that 'falling in love' is love or at least one of the manifestations of love."

—M. SCOTT PECK

People who are married or in committed relationships are healthier, wealthier, and happier. So why do more than 60 percent of marriages end in divorce? Why has the national divorce rate climbed more than 200 percent in the last thirty years? And why are fewer people getting married today than ever before?

The answers to these questions are plentiful, but the main reason is simple. *It's easy to "fall" in love, but very few people know how to stay in love.* Even though staying in love is our "smartest" choice all the way around! Recent studies on marriage prove it's one of the major ingredients in life-long success for men and women. **"It lengthens life, substantially boosts physical and emotional health, and raises income over that of single or divorced people or those who live**

together," reported an article in the *New York Times*. **Marriage has also been found to boost happiness, reduce the degree of depression, and provide protection from sexually transmitted diseases.**

So let's wake up, make up, and turn this trend around! One of the most startling pieces of evidence that shows people are not in touch with what's really going on in their partnerships is the fact that the majority of people who file for divorce say they didn't think there was a relationship-threatening problem *just six months* prior to breaking up. Another shocker is that *most couples wait six years or more to seek professional help* when their relationship is in danger. By the time they do wake up and smell the coffee, it's often too late.

Truly there is no reason to resign yourself to a bad relationship—whether you're dating or married. Rather than changing partners and ending up in this same predicament again, you can learn to have a fabulous relationship with the partner you already have! **I strongly encourage you to make the relationship you have work because there is a higher rate of divorce and adultery in second marriages.**

Getting rid of your partner does not get rid of the problem, because half of the "problem" is yours. You can walk out on your marriage, but you can't run away from yourself, no matter how hard you try! Rather than blaming each other, couples can learn how to work as a team and coach each other through the troubled times and power struggles. To do this, you must create a "safe" relationship so you can express your needs and fears and effectively resolve anger and conflict. More relationships break up because people don't know how to validate each other (that frustration escalates to become anger) than for any other reason. This is truly a shame, because the skills for "fighting fair" are very easy to master with just a little practice and patience.

One of the biggest causes of unresolved anger between people is a lack of understanding. Men and women have different strengths and weaknesses, different ways of expressing ourselves, and different "childhood wounds" that we're trying to heal. While it may seem like we're from different planets, **we are actually very much alike when it comes to our need and desire for love and intimacy. We behave differently only in our quests for closeness. Stop doing what you think is "fair" or "right"** and start doing what works! It's not about "working harder," it's about "working smarter."

The vast majority of relationships can and should be saved and revived. In almost every case, couples can learn how to keep their relationships alive and growing and reap the rich rewards of real and lasting love. **Twenty-two years of family therapy practice has given me the certainty that almost any relationship can be turned into a great one if the people involved are willing.**

I realize these are bold statements, but the statistics of my family therapy practice speak for themselves.

More than 98 percent of the married couples in my practice who learn the skills you'll learn in this book, make up instead of break up, and have very happy and love-filled partnerships.

More than 98 percent of the singles who use these same skills enter committed relationships or get married to partners they love.

Make Up, Don't Break Up also gives special tools for men—the direct and to the point help they need to find their way in a relationship—instead of running when their hearts are really pounding to stay.

Perhaps even more striking is the success rate of my **couples who have experienced adultery. Whereas infidelity causes 65 percent of break-ups nationwide, this statistic**

can be cut down to 2 percent if couples learn the skills to get to the root of the problem and work through it. Adultery is actually a dysfunctional attempt to stabilize a relationship. There are so many affairs because we all seek connection and we all need attention and validation. **This book will help** to heal the heart of **anyone who has suffered the agony of betrayal (or who fears she or he will) and those who have carried the guilt for being the betrayer.** I know it's possible because 98 percent of **the couples in my therapy practice who have experienced adultery discover their relationship is worth keeping.** These couples stay together because they wake up their love and need for each other and make a conscious choice to commit to the relationship, move toward forgiveness, and stay together.

Those of you who believe you've reached a dead end in your relationship or in your dating are actually at the perfect point to turn things around. *Whether you're struggling with a relationship stalemate, wounded by adultery, frustrated by not being able to get past the third date, concerned about your long-distance relationship, or grinding gears instead of enjoying the shifts and changes that go hand in hand with relationship building—you can learn how to make up, stay together, and move forward toward real and lasting love. The success rate of my patients who use these tools and skills in their relationships is so dramatically higher than the national averages that I felt compelled to share this information with as many people as I could—so that you can have as much success in your relationships as my patients are having.*

Too many people break up before they make up a solid couple. At the onset of a relationship or marriage, there's fascination, the promise of untold happiness, and the thrill of the chase. But at some point things begin to change. One partner may begin to withdraw for no obvious reason, leaving the once-pursued confused and insecure. At this point many relationships stop before they've really started. **There comes a point in every relationship where we either wake up or we break up.**

Every relationship holds the potential for "sudden shutdowns." What's both exciting and stunning is that this turn of events can actually solidify your partnership—if you know what to do. There is no perfect relationship or person out there, so stop looking for perfection and work with the partner you have—or the one you're about to start a relationship with. Don't wait for the "right time," move now! Every relationship offers the experience we need to perfect our skills. In fact, the relationship process offers the perfect opportunity for personal as well as relationship growth.

Make Up, Don't Break Up is a ground-breaking look at the intricate roles both partners play in the "relationship dance." From the thrill of the first touch, to the steps toward withdrawal and disconnection and back again to closeness and reconnection, this book offers readers a step-by-step approach for making "the dance" last forever. You will learn the basic dynamics and skills needed to have an intimate relationship so you can develop and improve your partnership without manipulative games, blame, or condescension toward each other. *You will learn how to fix it BEFORE you break it, sometimes by temporarily breaking up—to make up.*

In *Make Up, Don't Break Up*, you get complete information—everything you need to break unsuccessful relationship cycles and make the changes needed to develop solid partnerships. You will learn the critical dialogue skills for sharing your fears and learn how to coach each other through resolving emotional wounds that you have been carrying deep inside since you were a child.

Make Up, Don't Break Up **takes you by the hand and walks you step by step through a new understanding of relationships so that you can enjoy all the fulfillment that "connecting, disconnecting, and reconnecting" have to offer. I guarantee you that within seven days, you can make a dramatic and welcome shift in your love life or marriage and discover what my patients are already experiencing— saving and recreating their relationships.**

The myth is that somehow we're all supposed to know how to begin a relationship and keep it growing. The reality is that we know very little, and unless we learn, we will be forever frustrated. The guidance and "Smart Heart Skills" that have been working successfully for the single and married couples in my practice for the past twenty-two years are certain to work for you too!

Once you've mastered Smart Heart Skills and Dialogue and understand where you and your date or partner *are "stuck" developmentally,* you will be ready to face whatever comes your way. These invaluable skills, dialogue, and actions make the road to love much smoother and help you to climb the mountains and rise above the valleys with greater confidence, self-worth, and compassion for yourself, your partner, and even your parents.

Most relationships can be saved but you have to wake up, shake up—and possibly even break up—before you can make up. Married couples can learn how to stay together and reap the harvest of real and lasting love. Singles can learn how to keep a relationship growing, *instead of stopping it before it starts.* The truth is that men and women are actually very much alike even though the ways we behave and express ourselves can make it seem like "men are from Mars and women are from Venus." Both men and women are from Earth and we can all learn to change—and enjoy the ride!

The first step in beating the odds is to throw away your rule books! Misguided rules like "Don't make the first move," "Don't sleep with him (or her) until you get what you want," or the flip side of that: "Seduce him (or her) to get what you want," "Make her jealous," "Make him chase you," "Wait at least one week before you call back for another date," and "Play Hard to Get," are leading us further away from each other, instead of bringing us together. **These rules *may* appear to work while you're dating, but after you're married, just try playing "Hard to Get" when it's time to take out the garbage or the baby is crying!**

When you use rules that don't work, your anxiety level goes way up! We don't need rules, **we need tools:** straight answers, skills, dialogue, and action steps that work! I call these tools Smart Heart Skills because we must use our heads and our hearts to create the relationships we'd love to have.

Forget the rigid rules if you want to create and sustain a love-filled relationship. Thousands more relationships would be in full swing right now if women would *give up rules such as "Men have to make the first move."* Women are more prepared in many ways to make the first move. Our socialization and upbringing makes us more comfortable with connection skills. As children, while we were orchestrating a night on the town for our Barbie and Ken dolls, the boys were making battle plans with their GI Joes. While we were having tea parties, they were having plastic sword fights! In short, we've learned different skills and have strengths and weaknesses in different areas. That's why men and women complement each other in a relationship.

For single women, making the first move might be giving a man your business card or phone number, inviting him out for a date, asking him to dance, or sending a drink to his table at a restaurant or night club.

For married women, making the first move might be inviting your husband for a romantic evening, bringing home travel brochures to plan your next vacation, or calling him at work to tell him you have a fun surprise ready for him when he gets home.

Another old rule that wreaks havoc in a relationship is the idea of "using sex" to get what you want. Women have been unwisely taught to use sex as a way to get men to comply with their wishes. This is one of the most destructive rules around. Sex is a way to build intimacy and give each other pleasure. Having sex and withholding sex may work as a form of manipulation early on in a relationship, but sooner or later this technique will create resentment and bitterness.

Let go of your old rules and ways that don't work for you— or for him—and be creative in taking the initiative to get things going and keep them going strong. *Remember, tools not rules!*

So don't break up; wake up and make up!

2

Are You a Pursuer or a Distancer?

"For men, love is a thing apart, for women it is their whole existence."

—LORD BYRON

Men and women appear to be from different planets because most men emotionally distance themselves from relationships while most women pursue them. In general, women want to get close quickly because of their feelings of abandonment from childhood and previous relationships. Men try to keep a safe distance because of their fear of being suffocated in a relationship. This makes 80 percent of women "Pursuers" and 80 percent of men "Distancers." For the 20 percent of women Distancers and men Pursuers, relationships can seem even more daunting.

To Pursue means to follow a specified course of action, which is great! But if it's too extreme, it becomes imposing or demanding.

To Distance means to move away from in space or time.

Clearly, both of these behaviors have to be modified for two people to connect. **The role of the "Connection Guardian" is to bridge this gap.** You do this by "connecting," rather than "pursuing." Connecting means being available, making a move forward, taking a step backward, or standing still, depending on the circumstances.

The titles of Pursuer and Distancer, coined by my mentor, Dr. Thomas F. Fogarty, are not all-encompassing and should not be used to stereotype, but rather to describe someone's dominant manner of behavior in relationships. Since we all have some fear of abandonment and some fear of engulfment, we're much more alike than we appear to be on the surface. In addition, we can change roles under different circumstances. For example, many male Distancers may act more like Pursuers at the beginning of a relationship with sexual advances. Pursuers, who want nothing more than to be happily married, can turn into Distancers when the intensity of a relationship scares them, or when they are preoccupied with "predicting the outcome."

Distancers are minimizers and Pursuers are maximizers. Distancers are minimizers because they're logical and rational and always think they have plenty of time. Pursuers are maximizers because they're emotional, into their feelings, and think everything should be done yesterday. **Pursuers are also "movers and shakers"!**

Take the following quizzes to determine which relationship style is more prominent for you, and which is dominant for your date or partner and your parents.

Are You a Pursuer?

1. Do you obsess about being left, abandoned, or growing old alone?
2. Do you overreact, maximize, or mind read instead of finding facts?
3. Do you have high expectations of yourself and others?
4. Is one of your parents distant?
5. Do you think of others before yourself?
6. Do you dislike being alone?
7. Do you long for commitment or marriage?
8. Are you sensitive or emotional?
9. Do you thrive on having discussions of marriage or your relationship?
10. Do you get taken for granted or feel invisible?
11. Do you feel like you're not heard or taken seriously?
12. Do you resist setting limits or giving ultimatums?
13. Do you give in too easily because you're afraid or feel sorry for your date or partner?
14. Do you enable your date or partner to remain selfish by making excuses for him?
15. Do you feel like it's your fault when things go wrong?
16. Are you preoccupied with being betrayed?
17. Are you willing to take emotional risks?
18. Are you impulsive and do you jump into things?
19. Do you try to anticipate others' needs and fill them before you are asked?
20. Are you quick to attach to people and fall in love?

Scoring:

5–10 Yes answers indicates you are a *moderate* Pursuer.

11–20 Yes answers indicates you are a *strong* Pursuer.

Are You a Distancer?

1. Do you "stand still" in relationships rather than moving because you fear rejection?
2. Are you reluctant to invest in a relationship?
3. Do you say Yes when you want to say No, and then feel resentful?
4. Do you provoke your date or mate's fears?
5. Do you feel uncomfortable with "heavy discussions" and avoid confrontation at all costs?
6. Do you prefer to leave everything loose and up in the air?
7. Do you encourage people to come close, but then push them away?
8. Are you a last-minute kind of person?
9. Are you a workaholic?
10. Do you have trouble making decisions, or do you make unilateral decisions?
11. Do you "cop an attitude," moan, or sigh when you have to give?
12. Do you feel suffocated in relationships?
13. Do you long for more space but don't know how to ask for it (or feel guilty)?
14. Is one of your parents overbearing?
15. When sick, do you want to be left alone?
16. Do you dislike being told what to do?
17. When you're needed, do you feel pressured and try to escape?
18. When your date or partner has a complaint, do you check out, tune out, or refuse to respond?
19. Do you take your dates or partners for granted?
20. Are you cut off from your family?

Scoring:
5–10 Yes answers indicates you are a *moderate* Distancer.
11–20 Yes answers indicates you are a *strong* Distancer.

While you will always be more of either a Pursuer or Distancer, you can modify your behavior if you:

- Recognize your behavior and want to change it.
- Make your partner aware of your own behavior, gently help him to see his, and both agree to make some changes.
- Have a strong motive for change, such as wanting to stay together, or wanting to get into a relationship and sustain it.

Opposites Attract for Good Reason!

In general, a Distancer will be attracted to a Pursuer and vice versa. Pursuers need to encourage a Distancer to come closer, **by connecting, disconnecting, and reconnecting with him** slowly and with great kindness and patience. Distancers, on the other hand, need to trust Pursuers enough to take one step forward at a time.

When two Pursuers are attracted to each other, it's like dancing together with both of them trying to lead. It can quickly turn into an emotional battle for control. Plus, a Pursuer often has as many fears of being pursued as a Distancer has. **A woman Pursuer who is in a relationship with a man Pursuer will often reverse roles and begin playing the Distancer to balance the relationship dynamic.**

When a Distancer is attracted to another Distancer, connection can be even trickier. They both have more of a tendency to pull away from a relationship than to move forward with it. However, since everyone has both Pursuer and Distancer within them—with one being dominant—connection *is* possible for all of the various couple combinations.

The Female Pursuer

A Pursuer doesn't like to take "no" or "I don't know" for an answer. She can be the kind of woman men accurately describe as "demanding" or "high maintenance" in intimacy. If she moves in without leaving the Distancer any space, she gets rejected and blames the man or her lack of desirability, rather than her behavior. **Being rejected makes her pursue harder.** If she feels severely hurt or rejected, she may give up hope for the relationship or stage a revolt. She might even take on the role of a "Reactive Distancer" to withdraw from her pain. **But since she does this with anger rather than understanding, it pushes the Distancer further away.**

The moderate Pursuer thinks all relationship problems can be solved with "communication." She is the relationship talker. What are you thinking? What are you feeling? she asks her partner. And she wants to talk about **"the relationship,"** to analyze where they are, where they're going, and how quickly. Since she talks more openly and freely than the Distancer, she blames *him* for his "inability to communicate." By insisting that he talk, implying he's "dysfunctional" when he doesn't, and accusing him of emotional abandonment when he can't say what she wants to hear, *she makes him feel guilty*. The result? Both of their relationship styles become more pronounced and neither **understands the other any better.**

Distancers must set limits on what, when, and how their Pursuers can "communicate." Pursuers have to accept those limits and respect the Distancer's style. Blame and guilt don't change people or relationships. They create distance, which is why people fall out of love.

Rita, who is a Pursuer, came to see me because men never called her back after a few dates. Tears streaming down her face, she asked, "Why can't I connect with anyone?" In therapy, Rita learned she couldn't connect because she had never learned to disconnect. **The only way to connect with a Distancer is to disconnect.** She had to stop seeing spaces between closeness as a kind of deprivation, a form of abandonment. *When she learned that intimacy is precious because it isn't constant, she was able to stop clinging and scaring men away.*

A Pursuer's power lies in pulling back at the right time and to the right degree. A more secure Pursuer knows the power of pulling back because she appreciates her own value. She's not afraid of the back and forth movement of the Distancer, so if she hasn't heard from him in a while, she can call *him.*

A woman who fits into the category of Extreme Pursuer is the "smothering mother" of most men's nightmares. She will do anything to please, subvert any part of her personality that offends him, overlook and accept his most grievous behavior. Is she that loving and self-sacrificing? **No, she is that afraid of abandonment.**

"She says she 'gives and gives' but she's giving things I don't want to take," said Paul about his relationship with Rhonda, an Extreme Pursuer. "I want her to back off. If I want something from her, I'll ask."

Pursuers can modify their behavior with tools instead of rules!

Summary of Female Pursuer's Traits

- She can't take no for an answer.
- She can be demanding.
- She moves in without leaving the Distancer an inch of space and usually gets abandoned or rejected for this behavior.
- She has trouble with *disconnection and reconnection.*
- When she feels rejected, she pursues more.

The Female Distancer

Distancers like their freedom. They don't make demands and don't want any made of them. Most of the single women I see who are in their late twenties through early forties who have never been married are Distancers. Many of the married women I see or counsel over the phone who have been married for several years but are still not comfortable in their marriage are also Distancers. *As little girls, female Distancers identified more with their fathers or distancing mothers than with their pursuing parent.*

A woman Distancer cagily picks a male Distancer in Pursuer's clothing. He's showering her with gifts, calls, and promises, but not actually seeing her very much. She loves the attention, a throwback to when she was an infant and the apple of everyone's eye. At first she feels sexual, alive, attractive, and happy. But when it's her turn to respond, she can't. If she accepts the second date, halfway through the evening she begins to think about the possibility of a deep commitment. This usually sends the guy running. She then wants him back, but she makes no moves. She either assumes she did something "wrong," or she is repulsed and turns off. "He wasn't for me; if he really cared, he'd call back." **She's**

relieved because she's scared anyway, but she's lost some of her confidence for the next go-around.

A married Distancer has a bulging appointment calendar and seems to make time for everyone and everything but her husband. She says, "We really should spend more time together, but we're both so busy." She's terribly frightened of being smothered or losing too much of her "I" in the "we" of the marriage.

Alexis is a married Distancer who is learning how to meet her Pursuer husband, Nathaniel, halfway. Alexis was fearful of therapy because she felt it was "safer" to blame Nathaniel for the distance between them than to see her part in it. I instructed Alexis to do some family of origin work with her father so that she could see the part she played in keeping Nathaniel (and her father) distant. (You will learn how to do family of origin work in Chapter 11.) Alexis was accustomed to "checking out" when she felt controlled by Nathaniel, just as her father had done to her mother. Meanwhile, Nathaniel minimized Alexis's concerns or tried to "sell" her, provoke her, or control her. (Since behind every Pursuer there's a Distancer and vice versa, Nathaniel was "acting out" to get the distance he secretly wanted.) He steamrolled Alexis instead of validating her, and in turn, she had an affair. The affair was a big wake-up call for both of them. They both realized they truly wanted to save their marriage and called me to help them learn how to love each other without pushing each other away or "checking out."

The recurring pattern for women who are Distancers is to get rejected by men, then use it as a rationalization for not getting close. The husbands of female Distancers are prone to affairs to find the attention and connection they crave in their relationship, but also fear. As a female Distancer, your fear is making it easy for both of you to stay distant. You're not encouraging him to pursue you, so he either sees this as disinterest or he pursues you very strongly, which frightens you even more.

Tara is an example of a single female Distancer who had trouble "getting past the third date." She called herself "unlucky in love," because she picked very elusive men. Her unconscious motto was "I'll hurt you before you have a chance to hurt me." Tara had to learn how to desensitize herself to rejection, which all Distancers have to do. She learned it's okay to have needs and share them with her partner. She also learned how to create movement in a relationship by moving forward, backward, and standing still.

Vickie, another single Distancer, came to therapy because she thought she needed to learn "how to make better partner choices." Instead, she learned how to modify her own distancing behavior and coordinate her movements with those of a potential partner. She was a sexual Pursuer and used sex as a safe way to connect; a form of pseudo-intimacy. Delaying sexual intimacy was part of her behavior modification. By not immediately becoming sexual, she forced herself to pay more attention to other more productive ways to connect with men. When single Distancers tell me, "I can't find anyone good enough," I tell them, "You're not feeling good enough about yourself to find someone."

Summary of Female Distancer's Traits

- She looks for flaws in her date or mate, talks herself out of intimacy, **and stops relationships before they start.** This protects her from hurt and also from falling in love.
- She lashes out to hurt her date or partner before he can hurt her.
- She's not proactive; she waits instead of taking action because she fears being seen as needy.

- She rationalizes her behavior as "right" and "fair."
- She doesn't "Nail" the date or connection.

The Male Distancer

Most men are Distancers. The tendency to distance is built in from "caveman" days as a way to survive and prepare for "fight or flight." **Added to this are the wounds men suffer in early childhood, so it's no wonder men's natural tendency is to distance. They're prepared for flight at all times—just in case.**

In dating, during the "honey*moan*" stage, *the feel-good endorphins make men forget about this urge to flee.* They feel no danger. **When a relationship moves toward commitment, the stress makes the man physiologically uncomfortable and he takes flight. These are the times to give him more nurturing and soothing.**

Distancers are generally attracted to Pursuers, but want to keep them at arm's length. "Closet Distancers" are frequently attracted to women Distancers whom they can't have, because this feels safer for them. Married Distancers can be just as elusive with their spouses as single Distancers can be with their dates. The married **Distancer hides behind the newspaper, spends his evenings working, watching TV, or on-line on the computer—he is always too tired to "have a discussion."**

Distancers need time alone, time to disconnect. But don't give him so much time that he completely isolates from you because this makes *reconnection much more difficult.*

The male Distancer may be shy or not nearly as comfortable with verbal communication as his partner or date—which is another reason he makes physical moves. **He is drawn to the emotional qualities of a Pursuer—her vivacity, talkativeness, and warmth—that will in time drive him crazy.**

Luke, an attractive man in his late thirties who has had only a few brief relationships in his life, is a "worshipping Distancer." He either loves and quickly leaves, or he picks someone he can't have and worships her from afar. He's always in love with a twenty-two-year-old who looks like she's on her way to pose for *Vogue*. "If only I could have her," he says, "I would devote my life to making her happy. I'd do anything for her." If by some fluke he could have her, he'd run away—well before she turned twenty-three.

The "worshipping Distancer" often disconnects sexually. He may have sexual performance problems, difficulties with arousal or premature ejaculation, and lack of desire. After he's "had" a woman he loses interest in her because she no longer fits his idealized profile of untouched womanhood. A real woman with real needs, including sexual, overwhelms him.

Summary of Male Distancer Traits

- He does not like to be told what to do and feels suffocated in relationships.
- He is "allergic" to emotionality, discussions, and commitment.
- He gives the mixed message, "Come close, but move away." He is more comfortable with objects, sports, and work than relationships.
- When he feels physiologically uncomfortable, he withdraws or checks out.
- He is never sure and wants to be sure; he can't make decisions and says "I don't know."

The Male Pursuer

The moderate male Pursuer has lots of female friends, but can't hold on to a relationship because he holds on too tightly and scares women away. **He's all about too much, too soon.** He gives his partner flowers, cards, compliments by the dozen, and fishes for his own compliments too, because he is afraid of rejection and abandonment. *Men Pursuers are typically attracted to women Distancers and the more they pursue, the faster the Distancer runs away.*

The Extreme Male Pursuer is the guy who steps on your toes and holds you so tightly you can barely breathe. He desperately wants a close relationship and needs the love and acceptance of a woman because he felt very disconnected from his parents when he was a child. "I love women," he says. "I want a relationship. Why don't I have one? Why do women always pick the jerks?"

At first glance it's hard to see why women wouldn't love him too. He's often good looking, successful, generous, and willing to spend a lot of time with his date or partner. On the first date he'll say how much he wants a wife and children and a house in the country. He's saying "we" before she even knows who he is. "He's creepy," women say about him. "He comes on too strong. There's something wrong with him. He makes me nervous. I'm just not attracted to him."

Deep down, many Male Pursuers are actually Distancers. Hot pursuit is their unconscious way of keeping intimacy at bay. **A man who's a Pursuer often changes roles to a Distancer in the blink of an eye if he meets a woman who won't take no for an answer.**

The more secure Male Pursuer has learned to moderate his pursuit. Some of these men really are ready for commitment, while others are not. *You have to date this man for a while before knowing.* Because there's a Distancer inside every Pursuer (and vice versa), these people *also* have fears of being smothered or suffocated in a relationship, which began in early childhood. Thus, while a Pursuer's primary fear is that of being rejected or abandoned, they also worry about being confined or hemmed in.

Paul comes across like a Pursuer but is actually more of a Distancer. He gives what he wants to give and when he wants to give it—typical behavior for this type of man. He withholds something his date or partner wants to provoke her, confuse her, and push her away.

"He talked about marriage," his girlfriend Rhonda said. "When I asked for an engagement ring and a special vacation for my thirtieth birthday, he refused. I was crushed."

Paul said, "She's too demanding. I'll do what I want, how and when I want to do it. I feel too much pressure. No one tells me what to do. She's acting just like my ex; *it's never enough.*" Paul could not handle Rhonda's needs because his own needs were not met when he was a child. They broke up because he projected his issues with his withholding father onto her.

My patient Ziegefried, a Pursuer, had to learn to take it slower from the beginning and let the relationship warm up, the way a car warms up before you start driving and shifting gears. He charmed women into bed quickly so he could feel connected. Instead, he felt *too* connected and scared the hell out of himself. He'd retreat, wouldn't call, and felt guilty because he knew she was mad at him.

Since Ziegefried is a mountain-biker, I said, "When you're on your bike, you have to change gears for the ups and downs, and you have to do the same thing in relationships. Be as flexible as you are on the bike. Keep your balance by spacing out intimacy. Don't set a precedent to keep the relationship from accelerating. When the road of the relationship changes, shift gears whether you feel ready or not."

Ziegfried thought if a relationship wasn't quickly moving forward it would die. That triggered his abandonment wound, and he responded by pushing for fast intimacy.

Summary of Male Pursuer Traits

• He holds on tightly (or way too tightly).

• He calls you several times a day, wants to be with you all the time, and gives you no space unless you pursue *him*. When he's not with you, he wants to know where you are, and with whom.

• He showers you with gifts and compliments.

• He's generous when and how he wants to be and projects his needs onto you.

• He has suffocation wounds, so remember *he has a Distancer lurking inside.*

Different Strokes for Different Folks

Regardless of whether you or your partner have a dominant "pursuing" or "distancing" style, you both play varying roles at different times and in different situations. Many women become confused in a relationship because initially their Distancer partners appeared to be Pursuers. Men typically make the first phone call, assume financial responsibility for dating, initiate contact, and propose marriage. But it's the Pursuer who knows she wants the "relationship" first.

It's common for a man to be a sexual Pursuer, but an emotional Distancer. *For men, sex is an acceptable way of getting close.* To understand the Pursuer/Distancer dynamic you must separate sex and intimacy when you're examining and evaluating behavior. The typical scenario is for a woman to respond to a man's **sexual pursuit by moving closer toward him, at which point he pulls away.** This can be particularly agonizing when it follows on the *heels of a magnificent sexual encounter.* Women feel bonded and **their expectations go up. Men get scared and distance.** This leaves the woman feeling rejected, **but the feelings of rejection don't hurt as much when you know the man is acting out his own script. The key is to let the Distancer go with love and then reconnect so that he comes back again and again. This allows him to feel like he is in control, and helps him to know you welcome him back, which he desperately needs to feel.**

There are three types of movement in a relationship; *forward, backward, and standing still.* It's important to know which of these three moves to make, and when. Moving forward means being *quietly aggressive,* **without "pursuing." Moving backward, sometimes called "pulling back" is a move made when your partner is taking you for granted, or obviously needs some space.** Standing still refers to letting him come to you without taking a step toward your partner or away from him. While this sounds more like a *"nonmovement,"* it's actually a very important part of the relationship dance. Once you learn the basic skills that go with these moves in Chapter 6, you can step onto the "relationship dance floor" with anyone.

Smart Heart Skills for Balancing Pursuing and Distancing Styles

- Understand the Pursuer/Distancer dynamic. Identify your own behavior (and your parents, partner's or potential partner's) as either predominantly Pursuing or Distancing.
- *Go back home* to your parents and see how their behavior affected the way you relate to others in

closeness and intimacy. Also observe how you relate to your parents and how they relate to each other.

- Accept and forgive your parents and set realistic expectations for yourself and your partner.
- Connect with the parent from whom you are most distant. (You will learn how in Chapter 11.)
- Work together with your partner on modifying your behaviors to change the movement.

I began learning how to relate to men and their relationship fears and movements from my grandmother Sarah. Her advice has stayed with me through the years, and while it sounds "old fashioned" it's an important part of being the relationship's Connection Guardian.

As my grandmother Sarah always said:

"Never let a man know you're chasing him." (In other words, don't openly pursue a Distancer.)

"Always let him think everything is his idea, even if you set it up!"

"Chase him until he catches you." (This is my mother's favorite advice from Grandma, which she used to encourage my dad to ask her to "go steady.")

Times are changing, but certain dynamics in relationships remain basically the same and Grandma's rules are among them. Women and men are accepting different roles in life and relationships and many people value and want equality. But let's face it, it's going to be a long time (if ever) before those statistics of 80 percent of men being Distancers and 80 percent of women being Pursuers even out to 50/50. **So stop complaining about what's fair and start doing what works.**

~ 3 ~

Developmental Stages and Relationship Patterns

> *"To some extent, each of us marries to make up for his own deficiencies. In order to survive as children, we have all had to exaggerate those aspects of ourselves that pleased those on whom we depended and to disown those attitudes and behaviors that were unacceptable to them. What we lack, we seek and then struggle against in those whom we select as mates.*
>
> —SHELDON KOPP

Across a crowded room you will be attracted to a stranger because he seems familiar. The attraction is based on unconscious images of your parents, siblings, or even an aunt or uncle. It can be a mustache, a smile, the color of his eyes, a certain height or weight that triggers your attraction. (My husband, Jeff, wears a cologne similar to my father's and has a "candy drawer" just like Dad, even though he's a periodontist. I share a striking resemblance to his mother when she was my age.)

This image is what Dr. Hendrix calls the **"Imago."** It's an unconscious composite of your parents' positive and *negative* traits. When you meet your Imago, you unconsciously sense an opportunity to "fix" some of the "wrongs" of your childhood. It's the positive traits that make your knees weak, but *the negative traits are actually more magnetic on an unconscious level.* The chemistry that turns you on is reminiscent of someone in your childhood whose love and affection you are still trying to recreate. Your unconscious mind says, "Here's a man who can make all my troubles go away. He can make up for all the things that went 'wrong' in my childhood and previous relationships and recapture what went right!"

Everything goes smoothly until about the **third date or shortly thereafter,** which is when you begin to notice *his negative traits.* Your Imago's negative traits are powerful triggers that bring back unpleasant memories from your childhood and set off a cascade of painful emotions. **What initially attracted you begins to repel you.** The **image of the partner who is most attractive** to you is buried **deep within your unconscious mind.** You began sketching this picture soon after your birth and before you were a teenager the composite was nearly complete. Your Imago has a dominant influence over the type of partner you seek, the way you relate to him, and how happy you will be together. **The relationship script you wrote as a child is based on both the Imago you created and the childhood wounds you suffered.**

Many people break up because they think their partner should only display positive character traits, and they don't want to accept the negative traits. When I say *we pick the one who gives us the most trouble,* I mean that the love of our life is also our *crucible*—meaning a test or trial that will challenge us. (The term crucible was coined by David Schnarch.) Your crucible will be the one who will push your most tender emotional buttons and force you to stretch your comfort zone and grow. Guess what? That's the way it's supposed to work. **Choosing the partner who gives you the most trouble is Mother Nature's way of giving you a second chance to go back and heal your early wounds from childhood.** Your partner is your crucible because he brings you face to face with your old, and often buried, heartaches. The partners who sometimes make us want to pull our hair out (or theirs) are actually the ones who *teach us the most*. This may sound hard to believe, but it's one of the few things that is certain and predictable about relationships.

If your relationship history is filled with carbon copies of the same man in different packages, it's because these men are precisely **what you need most for your own development.** They may not be the "ones" you want to live happily ever after with, but they are sure to be important stepping stones. Plus they give you a chance to practice the skills you're learning, so *you are more confident when* the "love of your life" enters the picture.

According to **Dr. Harville Hendrix, bestselling author of *Getting the Love You Want*, relationships are created and should be nurtured and maintained so we can "finish our childhood with our partner, instead of running from our partner."**

Certain needs must be met in each developmental stage of infancy and childhood. **Needs that were not met—or that you perceived were not met—come out in frustrations with your partner.** Since your perception of the world as an infant and child was so narrow, the occasions when your parents didn't understand or meet your needs became exaggerated and imprinted in your mind. *From these experiences* *you formulated an unconscious picture of a "perfect parent or attachment figure." As an adult, you project this unrealistic image of your "perfect parent" on to your partner or potential partner.* Your hidden hope is that this person will meet your earlier unmet needs and somehow *magically* "complete you."

The trouble begins when you get angry with your partner or date for having the negative traits you associate with your parents and are trying to avoid. *Ironically, since the negative traits create a stronger attraction, if your partner didn't have them, you wouldn't have been drawn to him in the first place.* Fritz Perls, founder of Gestalt Therapy, suggests we all have "unfinished business" with our parents because all of our needs were not met all of the time. **He suggests this unfinished business becomes "frozen" at some point in our childhood, and begins to "thaw" in adulthood when we enter a relationship with someone who fits our Imago.**

For example, my patient Judy was attracted to one elusive man after another because her mother was overbearing and she was afraid of being smothered in a relationship. I was attracted to my first husband because he reminded me of my friend Barbara's father whom I considered "trustworthy, reliable, and nurturing." I was trying to avoid a man like my father because he was unfaithful to my mother when I was a child. I hadn't done family of origin work with my father yet and my first husband was an "over-correction." He ended up being just as distant as my father because I unconsciously picked someone who was not very interested in having a sexual relationship. **If you objectively look at your date or partner's traits, you can easily see them in your parents.**

When you look at the *stages of early development* and attachment, you can see where and why you got stuck in a certain stage and how these early pains created emotional wounds that you carry with you today. Understanding these early stages of life gives you valuable clues for your past, present, and future relationships. *A greater understanding will give you more compassion for your parents, your partner, and yourself.* No matter how great your parents were, everyone has some fear of being rejected or abandoned and some fear of being smothered or suffocated in a relationship.

Reviewing the Developmental Stages will help you realize that many of your "fantasies" about relationships revolve around your unconscious desire to "return to Nirvana," that early stage of life—beginning in the womb—*when all of your needs were met.* You may not want to admit it, but everyone has a fantasy of being an infant again. The hedonistic pleasure of getting what you want without having to give anything in return is hard to compete with. **But once you understand your history you can learn the necessary steps for connecting, disconnecting, and reconnecting with your parents and your partners in ways that nurture rather than end relationships.**

Your Relationship Fears Are Rooted in Your Early Development

The fear planted in most boys is that of losing themselves, their independence, or their masculinity. It stems from being stifled or confined, usually by their mothers, when they needed to be separate and being independent when they needed to be dependent. Consequently, as men they want to be free and unattached. These fears can be traced back to when they were toddlers, between eighteen months and three years old. Some of men's anxieties can also be linked to the Oedipal Stage of development, which typically occurs between age five and seven. **This is what makes 80 percent of men Distancers in their relationship style.**

The fear seeded in most women is that of being rejected or abandoned. This leads to their distrust and driving *need to gain "self"* through a close relationship with a love partner. For women, these early wounds are formed in infancy, between birth and eighteen months. They are manifested in the feeling of *"you're never there for me."* **This is what makes 80 percent of women Pursuers.**

When you review these developmental stages you can see how you became a Pursuer or a Distancer. You can also glean insight into why your relationship script reads like it does and how you formed your Imago.

Sweet Little Bundle of Joy: Birth to 18 Months

This is the attachment or "connection" stage of development. During this stage you are supposed to learn how to trust and connect. If your parents were warm and affectionate, were readily available to attend to your needs, and connected with you by holding you, making eye contact, and fussing over you by cooing, singing to you, and smiling (all attachment skills), you made a secure connection.

If your parents were inconsistent in their affection or pushed you away when you cried or needed their attention, you **developed a fear of abandonment.** The more you fear abandonment, the more you behave like a "Pursuer" in your adult relationships.

BIRTH TO 18 MONTHS

Developmental Stage	Connection and Attachment
Developmental Goal	To connect and learn to trust
Contrary Parenting	Inconsistent fluctuations between being affectionate and connected and being distant, unavailable, and rejecting. Slow to respond to your cries or needs. Pushes you away when you reach out.
Frightening Messages Child Perceives from One or Both Parents	"You can't depend on me." "I don't want you to need me." "You are invisible."
Childhood Wound	Fear of abandonment and rejection. Overwhelming need to connect.
Conditioned Response	Become a Pursuer
Relationship Script	"I want to find my 'other half,' get married, feel secure, and make sure I never get rejected or abandoned again."
Positive Partnering (how to help your partner heal his/her wound)	Be warm and affectionate, and available to meet needs. Connect and attach by holding and cuddling, responding to her needs, stroking her, and gazing into her eyes.

Terrific Toddlers and "Terrible" Twos: 18 Months to 3 Years

During this stage of development children are learning **how to separate, or disconnect from their parents or caregivers, and how to return or reconnect.** They want a little disconnection with their parents, but not so much that it's frightening. They want the freedom to hop off Mom's or Dad's laps to go play with a toy, but they also want to know Mom and Dad will welcome them back when they want to reconnect. Some parents, because of their own childhood wounds, feel rejected when the child begins to connect with other people and explore his or her surroundings.

Research indicates parents are better at disconnecting and reconnecting with their daughters than their sons. **This is the stage where 80 percent of boys and 20 percent of girls get stuck and feel smothered or suffocated by their parents.** This early childhood fear leads to *"distancing"* behavior in adult relationships. They avoid closeness because it *triggers these early memories* and makes them fear they're losing their independence.

This is when boys begin to disconnect with their mothers and identify with their fathers. They usually don't complete this process until they are between five and seven years old, but the **pain and guilt of separation begins here. During this stage of separation and then return, boys experience guilt. If they are not welcomed back lovingly or if they are held on to too long by their mothers, this manifests in having trouble with connecting, disconnecting, and reconnecting with partners in adult relationships.**

18 MONTHS TO 3 YEARS

Developmental Stage	Exploration	
	Disconnection & Separation	**Reconnection & Return**
Developmental Goal	To become an "I" To learn how to disconnect	To reconnect and be welcomed back
Contrary Parenting	Refuses to let go, or lets go without love; clings to you	Inconsistent, mixed messages Doesn't welcome you back or nurture you when you return
Frightening Messages Child Perceives from One or Both Parents	"Don't leave me"	"Don't depend on me"
Childhood Wound	Fear of suffocation and commitment Guilt for leaving	Fear of closeness, connection problems; Guilt for staying; ambivalence
Conditioned Response	Become a Distancer	Become a Pursuer or a "Reactive Distancer"
Relationship Script	Distancer: Closeness is frightening and suffocating. I'll lose myself.	Pursuer: I crave Closeness, and I want it quickly! I want someone I can depend on.
Positive Partnering (how to help your partner heal his/her wound)	To help your Distancer: Show you're available. Give him space with warmth, love, and support. Help him disconnect and reconnect without guilt.	To help your Pursuer: Announce your disconnections and reconnections and help her to prepare for them.

Dolls and Balls and Being Me: 3 to 4 Years

Between the years of three and four a child wants to prove he or she is an "individual," separate from parents, but still connected.

Children who get positive feedback and validation for their individuality develop their self-esteem and self-worth. Children who receive negative feedback or none at all develop shame, inadequacy, and a sense of being "invisible." *These children become adults who have a fear of intimacy because they feel shamed, inadequate, or rejected when close feelings are triggered.*

3 TO 4 YEARS

Developmental Stage	Independence, Self-Esteem, Ambition, and Encouragement
Developmental Goal	To be separate and connected with parents. To be an "I" and a "we."
Contrary Parenting	Negative or inadequate feedback, and failure to acknowledge and validate. Conditional love and approval with strings attached.
Frightening Messages Child Perceives from Parents	"Be who I want you to be, if you want me to love you." "You have no say-so here. Your feelings and concerns are not important."
Childhood Wound	Low self-esteem and self-worth. Inflexible and scattered.
Conditioned Response	Seek peace at any price. Say yes when you mean no. Self-sabotage.
Relationship Script	"I have to hide my "bad" parts and fears or I will be rejected and not loved. I will never be good enough."
Positive Partnering	Respond with positive feedback, acknowledge and validate needs and fears. Affirm his or her "I" and your "we." Give unconditional love.

I'm Good Enough, Aren't I? 4 to 5 Years

Between the ages of four and five, children make a decision about whether they are "adequate" or "good enough." *If parents expect too much, or too little, the child feels inadequate.*

Parents who behave inconsistently by praising a child for an action one time and getting angry another time confuse the child. This creates a paralysis where the child is afraid to take action and reasonable risks or make decisions for fear of making the wrong choice and being punished. Hello Commitment Phobia!

The conditioned response for either of these scenarios is for the child to become **competitive, self-sabotaging, or passive-aggressive.** Not surprisingly, these early wounds are carried with them into their adult relationships and *triggered by their dates and partners.*

The Oedipal Stage: 5 to 7 Years

Between the ages of five and seven, little girls are learning to separate from their fathers and identify with their mothers, and little boys are supposed to complete their separation from their mothers and identify solely with their fathers. Boys have to take an extra step in their development. To separate, or disconnect, they must give up their dependency on their mothers. Consequently they equate independence with distance.

I don't believe boys have a chance to truly separate from their mothers at this age because they are expected to make this change so abruptly and so easily. They secretly want to identify with their mothers and get nurturing and gentle reliance from their primary caregivers (in most cases), but they're afraid of merging with her and becoming feminine.

4 TO 5 YEARS

Developmental Stage	Adequacy
Developmental Goal	To determine they are adequate
Contrary Parenting	Confusing and inappropriate boundaries. Giving mixed messages.
Frightening Messages Child Perceives from One or Both Parents	"You are bad if you make mistakes." "Do as I say or I won't love you."
Childhood Wound	Fear of "not measuring up" and punishment; guilt.
Conditioned Response	Become competitive or self-sabotaging, passive-aggressive and distancing. Or, manifest low self-esteem by becoming a Pursuer.
Relationship Script	Pursuer and Distancer: "The people I love will reject and abandon me. Only if I cave in will I be loved." (conditional love) Pursuer: Since I'm not perfect, it's okay to be controlled—it's a way to be loved. Distancer: I won't be good enough, so why bother trying?
Positive Partnering (How to help your partner and heal his/her wounds)	Establish clear limits and boundaries by giving gentle reliance and coaching. Praise and compliment. Help them to make decisions, then validate and reward them for their choices.

They have to disconnect from the most important woman in their life. Before this time, they got most of what they needed from their mothers and were happy.

This abrupt schism includes:

- Separating from his mother, denouncing his dependency on her
- No longer having his dependency needs met and still yearning for that
- Identifying with his father—who is probably a Distancer
- Renouncing his mother—who is typically a Pursuer
- Trying to become an independent person by giving up the "we"
- Learning how to be masculine

Boys don't leap this schism gracefully and the wounds they incur affect their intimacy with women their entire lives. He's afraid of merging with you, and at the same time, that's what he *really* wants. That's why after a tender moment or a romantic vacation together, he may act distant and move away from you—either physically, emotionally, or both. **It's the same old childhood relationship script being replayed again on the adult stage.**

The pressures of this stage are generally **not as intense or lasting for girls** as they are for boys. Girls at this age are still connected to their fathers, even though they are identifying with their mothers. In fact, if her parents don't have a loving relationship, she may believe she can take her mother's place since all little girls fantasize about marrying their fathers. The same fantasy plays out for boys, but when they have this secret desire they feel guilty and ashamed. They keep this "deep, dark secret" to themselves because they are afraid their fathers will renounce or punish them.

Some boys in this stage must also face the abandonment wounds of their mothers. **Some mothers have a hard time letting their little boys go, and this can make the boy feel guilty for "leaving" or distancing from her. A man with this**

5 TO 7 YEARS

	Boys	Girls
Developmental Goal	Separate from mother Identify with father Overcome need for mother	Separate from father, but stay connected Identify with mother
Contrary Parenting	Mother clings to the boy and makes him feel guilty for separating from her.	Father rejects daughter, or is too close, mother is competitive.
Frightening Messages Child Perceives from One or Both Parents	"Go! Don't leave, stay."	"You have to meet my needs. You shouldn't have needs of your own."
Childhood Wound	Fear of dependency and commitment	Fear of being alone
Conditioned Response	Ambivalence; Distancer who runs from intimacy and commitment.	Pursuer who desires a Distancer to help her rewrite her script with her father.
Relationship Script	"I can't be vulnerable." "Come close, move away." "I can't be an 'I' & a 'we.'"	"I can get someone to love me if I give up my 'I.'"
Positive Partnering	For a Distancer: Show him you are not going to smother him or make him feel guilty when he needs his space. Teach him to announce disconnections. When he learns you are "safe," he can allow himself to depend on you without fearing a loss of his independence or masculinity. For a Pursuer: Announce disconnection and reconnection to minimize her abandonment wound and check in to see if she is feeling loved.	

**early script will disappear from a relationship if a woman
makes him feel guilty about not meeting her needs or if he
fears he can't meet her needs.**

Boys who move through this stage most easily stay emotionally connected with their mothers even as they disconnect physically. These men are still Distancers, but they can sustain intimate relationships. My husband Jeff is a great example. When we were discussing this topic Jeff's mother said to him, "You left when you were about one and a half years old!" My husband lovingly responded, "Mom, I've never left you." (Since he was able to leave, he could stay.) He's always been emotionally connected to her, which is why he is able to connect with me and have a normal level of dependence on me.

HOW CHILDHOOD WOUNDS ARE TRANSLATED INTO ADULT BEHAVIOR

	Distancer	Pursuer
Self-Talk	"I can't get close to you because you'll smother me and complicate my life. "I'm afraid to depend on you and afraid to want to."	"You don't love me unless you want to validate and meet my needs. "I can't depend on you."
Scripted Behavior	Distancing, disconnecting, passive-aggression Avoidance of intimacy and commitment Ambivalence and withholding	Pursuing "Reactive" distancing Craves intimacy and commitment Clingy and needy
Complaints	About the Distancer: "He's cold and unfeeling." "He won't connect." "He doesn't announce it or check in with how I feel when he disconnects or reconnects." "He says yes, but means no." "Avoids discussion like the plague, especially about the relationship; he's allergic to my upset."	About the Pursuer: "She's too emotional and needy." "She never gives me space." "She doesn't announce when she's angry. She expects me to know." "She won't take no for an answer." "She always wants to talk about the

	"He says the opposite of what he feels." "He mind-reads instead of fact-finding." "He's selfish."	relationship." "She gives too much, so I feel guilty."
Highest Values	Distancer: Independence and freedom	Pursuer: Partnership and close connection
Response to Conflict	Disconnects and distances Blames and punishes Physiological discomfort Invalidates Wants peace at any price Avoids reconnection	Demands, blames and chastises as a way to get movement Invalidates Wants resolution at any price Feels anxiety and pushes for reconnection too soon
To Rewrite the Script	Distancer: Learn to connect, disconnect, and reconnect more smoothly and by announcing and preparing partner for your movements. Announce your need for space, with love. Move forward, when you want to go distant. Express your needs and fears. Share your wounds. Validate your partner's needs even if you don't agree with them. Don't get hurt by Pursuer's words or upsets. Risk and confront, even if she's upset.	Pursuer: Learn to get comfortable with movements between connection, disconnection, and reconnection. Announce your need for connection. Move back, when you want to pursue. Express your needs and fears. Share your wounds. Validate your partner's feelings even if you don't agree with them. Desensitize yourself to rejection and abandonment to ease your anxiety.

In the next chapter, you'll learn how to take charge of your relationship and make it move!

⤙ 4 ⤚

The Eight Stages of Relationships

> *"Marriage is not a static state between two unchanging people. Marriage is a psychological and spiritual journey that begins in the ecstasy of attraction, meanders through a rocky stretch of self-discovery and culminates in the creation of an intimate, joyful, lifelong union."*
> —HARVILLE HENDRIX, PH.D.

Every relationship moves through predictable stages but for some reason people believe that a "good" relationship is one long honeymoon that endures until death. By this definition there are no good relationships!

The reason relationships stop before they start and so many singles and couples break up instead of make up is because we change partners instead of shifting and changing gears. Change is a built-in component of moving from one stage of a relationship to another. Many singles never get past the third date and many couples never make it to the stage of real and lasting love because they don't know how to shift gears to handle changes.

Couples move back and forth between the various stages of love until they reach real and lasting love, or until one or both of them give up and they break up, divorce, settle for a mediocre marriage, or end up in an emotional divorce. It's unrealistic to think a relationship can blossom without some growing pains. Strong relationships have problems and troubles, so **strive to have five times as much positive interaction as you have negative.** *(According to John Gottman's research, that's the "winning" ratio. Gottman is a psychologist who specializes in relationships and has conducted numerous research studies.)*

Understanding the Stages of Love

Many therapists refer to three traditional stages of relationships—Honeymoon, Power Struggle, and Real Life Love. However, I have observed there are actually eight stages of love and couples move back and forth through these stages. There is no specific amount of time that each stage takes (or should take) and some couples can go through many of the stages within weeks, while other couples may take a lifetime. In general, the Euphoria Stage lasts three to six months, but some people are out of Euphoria by the second date, while others skip the Euphoria Stage altogether.

I. Euphoria Stage—The Honeymoan

You are gazing into each other's eyes with little care for anything or anyone else. You feel blissful and everything seems to spontaneously flow and take care of itself. The first stage of a relationship, which I call the **Euphoria Stage, isn't supposed to last.** It's at the beginning for a good reason. You feel this way because your brain is stimulating the release of powerful "feel good hormones" called *vasopressin and oxytocin,* which overpower your fears.

This somewhat superficial stage is very powerful because if we couldn't put our fears on hold, **few of us would ever truly connect.** The Euphoria Stage is a spontaneous "falling in love" feeling, but it is **not a conscious decision to love each other.** During the Euphoria Stage we are virtually blind to each other's negative traits. We're driven with our heart and our hormones, not our heads. We can't make wise choices under these circumstances. How many times have you said, "I can't believe I didn't see that in him!"—referring to one of his negative traits that you were virtually blind to during the Euphoria Stage of love?

At this early stage of a relationship we don't recognize any troubles, problems, conflicts, or need for change. For that reason, we don't see a need to learn how to resolve conflicts or deal with changes until the "high" wears off. That's why it's so important to use Smart Heart Skills and dialogue at the *beginning* of a courtship and throughout your relationship. Otherwise we are utterly unprepared to manage the relationship once the stars fall from our eyes. Forget everything you've learned about how men and women are "supposed" to act and trade in your polite small talk for dialogue that opens the door for true connection. **It's not only okay to let a man know your needs and fears (and to give him a safe way to express his own), it's essential.**

The trouble is that we mistake the Euphoria Stage as real love. In America, romantic love is the cause of many break-ups. Some studies show that our parents would pick better partners for us than we can pick for ourselves because we're not thinking clearly when we're in this stage. Many people believe love should be like taking a vacation—a marvelous, mystical experience in which we leave our problems behind and wonderful things happen to us without any real effort. But even vacations have to be planned and guided if they are going to be everything we want them to be.

We say, "I've fallen in love," but in reality we have fallen in lust! One of my patients wisely said, *"We don't fall in love, we climb in love."* When we are in Euphoria, we are blinded by our infatuation and fooled by the popular belief that this surge of emotions and hormones *is* love. We want to savor it and prolong it because it feels so good. Many relationships end right after this stage because people think they have "fallen out" of love when in fact, they are actually moving toward it.

To give up on a relationship because you think you're supposed to stay in Euphoria forever would be like giving away your baby when he or she reaches the predictable and natural stage of the "terrible twos." Just like parents have to shift gears to accommodate this stage of child development, partners have to shift gears to accommodate the stages that naturally and predictably come after Euphoria. This is the point where you shift gears and make a "conscious," rather than an emotional, decision to love each other. **If you give up when the hormones subside it is truly a cop-out based on your own fantasies. It's your fear of commitment talking, not your mind and heart.**

For couples who are living together or newlywed, the Euphoria typically begins when they start dating and continues for three to six months into the relationship or marriage. But that doesn't mean they don't face some power struggles along the way. Singles often begin to experience Euphoria on a first date if it's going well.

To give you an example of what happens during this stage, here's a short summary of Joyce and Kevin's Euphoria: They both did nice things for each other, acknowledged each other without announcing or asking, and mind-read. It appeared to be working. They were meeting all of each other's needs without asking. By the fourth date they both wanted to get married. They were having no problems, felt blissful, and reminded each other of the "positive" traits of their parents.

Two months later they were both disenchanted. They had no endorphins flowing and no problem-solving skills. *(In the Euphoria Stage endorphins take the place of problem-solving skills.)* They were judging each other by weaknesses, rather than strengths, and their negative traits were coming out with a vengeance. *Hello Power Struggle.* They were still attracted to each other but they were both becoming resentful and filling up their "bitter buckets." The parts of themselves they hid were showing up in each other. They got angry with each other, but they were actually (unconsciously) angry at themselves and their parents.

Smart Heart Skills for the Euphoria Stage

- Enjoy the bliss, but don't expect it to last forever. If it did, you would both burn out from exhaustion!
- See both sides of your date or partner. Don't idealize him or her, or you will surely be disillusioned in the near future. Look for the negatives and get comfortable with them.
- Begin sharing your wounds by using Smart Heart Dialogue.
- Start practicing problem-solving skills now with small and benign issues so you will be prepared when the real power struggles begin.

Kim and Steve (my friend Barbara's daughter and son-in-law), are an example of a couple who wisely walked through the Euphoria Stage hand in hand. They are children of stable families with parents and grandparents who reached real life love. Kim and Steve had relatively few childhood wounds because they received the type of parenting they needed. Even though they were somewhat "blinded" when they first met and fell in love, they were also realistic enough to know that all honeymoons end, and real life love lasts forever. They had role models who proved that the honeymoon couldn't even compare with the true bliss and heart-melting experience of real and lasting love.

II. The Magical Thinking Stage

The "feel-good hormones" or endorphins begin to subside. Rather than seeing the reality of our similarities and differ-ences, **we try to gloss over them with magical thinking,** rationalizing, and making excuses for ourselves and our dates or mates. However, I have never seen the "Abra Cadabra" type of magical thinking work. **This is the thinking of a child—the wishful but unrealistic idea that somehow things will magi-cally work out.** The longer you stay in magical thinking the bigger the problems become and the *more disconnected* you get from your partner. **There are times for a positive form of magical thinking such as during the break-up and make-up stages, because it helps couples have the confidence to go on. But otherwise, magical thinking is best avoided.**

This is also the stage when many affairs occur. People are trying to recreate the Euphoria Stage which is reminiscent of Nirvana when our parents cooed at us, looked lovingly into our eyes, and everything was given to us without us having to give anything in return. Of course, adult life doesn't work this way. If we want to get something, we have to give something. To succeed at a relationship, **you need to leave the wishing and hoping of magical thinking behind once and for all.**

If you want to develop love, climb into the driver's seat instead of being a passenger in your own relationship and hoping the car ends up where you want to go. People don't want to do this because they're scared. On the surface it appears safer and easier to be defensive and reactive than it does to be proactive. **This is when you have to "go counter-intuitive,"** and do the courageous things instead of the comfortable things.

Smart Heart Skills for the Magical Thinking Stage

- **Replace Magical Thinking with connection, Smart Heart Skills and Dialogue.**
- Problem-solve and fight fair; problems that are ignored get bigger and cause temporary or permanent disconnection.
- The chances of pulling a magical solution out of thin air are slim to none, so don't wish or wait for your partner to change. When *you* change, *he* will change.
- Don't look for love in all the wrong places, like so many people do when they are in this stage. Having an affair, working late at the office, or avoiding your date or partner by other means will not solve the problems.
- Learn to give to your partner because you want to make him happy, not because you expect something in return.

III. The Power Struggle Stage

After the mist clears and the flow of endorphins slows to a trickle, you begin to see each other more clearly. During the power struggle couples tend to focus on their differences, rather than their similarities, as frustrations from their parents are projected onto each other. *The tricky part about this stage is the closer you get to your mate, the closer you get to your childhood wounds.* Instead of sharing, you are now competing.

This is when you have to give up "being right" and give in to "what works." If you don't move through this stage, your life can become a cycle of alternating Euphoria, Magical Thinking, and Power Struggles and you will never make it to real life love. Predict and expect the Power Struggle Stage. People bail out of relationships too quickly when they experience a power struggle. That's another reason why there are so many break-ups. This is precisely the time when couples need to work smarter, hang in, nurture, and connect with each other—*even more* than at other times.

During this stage, you have to do the opposite of what your emotions may be leading you to do; go **"counter-intuitive."** If you want to disconnect, you need to connect instead. If you are desperate for a connection, give your partner space instead. (The idea of going "counter-intuitive is based on Sunny Shulkin, Imago therapist's work on going "counter-instinctual.") During changes and times of stress, people tend to do more of whatever their natural tendencies are, based on their childhood wound. **Pursuers need more nurturing and Distancers need more space.**

Smart Heart Skills for the Power Struggle Stage

- Predict and expect conflicts and struggles.
- Identify and define the struggle.
- Find solutions with problem-solving dialogues and by fighting fairly.
- Prepare for the change by coaching each other.
- Balance stress with pleasure.

- Announce connections, disconnections, and reconnections with love and no anger.
- Incorporate stress-reducers in your relationship like exercise, music, massage, cuddling, and making love. (By the way, watching TV doesn't reduce stress, but sex does!)
- See your partner as a wounded child.
- Struggles occur at all points in a relationship. Use the struggles to make each of you and the relationship stronger and more secure.

When my patients Larry and Marlene, Vanessa and George, and Tracia and Wayne entered the Power Struggle Stage, they all thought their relationships were ending. "No," I told them, "it's just getting good!" We need the Power Struggle Stage to take our love and commitment to the next level and to cement the bond we already have. *It's a second chance to finish our childhood the right way.* Power Struggles teach us about ourselves and each other. They are opportunities to grow closer and heal more of our wounds. All of these couples needed to change and shift gears, not change partners!

IV. The Transition Stage

This is an opportunity to make true and lasting transformations in your relationship and also in your families of origin. Relationships change daily and they also go through predictable cycles of change, like the seven-year itch. Big changes require moving back into the Transition Stage so you can make the needed behavioral changes and move on to another stage. If you're willing to see the part you both play in the power struggle, and walk in each other's shoes (and baby booties), you can spread your wings and fly together—without colliding!

Changes like getting or losing a job, having a baby, moving to a new city or town, buying a house, going back to school, moving in together, getting engaged or married, and even getting a raise or receiving a pay cut are all parts of life that require gear-shifting. These are the perfect times to use change to your advantage, rather than letting it throw you off course. See each change as an opportunity for relationship and personal growth and coach your date or mate to do the same. *Don't believe that you can't change, and don't wait for your partner to do it first.* When you change, you create the space in the relationship dynamic for your partner to change. Do what needs to be done and be cooperative—even if you don't like it.

Sometimes a temporary break-up is needed to create a change because the fear of loss is a great motivator to make the change that is needed. It also helps couples to appreciate the relationship more and work on making it better. The pain of the break-up is used for positive change and growth. If a couple is motivated and learns fast, a break-up may not be necessary. Remember, almost anyone can change if they want to, and we are all changing in one way or another all the time.

For example, my patients Tracia and Wayne were struggling with the Transition Stage. They had been living together for four years and could not form a commitment. He was afraid of suffocation and she was afraid of abandonment. They had to build their trust so they could feel safe and move forward. They broke up to make up, but he decided he couldn't marry her because he was afraid of losing himself. She felt rejected and unlovable and disconnected from him.

Shortly thereafter, he woke up to the realization that he didn't want to lose her. His fear of losing her made him re-evaluate his own thinking and behavior and he discovered he really was afraid of commitment. As days dragged on, he entered the "pit of his emptiness"—an emotional state that is painful but also very revealing. Many people don't wake up to their own reality until they go deeply into this sense of emptiness (which is explained in detail in Chapters 14 and 16). Wayne realized that his fear of losing Tracia was greater than his fear of commitment and he professed his love and need for her. Tracia was still holding a grudge since he hadn't wanted to marry her earlier. Instead of supporting him, she used his earlier fear of commitment against him.

They both had to learn not to blame each other and to provide safety for their fears through Smart Heart Skills and Dialogue, validation, and showing their affection for each other. These are the skills that moved them out of the Transition Stage and into marriage.

My patient Janice said to her boyfriend, Frank, "Anything good and worth having is hard." You need the courage to face the new changes and shift gears to minimize your power struggles. I told them, "The only way for your relationship to survive is for both of you to shift gears. You both need to be willing to change and you have to change the relationship."

Janice and Frank needed to start fresh, by wiping the slate clean and using the good things in their relationship as the foundation on which to build. *Frank and Janice needed to break up so they could shift gears and make up.* They were afraid to shift gears because they both wanted to avoid confrontation, anguish, and heartache. I helped them understand that the pain of shifting gears is much less severe than the pain of a permanent break-up, which was exactly where they were heading if they didn't make the needed changes.

If you don't shift gears, you enter a vicious cycle and one or both of you will do what Frank did, which was to say, "Stop the relationship, I want to get off."

Smart Heart Skills for the Transition Stage

- Predict going backward (it's guaranteed to happen sometimes).
- Prevent it by being aware that it's about to happen.
- Expect change and prepare for it.
- Don't expect failure.
- Don't take changes for granted. Appreciate them and use them to the relationship's advantage.
- Do not coast or become resigned.
- Continue to respond in new ways and try different things to make the changes work.
- Don't make it harder than it has to be.

When you worry about the transition stage, *let your anxiety work for you.* Make the changes in this stage new habits. I remember when my tennis coach told me I needed to change my backhand. I said, "I'll try." He said, "Trying is lying. Don't *try* to change it; change it. You won't change until you commit to do it."

V. The Break-Up Stage

Most couples reach a point in their relationship where they wonder if they should break up, one of them wants to break up or fantasizes about breaking up, or they do break up, even if only for a few hours or a day. Break-ups can also happen emotionally, even if the couple physically stays together. If a couple breaks up and gets stuck in anger and grudge-holding, they will probably not make up. But *if a couple breaks up with love, as a proactive rather than reactive step, the relationship can be revived and gain momentum.*

If the break-up is used as a temporary "Brush with Death" to create a crisis and motivate change and movement in the relationship, most couples can make up instead of breaking up permanently. In my professional (and personal) experience, I have observed that *most couples need this stage to move their relationship to the next level of commitment or intimacy.* In addition couples who have experienced adultery can heal their wounds and start fresh by breaking up to make up.

The Break-Up Stage can last a few hours, a day, weeks, or months, but it usually takes about six weeks for the Distancer's "emptiness" to set in. While this sounds negative, it's actually positive, because it is the feelings of emptiness that propel us to shift gears, go into the Transition Stage, and make the changes we need to make love last.

For example, my patients Beth and Don needed a temporary break-up. Don's early wounds with his mother made him distrust women. He spent the first twenty-five years of his marriage to Beth being unfaithful. His affairs made him feel safe because they kept him from moving to the next level of intimacy with Beth, whom he truly loved but was afraid to trust, for fear she would abandon him as his mother did.

During the break-up, Don came face to face with his abandonment wounds (his mother was very ill when he was a baby and he never attached to her), which were buried beneath his fears of engulfment and his anxieties about being smothered. He was able to heal his wounds, stop cheating, and emotionally commit to his marriage. This worked so well for them that they referred my patients Jerry and Linda to me. They taught Jerry and Linda, who were on the verge of divorce, some Smart Heart Skills. When Jerry and Linda used the skills and saw how great Beth and Don were getting along, they committed to therapy so I could help them make up.

Smart Heart Skills for the Break-Up Stage

- When emotions are triggered by something you or your partner does or doesn't do, ask "When has this come up for me (or for you) before we met? You need to look at your families of origin and previous relationships so you can shift gears and not project old wounds and fears onto your partner.
- Don't leave anything to chance. Don't assume next time will be the same as last time. Accept that circumstances are different now and act accordingly.
- Don't take anything for granted. You need to fact-find and dialogue it out, even if you think it is self-evident. Communicate in detail, as you would with a professional colleague.
- Guard against invading each other's boundaries.
- It's not about "saying" what you will do, it's about shifting gears and doing it!

In Part IV of *Make Up, Don't Break Up* you will learn all the steps to revive or cement your relationship with a time-limited break-up.

VI. The Make-Up Stage

After a temporary break-up, the Make-Up Stage is your second chance for love. It's also your second chance to make a first impression and start fresh. *Couples who break up to make up and work through this stage develop the strongest and most connected relationships.* They don't forget the "brush with death." In the Make-Up Stage, you both change and agree to keep changing. You are willing to make changes that you may not want to make because your partner needs you to make them, and vice-versa. Many people divorce or break up to avoid this stage, because they don't have the skills, commitment, and belief they need to make it through.

During this stage you move through the power struggles and resolve conflicts by using "fair fighting" and coaching each other. You both commit to creating a connected, satisfying, and fulfilling relationship. When you make up, *the conflict and tension from the break-up causes passion, which is why the sex is so great at the onset of this stage.*

Smart Heart Skills for the Make-Up Stage

- Announce it when you want to give your partner affection (attachment skills), or when you need some yourself. Check in and see how he feels about your announcement.

- Announce it if you need space, and determine a specific period of time.

- Announce reconnection, and reconnect with love and warmth, even though you are feeling anxious from the change and shifting gears. (Announce these feelings and check in with partner's as well.)

- Do not blame or get angry; use attachment skills and validation instead. Deal with your anxiety by "going counter-intuitive." (Going counter-intuitive means going against the grain of your pattern. Being more of a Distancer if you're a Pursuer and vice versa. If you're anxious or confused, then you are changing, which is good.)

- Tell each other your scripts (the truth about how you feel and what you need or want); don't get emotional if they're different.

You will learn all the skills to make up successfully in Part IV, and I'll share the stories of some patients who have triumphed in this stage.

VII. The Re-Romanticizing Stage

Whether you're making up after a break-up, or your relationship has stalled out or is about to, it's time to shift gears and enter the Re-Romanticizing Stage. This is the time to pull out all the stops and really go for it! It's up to you to recreate the magic and romance in your relationship by doing all the things you did when you first met and couldn't take your eyes off each other. (Re-enact how you met and your first dates together.) This stage is very important for all couples and it is also challenging. But the results are more than worth the effort.

Two of my patients, Sandy and Guy, came to me as a last hope after they had experienced adultery and had been separated for five months. Sandy saw me on *Oprah* discussing my first book, *Adultery, The Forgivable Sin*. Sandy and Guy's former therapist hadn't been able to get to the root of the problem and told them divorce was their best option. But after just one session with me, they both had a new sense of hope. I helped Sandy to see that Guy felt abandoned in their marriage because she put her family of origin before him and he really needed to be first.

I helped Guy link his feelings of abandonment in his marriage to his childhood, when at the age of five his parents split up and left him with his grandparents. Sandy triggered these old abandonment wounds when she put her family before him.

Sandy said, "It is such a relief to be working with you because you have a game plan and I know you can help us." Guy said, "I feel relieved to know we are in your hands and you are going to guide us through this."

Once we worked through their wounds and it was time for them to make up and get back together, it was very important for them to shift gears and move into the Re-Romanticizing Stage.

Sandy said, "At first it was really hard. I didn't want to make love with him, but since you told me that the feelings would come back by connecting with him and seeing sex as connection and nurturing, I was able to do it. It took awhile before I actually felt comfortable with him again, but you were right, the more we made love, the more our feelings for each other came back and the more we wanted to be romantic with each other. I acted 'as if' and tricked my feelings into coming back."

It's been four and a half years since I worked with Sandy and Guy, but she called the other day to let me know they are doing great and have a six-month-old baby. They were willing to shift gears and make the changes they needed. Sandy said in our last phone conversation, *"I never thought I would say this, but because of what you taught us, the affair ended up being one of the best things that ever happened in our marriage.* I thank God for it because we have the most amazing marriage now! Our relationship is so much deeper. We know how to shift gears and we have a much more realistic idea of how marriage works!"

Trust and forgiveness—including letting go of grudges—are very important during this stage, and so are courage and connection.

Smart Heart Skills for the Re-Romanticizing Stage

- Don't be defensive; validate and fight fair. Find solutions instead of getting or staying stuck. Defensiveness leads to escalation and dirty fighting.

- Hug when you want to stomp your feet and walk away.
- Coach each other to stay on track.
- Modify your own behavior so your partner can modify his or hers.
- Be prepared to have your wounds triggered when you or your partner changes.
- Use a sense of humor when one of you starts to go back to the power struggle. Like my mother told Jeff and I to do, *take each other's hand in the darkness and find the light switch together.*
- Don't throw the past back in your partner's face. See your partner as new each day.
- Be prepared for some regressions and welcome them so you can find out what new work needs to be done.
- Be responsible for yourself—and treat your partner as your equal.

You will get the skills, guidelines, and lots of romantic ideas for the Re-Romanticizing Stage in Chapter 20, Restoring the Magic.

VIII. The Real and Lasting Love Stage

In the Real and Lasting Love Stage, you continue to grow, together and individually. You keep the love light glowing by using Smart Heart Skills, fighting fairly, and using attachment skills. When you reach this stage, the relationship no longer creates deep emotional pain. You know how to resolve conflicts so there are no power struggles, and you don't take each other for granted. You make the time for romance, fun, and playing together, and you share in each other's troubles as well. You respect each other and accept your partner's negative traits and use them for growth.

Real Life Love outshines Euphoria because it is eternal. The romance and sizzle comes out of the safety and bond that you have created with each other. You still set up sexy dates and you still turn each other on. When you are in Real Life Love, you coach each other, support each other, and work together as two people riding a tandem bicycle, shifting gears together and truly enjoying the ride!

For example, despite my father's wandering ways in the first twenty-five years of marriage to my mother, he was able to learn through therapy and the break-up that his bond with my mother was the most valuable bond in his life. This revelation gave him the courage to change. Had he not possessed the courage to change, he and my mother would not have been able to spend another very happy twenty-five years together.

Smart Heart Skills for the Real Life Love Stage

- Keep working as a team.
- Keep fighting fair to build even greater safety into the relationship and to fuel passion.
- Make sure romance stays at the top of your list.
- Continue to introduce newness into your relationship.
- Enjoy!

Just like a car needs to shift gears to start, get up to speed, and go up and down hills, relationships need to shift gears too, and for the same basic reasons. If we try to take off too soon, or if we don't give the engine enough power, we can stall out. When we push our way through the gears, or stages of love, before we're really synchronized and connected, we grind the gears and take chinks out of our hearts.

Shifting gears through the relationship stages can be fun, playful, romantic, exciting, and very rewarding. Using Smart

Heart Skills will empower you to shift gears and make relationship-building easier.

Understanding the relationship stages is important because failing to master each stage is one of the biggest reasons couples break up, when making up is easier and makes a lot more sense. Love is a short word, but it has so many different meanings at different points in our lives. It only stands to reason that falling in love is a different feeling than staying in love with a partner you are married to or have lived with for many years. Mastering each stage of love requires specific and different skills.

By learning about the stages of a relationship, you can predict them, prepare for them, and be ready to shift gears to get to the next stage. Think of it like riding a mountain bike. The uphills are challenging, but when you get to the top, the view and sense of accomplishment are worth it! The downhills can be scary, but they're also exciting because your adrenaline is rushing and when the road levels out, you have a chance to catch your breath. If the road ahead were always straight and flat, you would probably die of boredom. Rather than cursing the uphills, downhills, and curves, learn how to enjoy the ride.

It may sound difficult to do, but do you remember how daunting learning to ride a bike and shifting gears was when you first tried it? It takes some focus and concentration at first, but eventually it becomes second nature. This is the same way learning to shift gears in a relationship takes place. Another mystery of learning to ride a bike that has a lot in common with relationships is the word "balance." Remember when your parents ran alongside your bike, holding it up straight and saying, "Balance. You have to balance"? The concept of balancing your weight on the bike did not become clear to you until you actually did it the first time. Aha! The mystery was solved. The same holds true in riding your relationship bike.

You need to learn how to *balance the fun with the problems.* Finding this balance takes some time, and you are sure to make some mistakes. But once you experience this "balance" you never forget, just like you never forget how to ride a bike once you've learned. You also have the added benefit of learning from the mistakes you make so you can avoid repeating them.

It's not surprising that everyone behaves a little differently during the various stages of love. Some of the stages are more comfortable for one partner than the other. That's the beauty of working as a team. You and your date or partner will often be in different stages at the same time. For example, you may be in the Euphoria Stage while your date or partner is in the Power Struggle Stage. Be aware of these differences so you know how to relate to each other. *Help each other to learn how to do the things you don't know how to do, and don't punish each other for what you haven't yet learned.*

A funny story from my own relationship occurred after Jeff and I had been dating for several months. Each night when he came to my apartment he brought his shaving kit and clothes for the next day. He wouldn't leave anything at my apartment, not even his toothbrush, even though I left things at his house and he gave me some drawers and closet space. One day I was on the phone with a friend while Jeff was at my apartment. My girlfriend asked how my relationship was going and I said, "Oh, it's great! Jeff and I are living together and it's wonderful." When I hung up the phone Jeff came into the room with his face as white as a ghost. He said, "We're *living* together?" I said, "We're *not?*"

My interpretation of spending every night together, whether at his place or mine, was that we were living together. Jeff purposely didn't leave anything at my place because he was afraid of commitment and that was his way of feeling comfortable. He figured if he didn't keep his things at my place that meant we weren't living together.

I was in the Euphoria Stage at this point and he was in denial—a form of Magical Thinking. We had to bridge this gap with a great deal of sensitivity for where we each were. The term "living together" scared Jeff, so I said, "Okay, if it makes you feel better, we're not living together," even though in my mind we were.

❧ 5 ❧

Connection, Disconnection, and Reconnection

"Let there be spaces in your togetherness, and let the winds of the heavens dance between you."
—KAHLIL GIBRAN

Opposites attract so we can bridge the gap with our different strengths. If we refuse to use our strengths because we don't think it's "fair" for us to be the ones to keep a relationship going, we hurt ourselves more than anyone else. *Your strengths make you the perfect "Connection Guardian."* The key is learning how to connect, disconnect, and reconnect with your date or partner. Only when you learn these movements will you be comfortable in your role.

For married couples, connecting is saying hello in the morning, touching base during the day, and greeting each other at the end of a day's work. For singles, it's saying hello to new opportunities, and connecting with your date when you're together and when you're apart. Each time we say hello we make a connection. Most women have a much easier time connecting than most men, so it's usually up to us to reach out and say hello. This may sound like we're letting men get off easy, but that's not it at all; we're simply using our strength of having better connection skills.

If women truly want to keep a relationship alive we have to accept the role of Connection Guardian and stop blaming men for not doing what they don't know how to do. Couples who stay together learn how to connect, disconnect, and reconnect. In fact, Dr. John Gottman, author of *Why Marriages Succeed or Fail,* says: "Contrary to popular belief it is the mundane events of everyday life that build love in marriage. Connecting in the countless 'mindless moments' that usually go by unnoticed establishes a positive emotional climate."

Our role as the Connection Guardian is to help men connect by giving them "gentle reliance." We do this by taking the initiative, setting limits, and giving them loving ultimatums. We connect with them in fun ways like quick no-pressure phone calls, funny cards or e-mail messages, or invitations to get together and have fun. A man in one of my "Getting Past the Third Date" seminars said, "I want a woman to be a Pursuer when she calls me and a Distancer when she hangs up." So reach out and connect, then pull back again.

Start your conversations with a connection and end with a solid and specific plan for reconnecting, so that your disconnections can be bridges instead of barriers. Whether you're married or single, it's paramount that you understand and accept that men need time to chill out—to disconnect—before they can come close and connect with you again. If you don't give them this time, you will never get the connection you want.

For example, my patient Becky complained, "We never do anything together." Her husband Leo lamented, "I never get any chill-out time." I told Becky it's not fair, but to connect with Leo, he needs chill-out time. Becky had to give Leo what *he* needed to get what *she* needed. Most men are unable to connect with women without having some built-in time for being disconnected or separate. It's not bad or wrong that they're this way, it's just the way it is. Rather than fighting a losing battle by trying to "change them," it's smarter to work with what you have. Maintain your position as the Connection Guardian by giving him space and planning times to connect that are fun for both of you, instead of trying to compete with his favorites.

Even though men and women appear different on the surface, we can all connect because we have one common bond that's stronger than our fears. **That bond is the human desire to connect and attach in a loving relationship.** Deep down inside, it's what we all need, whether we know it or not. Once we understand the dynamics of connecting, disconnecting, and reconnecting, the road to real life love will have fewer potholes and many more bridges.

To help a man to connect, you have to learn how to "disconnect" in ways that make reconnection smoother and easier. The most helpful thing you can do is to disconnect in a loving way from a man *before* he begins to feel smothered and pulls away. Announce your disconnection and let him know when you will be available again.

Smart Heart Dialogue to Give Your Partner Space

- "I'd love to see you again next week, but my schedule is packed until the weekend."
- "I'd love to spend the afternoon with you, but I need to take the kids shopping. Why don't you enjoy the solitude. I'll get a baby-sitter and we can go out tonight alone."

This gives him a sense of comfort because you are creating space in the relationship. It also gives you comfort because you've "nailed" the next connection and don't have to feel anxious wondering if he'll call or when he'll make time for you.

Smart Heart Dialogue to Establish a Plan for Reconnecting

- "Would you like to go to the ball game together next Saturday?"
- "You've taken me out for so many nice dinners, why don't I treat you next Saturday?"
- "Why don't you relax and watch the ball game this afternoon and tonight I'll take you out for dinner and a movie?"

Disconnect and welcome him back with a set plan to reconnect. When you give your partner the disconnection he needs, he can reconnect with you later. When you don't demand his attention each night of the week, he looks forward to spending pre-planned evenings or outings with you.

If you and your date or partner disconnect without a plan, take the initiative and make the first move for a reconnection. *For some men, the cliche "out of sight, out of mind" really does apply no matter how much he likes or loves you when you're together. If you're single, give the disconnection a few days and then call him up and reconnect.* Men disconnect naturally; connection is not a natural state for them. The problem is that many men disconnect abruptly. **It is precisely this abrupt disconnection that makes women respond with**

extreme hurt, rage, and helplessness. These emotions propel them to seek vengeance or bring men down, as we've seen repeatedly in the media over the past few years.

Don't pressure him and don't make him feel bad or guilty if he says no. Show him that you want him and enjoy him, but you don't need him. This is the only way for him to move closer to you without getting scared away. **If a man disconnects and doesn't call for a few days or even weeks, the way you handle the phone call is critical.** No matter how your emotions are bouncing around, be *positive and welcoming.* Don't even mention that you haven't heard from him in a while. Just let him know it's great to hear from him and keep the conversation light. Comments like, "I thought you died," or "If you were interested, you should have called sooner," are certain to trigger his old childhood developmental guilt and dependency wishes and fears, and push him farther away. If he, out of his own guilt, apologizes or mentions that he hasn't called you in a while, use the "act as if" approach: "Oh, I didn't realize it's been that long, I've been so busy lately."

Leave the door open for him to invite you out, and if he doesn't, Nail it! He needs structure, so invite him out with a specific plan: "How about Wednesday at seven, I know a great restaurant."

Smart Heart Dialogue to Reconnect— For Married Couples

- "We both have been so busy lately and our schedules are packed for the next week. Let's set a date to go out dancing next Saturday night."
  If your husband agrees, Nail it with a time and place.

If your husband disagrees:

- "It's okay that you don't want to go dancing on Saturday night. That's perfectly understandable. What night or activity would be better for you?" This allows him to be in control and gives you a second chance to Nail the date.

We can all learn to connect, disconnect, and reconnect in ways that work for both people involved in the relationship. *We all have something very powerful in common—an innate desire to connect and attach in a loving relationship.* For most women the desire to connect is apparent on the surface. For most men it's buried under years of fear.

Help a man get in touch with his deep desires by being patient, understanding, and nonjudgmental. At the same time, *you have to help him be accountable because he is learning from you and counting on you.* You can't let him walk all over you or take you for granted because he'll lose respect for you. It's a bit of a tightrope walk at times, but with Smart Heart Skills and Dialogue, you'll have a big enough safety net to walk the finest lines with self-confidence.

Problem-Solving Can Save Your Sanity and Protect Your Heart

You can't take charge and be the Connection Guardian if you don't learn how to problem-solve. Some people never learn this skill and others put it off until they're knee-deep in a relationship crisis. Don't wait until you're in the middle of a crisis to wake up! Learn how to solve problems together now. Begin with smaller, less emotionally charged issues; that gives you practice so you're ready when you hit "the biggies."

One of the biggest mistakes people make is starting a discussion about a problem when their date or partner is not physically or emotionally available to have the discussion. This usually ends up in a fight of frustration. Don't dump your issues on your date or partner when they walk in the door, during dinner, or when it's obvious they don't want to talk about it. *Learn to schedule short, time-limited appointments to discuss problems and also good things (separately of course), so you both know what's coming and you're prepared.* **I tell my patients to remember this bit of advice by thinking of it as the Three Ps—Prepare, Predict, Prevent!** In Chapter 10 you'll learn dialogue skills for fighting fair and problem solving.

~ 6 ~

The Distancer/Pursuer Dance

"Connectedness is the only need in life."
—THOMAS F. FOGARTY, M.D.

A relationship is like a dance because they both require movement, skills, coordination, and timing. To dance with your "crucible," you have to know all the steps and how they all work. The basic movements of the relationship dance are moving forward, pulling back, or standing still. A man in one of my seminars made the picturesque comparison between relationships and the tango. He said, "The more involved you are in a relationship, the better the two of you can dance the tango. People who are afraid of intimacy, who are pulling back from their partner in life, can never let go in the tango." But when a relationship begins or after a big change, the "dancers" are tentative—not sure of each other's steps—and may be afraid to step on each other's toes or get stepped on. The novelty is exhilarating, but the lack of trust can be agonizing. To make matters a little more complicated, the potential for misinterpreting each other's moves is sky high.

"He doesn't call when he says he'll call. Does that mean he isn't thinking of me?"

Not necessarily. Think of the steps of the flamboyant tango with its wild and beautiful ups and downs, unions and separations. Imagine the male dancer after he has whirled to the opposite side of the floor, his eyes on his partner, his body tense in preparation for dancing back to her. He retreats while she clings after intimacy or lovemaking.

"Is he playing hard to get and winning?"

"Is he a cruel man who only chases when she runs away so he can keep her forever on his string?"

Look to the dancers for another explanation. The woman who has just broken away from her partner in a flourish of skillful steps strikes a seductive pose, while from several paces away he admires her before rushing back to her side.

In the Relationship Dance the disconnections can be as powerful as the connections. The basic steps of the relationship dance are simple, but synchronizing your steps and movements with your partner is more of a challenge. You probably like the idea of dancing gracefully together, but you may be afraid to try the steps that scare you—like pulling back when your emotions are urging you to move forward. That's perfectly understandable. With practice, you will become skillful at quietly choreographing the movements of your relationship to guarantee the dance will go on!

If you're hesitant to try new steps, motivate yourself by considering the alternative of frequently changing partners— not a very satisfying resolution. The constantly changing couples never learn the basic steps, so they never enjoy the pleasures the dance can bring. If you practice, you will discover you are capable of doing and saying things you'd only dreamed possible. Your relationship (or potential one) will be much more fun, playful, and secure for both of you.

It took me twenty years to find my husband Jeff. When I was ready for him and he was ready for me, we found each other. Like every other couple who stay together, we had to learn the dance. I taught Jeff the same Smart Heart Skills and Dialogue I'm teaching you and together we learned how to choreograph our dance. That doesn't mean we didn't trip or stumble along the way—we did. And it wasn't always pretty! *But we did it, and you can too!*

Let's Clear Up the Confusion

Too much relationship advice has been based on misconceptions about men and women, oversimplifications of their needs and motives, and misinterpretations of their behavior patterns. Once we understand the basic moves of the relationship dance, all that confusion is cleared up. When women are told to "play hard to get," wait to have sex, not call him too soon or too often, they're really being told: *Practice some distancing techniques because your pursuing style is scaring men away.*

If you understand the Distancer/Pursuer Dance, you will be able to modify your behavior, without experiencing an overload of pain or anxiety. *If the partners don't understand their roles as Distancer and Pursuer, they never really connect.* They are either afraid to get close or afraid to pull apart. In the strongest relationships, the partners achieve a balance of Distancer and Pursuer within themselves and change roles.

We're all growing, and relationships are the best way to stretch ourselves, overcome our fears, and learn to be more than we thought we were. A couple is strongest in their relationship when the strengths of one person complement the weaknesses of the other. This allows for a give-and-take partnership where each mate is nurtured and challenged to grow by the other. **In many ways, the more incompatible you feel,**

the more compatible you are. When you "dance" with your Imago—your crucible—the potentials for growth, expansion, enlightenment, and love are unlimited.

What Happens When a Pursuer and Distancer Dance?

The Distancer/Pursuer Dance often begins with the Distancer acting more like a Pursuer. He is high on endorphins, moves in with intensity, and hooks the Pursuer with romantic, heavy-duty courtship. He calls frequently, sends flowers, and wants to see her several times a week. This behavior is almost suffocating to her, even though it's what she claims she wants. The Pursuer either believes this type of movement will continue, which raises her expectations, or she feels unnerved by getting too much too soon, waits for it to end, and panics. She also might question the Distancer's authenticity. This is where the dance can take a nose dive if you're not smart! I say, *enjoy the attention and the flowers and keep in mind that things will soon be changing because the Euphoria Stage is short-lived.*

If the Pursuer stands still or withdraws, the Distancer feels safe. If she steps forward, he panics and withdraws. This two-step goes back and forth with extreme ambivalence on the part of the Distancer. Married or single, the more the Pursuer strives for closeness, the more remote the Distancer becomes. Whereas you were spending every Friday night together, he suddenly has reasons why Friday night doesn't work for him. He uses excuses that you both buy into, all the while claiming "nothing is wrong, it's just that he's so busy."

This change activates the Pursuer's abandonment wound. She panics, and her panic creates an *even greater panic* in the Distancer. She blames herself for acting too desperate, clingy, or needy, and he blames her too. He says if she would only be more reasonable things would work out. The more "reasonable" she tries to be, the more angry she becomes, and the more suffocated the Distancer feels. He fears she's trying to "pin him down," and runs farther and faster. *There's really no way to pin down a Distancer and even the most valiant attempts will eventually hit a brick wall and crumble into pieces.*

Your best course of action is to hold on and be patient. Don't let his words or actions provoke you into playing the role of the "bitch" or "martyr." Remember that when he acts like a little boy by throwing temper tantrums, pouting, or lashing out at you, he is reverting back to his early programming. Rather than getting mad or shaming him for his behavior, deal with him as you would a child who was behaving in the same manner. Be kind and firm at the same time. **Help him feel comfortable with his feelings for you so he won't be so terrified of "depending" on you or losing control.** Let him lead the dance for now. Once he becomes more comfortable you can throw in a few steps of your own.

Smart Heart Skills to Invite a Distancer to Dance

- Reach out and be kind; be playful, light hearted, warm, and compassionate.
- Avoid extreme emotionalism, explosive topics, and lengthy discussions.
- Make him feel attractive and let him know you're interested in him.
- Make him feel like he's in charge.
- Respect him and look up to him, *but don't lose yourself in him.* Show your independence.
- Accept him as he is; don't try to change him.
- Be available and there for him—but within reason.

Smart Heart Skills to Help Him Move Forward in the Dance

- Accept that he was emotionally "wounded" in his childhood, and keep his wound—where he is stuck in his developmental stages—in mind when you interact with him. (He may not know or be willing to accept that his behavior is linked to early painful memories. Regardless, *you* must know, understand, and accept his wound, even if *he doesn't*.) If you know his wound is based in a fear of being suffocated in a relationship, by all means don't aggressively pursue him. If you know his wound is based on a fear of being rejected, make sure you reach out to connect and reconnect with him, and when he reconnects with you, welcome him back so he doesn't feel guilty for his disconnection.
- Help him with his fears by validating him and showing confidence in him and the relationship.
- Don't worry about what's fair; do what works!
- Put his wound first, and yours second. (**This will give you a second chance to work out your unresolved abandonment issues.** He'll be willing to help you with yours once you've helped him with his.)

Smart Heart Skills to Keep the Dance Moving

- Make sure he's connecting and reconnecting.
- Make him reach for you, as in the tango, but keep some space between you.
- Show him it's okay for him to lead (he never wants to feel controlled).
- Keep your movements in balance with his so that you're blending together slowly. (**This will make him feel safe—even though he's depending on you a little.**)

- Show him that if he's willing to stand still, you can blend in your steps without controlling him.
- Don't let him use his wound as an excuse. Help him take responsibility and be accountable for it. Your mutual goal is not to use the wound as a crutch, but rather to work *with it to create movement*.

Distancers can drive Pursuers crazy because they trigger your abandonment issues. *But remember that behind every Pursuer is a Distancer and behind every Distancer is a Pursuer.* The truth is that Distancers fear rejection or abandonment more than Pursuers since most men are stuck at the "separate and return" stage of development. They feel guilty when they disconnect while dating or after a fight. *If he feels rejected, punished, or shamed, the guilt can drive him away from you.*

Pursuers are more *literal* than Distancers so you can't always trust a Distancer's words. He may not be intentionally lying as he hides his true feelings and desires, just unconsciously protecting himself or masking unsure feelings. A male patient told me: "I want kids, but on a first date I always say I don't want them. The woman I'm seeing now called me on that. She asked me why I lied. I realized I'd probably been trying to turn her off at the start."

Choreographing Your Movements with a Distancer

To choreograph your dance with a Distancer, *knowing when and how to pull back is very important.* You also need to learn the difference between pulling back and distancing, which I explain below.

When to Pull Back

- You want to create movement.
- You're not getting heard and your needs aren't being met.
- He's taking you for granted.
- You want to take the relationship to the next level. The way to cement the relationship and see each other more is to pull back so his desire to see you increases.
- When all else fails. (You've talked until you're blue in the face, and as a result, he's pulling away.)

How to Pull Back Without the Threat of a Break-Up

All Pursuers need to learn how to pull back. If you do it right, it almost always works. If you do it with anger or in an attempt to manipulate a man, it nearly always fails.

First of All, Here's What NOT to Do:

- Don't ask when you're getting together, or "When are you seeing me?" This reeks of desperation. Don't beg.
- Don't apologize for wanting to see the Distancer or wanting to get married.
- Don't buy into excuses.
- Don't act rude or mean or "over-correct" by rejecting *him*. Distancers fear rejection more than you do. You can pull back without rejecting him. Help him reach for you. Now is the time to become mysterious.

Here's What TO DO:

- Be firm and kind when taking a stand. Don't let him "sell you," steamroll, or bulldoze. Don't waver. Get your needs met.

- Make a move away from him and stay there, *torturous as it is*. Put off short-term gratification for long-term love.
- Make him get to know you and what's important to you (your needs). He'll get to know you a lot better when he's in his emptiness and when you're gone, than when you're together and he's tuning you out and taking you for granted.

Pulling Back Versus Distancing

When you pull back to bring about change, you are doing it *to create a fear of loss* in your partner because you've been too available. When you pull back out of *reactive distance* you do it because you're angry or holding grudges. Anger doesn't solve a problem and reactive distancing doesn't work.

There are many factors that contribute to fears of closeness. Isolating which factors affect you and your date will help you to reduce your fears.

Contributors to Fear of Closeness:
- You or your date or partner are too close to your family of origin and feel like you don't have any space.
- You or your date or partner are not close *enough* to your family of origin, or you are cut off from them and therefore can't connect to a date.
- You or your date or partner had to care for aged parents so you feel smothered by love and nurturing.
- You or your date or partner see closeness as dangerous because of family ties or responsibilities, fear of divorce, history of divorce or fighting in your family of origin, fear of abandonment or suffocation, or insecure connection with your attachment figure when you were a child.

- You or your date or partner never disconnected from your family of origin, so you've never reconnected with them properly.

Here are some Smart Heart Guidelines to help you choreograph your day-to-day relationship with a Distancer.

What Doesn't Work:
- Pursuing, "selling," or arguing; it makes him distance more.
- Getting angry when he distances.
- Feeling victimized or burdened as the Pursuer.
- Confusing connecting with pursuing. Connection and movement are necessary for closeness; it's okay to connect, but not to pursue.
- The three D's—don't be desperate, demanding, or domineering.
- Going overboard in an attempt not to pursue by presenting obstacles to getting together. The Distancer will feel there is no time for him and he'll go to another Pursuer.
- Playing games or "hard to get." Practice movements that will work forever—don't employ short-lived manipulative techniques.
- Taking him too literally. They're not literal like Pursuers. "I'll call you soon" could mean tomorrow or two weeks from now. *If it's two weeks, don't blast him!*

What does work:
- **Watching his movement more than listening to his words.** (Advice I learned from Dr. Fogarty.) At the

same time my husband Jeff (who was then my boyfriend) was saying things like, "Maybe I should leave before I hurt you," he was calling, moving toward me with dates, cards, and flowers, and spending more time on weekends with me.

- Validating his need for space and giving it to him. Predict his need for space and suggest it before he does. **Take space from him even if he insists he wants closeness. Otherwise it will boomerang later.** *Use your power as a Pursuer to move away. In a workable relationship, the Distancer will move in.*
- Using behavior modification as you would with a child. Reward positive behavior. When he could take space, but doesn't, reward him by offering him space at another time. Ignore negative behavior. When your partner sighs or acts childish, pretend you don't notice and keep being your same cheerful self!
- Being accepting and understanding of his schedule.
- Compromising and overlooking minor flaws. Treat him as a friend and an equal.
- Making him reach, but not too high. Make him accountable in a kind, loving way. Be firm but loving. Set limits within a *loose* structure.
- Pulling back, if he's interested in someone else. Don't compete, but stay connected. If he's yours, he'll come back.
- Drawing him out with fun and activities.
- Accepting his style and learning from it. Then, teach him yours. Show him opposites are really alike.
- **Differentiating between what you need from him and what you can give to yourself.**

Points to Remember

- **Distancers and Pursuers have different rhythms**. Speed up the process without pinning the Distancer down. Set up a loose dating structure to offset the Distancer's ambiguity about time and movement. **He waits for you to set the pace but needs to feel in control. If you don't connect, he may not either.**

- **If a Distancer doesn't call or act like he cares, he may be shy, scared, or even in love with you!** Reach out to him and help him reach out to you.

- **No one can control you if you don't let them.** Tell this to your Distancer. When either of you feels controlled, remember it's only a feeling, and it's your choice (or his) to feel that way.

- **Distancers are last-minute people**. Appreciate his spontaneity.

- **If you're being taken for granted, you may be pursuing too much.** Pull back and make yourself a little less available—but just for a while.

- **If he seems scared, but isn't distancing, don't pull back.** *He needs encouragement and reassurance.*

- **Men do not like to be manipulated.** They fear being tricked, duped, or made a fool of, so avoid those behaviors at all costs.

- **After sex, connect with him, but give him room—especially for a day or two afterwards and maybe even a week.** This is the most intense feeling of suffocation he has because of the fusion from the sexual experience. He knows his childish distancing behavior should provoke a reprimand from you—as if you were his mother. Don't reprimand him, it will only give him reason to distance further. Don't buy into the "bad boy" behavior.

- **The connection the Distancer wants the most, scares him the most.** One man I was living with told me, "I can't imagine life without you." The next day he was gone. He scared himself away.

While a Pursuer may hang on to a relationship that is not working for much too long, Distancers are more likely to opt out too soon. They have one foot on the dance floor and one foot out the door. When things don't go well, *cutting out* is their strongest emotional response.

Smart Heart Toolbox for Men
Tips to Avoid Sabotaging Your Relationship

- When you need space, announce it as early as possible to prepare her and disconnect gracefully and gently. Reassure her that your distancing is *your* problem and separate it from her problems. **Offer her closeness before you disconnect and when you reconnect.**

Scenario #1

You're supposed to spend the weekend together, but you can only spend Saturday together. *Don't wait until Saturday night to tell her you're leaving early Sunday.*

Scenario # 2

You're supposed to have dinner at 6 P.M. with your Pursuer. Now it's 2 P.M. and you're starting to feel so suffocated that you have to run away. *Share your feeling at that moment so she can prepare to handle her abandonment wound before the actual abandonment.*

Smart Heart Tools for Men

- Announce when you're planning to *reconnect*; she'll be less hurt by the disconnect:

  "I need space this week. How about if we spend the weekend together instead?"

- Deal with her emotionalism. (It only hurts for a little while.) When you purposely avoid addressing her needs, you add more pressure to yourself. By listening to her, validating and addressing her, *you stop the problem from escalating.* You don't have to "agree" with her, just walk in her shoes and let her know you understand.

- If you feel guilty when you "abandon" her, don't be mean. If you think she wants to move faster than you, talk it out, don't act it out by distancing.

- Appreciate her enthusiasm, fun, playfulness, creativity, and love. (That's why you chose her!) **Be careful not to squelch that.** *(One of your childhood wounds stems from being squelched for similar behaviors.)*

- When the Pursuer pulls back, ask yourself why. Allow yourself to miss her. *Take responsibility for the impact of your distancing behavior.* Don't minimize her pulling back. (That could have serious consequences.) If you care about this relationship, move toward the Pursuer.

- Don't make promises, but show movement. Give more easily without acting as if you're doing the Pursuer a favor.

- Occasionally, bring up talks you had previously shelved. Let the Pursuer vent and don't let yourself get angry or make her feel guilty. She is entitled to her feelings, so validate them even if you don't understand them or agree.

- Make short—as well as long-range plans with her. Follow through and be consistent.

- Try to shelve your ambivalence about the relationship sometimes. Don't barrage her with your insecurities, making her feel worse and you better. Avoid statements like, "I don't think I like (or love) you as much as you like me." "I could hurt you." "I don't know how I feel." This is *your* anxiety; don't make it hers.

- If you must share your ambivalence to stay in the relationship, do it in a nonthreatening way. Reassure her of your positive feelings and confidence in the outcome of the relationship. Ask her to help you sort out your feelings, without making it her problem.

- Go counter-intuitive! Instead of distancing when you feel pinned down or pushed, speak up and take charge.

- Don't say "yes" or "maybe" or "I don't know" when you mean "no." Say no. Be prepared for her upset and learn how to cope with it.

- Give up your motto of "peace at any price." It doesn't work in the long run and eliminates any chance of problem-solving together.

A Behind-the-Scenes Look at the Pursuer and Distancer Dances

Female Pursuer and Male Distancer

Distancers are often passive-aggressive, and like my patient Larry, act innocent and smile even when they're feeling hostile and angry. While his wife Marlene is a Pursuer and craved closeness, she was also afraid of being too close. Marlene pushed Larry away because she was afraid to be vulnerable or get hurt if she really "let him in." She put him in a no-win situation by getting angry when he didn't initiate connection and closeness with her, and pushing him away when he did. In addition, the more Larry did for Marlene, the more she expected. As a result, Larry did not feel appreciated or acknowledged by her. He was ready to give up and asked me, "Why is she making it so hard?"

I explained to Larry that *we often don't let our partner in the way we should, for fear they will leave us.* He wanted to know if Marlene was punishing him and I helped him see that she was, but she was also punishing the part of herself that yearned for closeness but was afraid to have it.

Here are some of the steps Marlene and Larry are taking to create a better dance:

- Announcing their feelings and telling each other what they need.
- Accepting that they don't always know what they're feeling.
- Giving each other space when either one needs it.
- Accepting that they both have to change.
- Staying instead of running.
- Not getting angry at each other when one of them moves too far forward or too far back, but staying connected through these times.
- Coaching each other (and being coachable) to announce connection, disconnection, and reconnection so Larry can learn to give more of what Marlene needs.
- Announcing their "scripts" by telling each other what they each expect or want, without getting hurt by each other's feelings, needs, or script.

They have the will to make it work and they're succeeding. As Dr. John Gottman says, "If you think it's worth the struggle to work out conflict in your marriage (or relationship), it's likely to last." **You may feel you've lost control in the relationship dance because you aren't always sure**

where to follow, since he isn't always sure where to lead.
But as long as you make him feel safe and give him enough
space, he'll want to return to that connection with you.

Female Distancer and Male Pursuer

Alexis and Nathaniel, whom you heard a little about
earlier, are a good example of a relationship between a female
Distancer and a male Pursuer. While they both have their
dominant styles of behaving, they also switch roles under
varying circumstances in their marriage. When things didn't
go Alexis's way, she checked out, disconnected, or predicted
the future—all of which stop the relationship dance before it
starts. Both Nathaniel and Alexis were using dysfunctional
ways to handle their upsets and fears.

Here's what they were doing wrong, so you know what
not to do!

Alexis was:
- Checking out and not checking in. She had to "close
  the exits" of leaving the relationship. When she
  checked out, she gave Nathaniel an excuse to check
  out too. (They had no trust, connection, or safety built
  into their marriage.)
- Punishing and disconnecting from Nathaniel when
  she felt hurt (which made it much more difficult to
  reconnect).
- Predicting a negative outcome.
- Refusing to see things Nathaniel's way.
- Holding grudges.

Nathaniel was:
- Punishing Alexis as a way of disconnecting.
- Checking out when he thought Alexis "made a mistake."

- Cutting Alexis off, disregarding her feelings and steamrolling her.
- Trying to "sell her" on his relationship style rather than validating and working with hers.

The way you handle upsets, problems, and stormy weather is the key to making or breaking a relationship. **If you don't make it safe to speak up and tell each other what is important, you begin to pick away at each other for all the "little things"** that get exaggerated into "big" things. Alexis and Nathaniel are learning new skills to replace the dysfunctional methods they were using in the past.

Distancers are attracted to Pursuers because they actually want to be connected. Pursuers are attracted to Distancers because they secretly want space and alone time. You're looking for a balance, rather than repeating the same "comfortable" but ineffective behaviors. When you attack your partner, you're attacking yourself. You're the hardest on your partner in the areas in which *you* are struggling.

Distancer with Distancer

One of my patients, Donna, realized she was a Distancer who was trying to behave like a Pursuer. She pushed men away by being too honest and too vulnerable, traits she regarded as "feminine" and took to an extreme to overcompensate for how she really felt. "I see now that I was really trying to push men away and telling myself I was trying to get too close."

Like many female Distancers, she didn't know how to be close without using sex for pseudo-closeness to calm her fears. Typically her sexual encounters were intense, and often having "intense sex" too early in a relationship scares men.

"Dating is tough," Donna said. "You can't run and you can't hide. You see your flaws and fears as well as his." But Donna did try to hide. Depressed when she comprehended her distancing behavior, she asked for medication. I insisted she use her Smart Heart Skills to deal with her wounds in a way that doesn't scare people and gets her what she wants. Donna was finally willing to begin the process of connecting with her father after twenty years of separation. This disconnection was the biggest obstacle in her adult relationships. **It's impossible to have a close relationship if we don't resolve the issues we have with our parents.**

Another one of my patients, Jill, is an extreme Distancer like her father, who was a selfish and withholding man. She had to beg for his attention. She got involved with Marty, who had the same kind of father as she did and also had an ex-wife who fit the Distancer profile. When they got together, Marty was afraid of being "ripped off" by another woman. But he wanted to learn how to connect and ask for what he wanted—something he never felt safe doing in his family or first marriage. Jill was working to keep up with Marty. "Now that I understand these dynamics I recognize when one of us is pushing too close or backing away too far, and I can do something positive about it," said Jill.

Pursuer with Pursuer

This relationship can go two different ways. It is sometimes a low-chemistry and somewhat boring combination that people force themselves into because they feel safer, due to the lack of passion. Power struggles create passion and these Pursuers rarely have power struggles, and consequently don't have fire and passion to fuel their intimacy. They will slowly fizzle out unless one of the partners changes roles and becomes a Distancer. The other way a Pursuer/Pursuer relationship can go is toward "burn-out." This happens when both partners struggle for control and tire each other out.

Don't let the Phone Disconnect Your Dance

The phone can help to make or break a relationship. Most Distancers either hate talking on the phone or use it as a tool to keep space between you. It's easy for them to hide behind the phone.

- Don't stay on the phone for more than fifteen minutes. If you drag out the conversation it becomes a "Pursuing" phone call, even if *he* called *you*. Be a Distancer when you hang up.
- Don't exhibit clinging behavior on the phone; it's just as bad as doing it in person.
- Be understanding and *initiate* hanging up, so he can miss you and want to see you.

If you suffocate a Distancer with calls, he'll have no desire to see you. *Married or single, use the phone as a tool, like busy business people.* Get to the point, make an appointment, and hang up.

The phone presents a problem in relationships because the Distancer's indifferent phone behavior triggers your abandonment wounds and perpetuates your anxiety. Keep in mind that your Distancer is unable to be demonstrative in person, let alone on the phone! Don't ask: "Do you miss me?" "Do you wish you were here?" and "When can we see each other?" Other pursuing phone behavior to avoid is leaving sexy, needy messages on his machine.

· 7 ·

Why Intimacy Is Hard to Achieve

> "For one human being to love another: that is perhaps the most difficult of all our tasks, the ultimate, the last test and proof, the work for which all other work is but preparation."
>
> —RAINER MARIA RILKE

Intimacy doesn't just happen and it doesn't come "naturally." It takes time and skills to create a truly close connection. Intimacy means sharing, trusting, confiding in each other, and bonding—without fusing. The fear of intimacy is directly related to the fear of invading each other's boundaries. **Like two porcupines in an igloo, you want to get close enough to stay warm, but not so close that you "prick" each other.** This balance takes time to achieve because a Distancer tries to maintain his "I," while a Pursuer wants to create a "we."

Gauge Your Quotient for Intimacy

The following questionnaires are designed to help you gauge your quotient for intimacy, and your partner's.

1. Are you carefree; can you escape and play?
2. Do you use "Kodak moments" wisely?
3. Are you concerned for others' feelings?
4. Do you like going to parties or other events, or do you prefer to be alone?
5. Are you friendly and welcoming?
6. Do you express your needs?
7. Are you willing to give up control?
8. Do you need excessive space and push people away?
9. Are you comfortable with affection and attention?
10. Do you enjoy sharing thoughts and feelings?
11. Are you coachable?

What Is Your Partner's Quotient for Intimacy?

1. Does he withdraw and seek more space than closeness?
2. Can he be spontaneous and playful?
3. Can he give up some control for connection or does he sabotage closeness?
4. Does he move toward you, treat you with affection, and show concern for you?
5. Can he express his feelings and listen to yours without "checking out"?
6. Does he spend enough time with you?
7. Does he stretch to meet your needs and come when you need him?
8. Can he say no?
9. Does he distance from you, or punish you after close moments?
10. Is he able to think about you and what is important to you?
11. Is he "coachable"?

If you answered "no" to more than five questions on either list, it's an indication that you or your date or partner have some work to do to make yourself more open to intimacy and closeness. **Doing family of origin work and healing your developmental wounds will make a major difference in your ability to be intimate.**

Take small steps, one at a time, toward greater intimacy so you feel safer and your date or partner learns to trust you and himself. Press the mute button on your rejection fears. Acknowledge your fears, but don't give them more power by dwelling on them. "Act as if" the fears are not prominent. Acting as if does more than make your partner comfortable; it's a very *powerful* way to change your own state of mind. For example, if you feel sad, but smile anyway, you can shift your emotional state and eventually your mood will swing up to match your smile. The same idea works with acting as if. When you practice being courageous and self-confident, your fears begin to subside. You "trick yourself" into feeling confident.

Master the Porcupine Analogy

Women fantasize about joining together with a lover and becoming "one." Movies and romance novels make this scenario look romantic, breathtaking, and exhilarating. *Unconsciously we think this "joining" or "fusion" is the best thing we can hope for, but it's actually the worst thing that can happen!* Used in this way, fusion happens when two people get so close that they start invading each other's boundaries and inevitably "prick" each other. It's an attempt to turn two people into one, which of course is not possible, and is certainly not in the best interest of the relationship. *The closer two people get to each other, the greater the intensity of emotional attraction and the greater the tendency toward fusion.* The more emotional you are, and the more you believe you need your partner, the more likely you are to push for fusion. The less emotional you are, and the more you fear intimacy, the more likely you are to pull away and distance.

Creating a comfortable balance helps you avoid pricking each other. It also helps you both to achieve a greater level of intimacy because you feel safer. **The more you force fusion, the more distance you create. The more you open the space between each other, the more closeness you create.**

A person pushing for "quick intimacy" has confusion about what she should get from "self" and what she needs from "others." This leads to fusion. According to Dr. Fogarty, "the force behind fusion is the desperate hope of filling one's 'emptiness' by uniting or taking something from someone else." A Pursuer tries to fill her emptiness with her partner. A Distancer maintains his sense of self through work, sports, hobbies, or other movement *away* from his partner.

Move toward closeness, but pull back before you "prick" each other. Each partner will invade the other's space a little. Learn to be comfortable with the flow *toward* fusion, but conscious enough of it that you can prevent it before it happens. *Keep the movement going by connecting, disconnecting, and reconnecting.* **Optimal distance is necessary to have closeness.** When the distance, or closeness, is greater than one of the partners can handle, the relationship may "triangle." The third party can be work, children, in-laws, affairs, television, the Internet, drugs, or anything that allows or creates avoidance of the partnership. Triangles prevent the resolution of problems by *avoiding* confrontation. Insight is not enough to create change because all members of the triangle will try to get the others to stop rocking the boat—and hold the status quo. Actions and movement are needed to stabilize the primary relationship and create lasting changes.

Be proactive, rather than reactive, and you will enjoy the same success as my patients. Whether you're going on your second date, are involved in a long-distance relationship, or have been waking up in the same bed with your mate for years, each time you connect you're seeing and experiencing a slightly different person. Every time you see your partner, look at him and listen to him as if it's the first time. See him with a "new face," to stop yourself from making assumptions based on what he did or didn't do in the past. When we pigeonhole someone as "always the same" we miss out on who they really are, or are becoming.

Respect is the foundation of intimacy and love. You need to respect each other's feelings and behaviors and be friends while you improve your relationship. Experiment with the process of connecting, disconnecting, and reconnecting until you find a balance that works for both of you. On average, men are more ambivalent toward intimacy because of the female authority figures in their early lives. Most young boys felt controlled by their mothers, grandmothers, aunts, teachers, nuns, or babysitters at the very time they were trying to become masculine and identify with their fathers. *Later in life these feelings resurface and affect their ability to be intimate with their partners.*

Women have more experience with empathizing, so it's often easier for us to imagine what our partner is going through than for our partner to understand what we're going through. Men have to learn how to validate, *but we have to be willing to teach them and be patient* (without making them feel like we're teaching them). One of the biggest reasons for break-ups is that men withdraw when their partners need or want them to be more giving. When they feel like they're being controlled, they disconnect and the connection is broken.

People with intimacy problems had problems when they were discovering who they were, usually in pre-adolescence, and also earlier in their childhood. Because of their fear of getting back into a relationship that would make them feel as they did as children or pre-teens, they protect themselves by keeping partners or potential dates at arm's length. They also have a hard time giving, because they are afraid if they give an inch, their partner will take a mile. On a subconscious level many people who struggle with intimacy use selfishness as a form of protection. They often rationalize their actions by thinking or saying, "No one ever did that for me." But to keep a relationship going, they must be willing to learn how to give what their partners need from them.

Partners need to be separate circles, close together but not overlapping, to be ready for the Kodak moments of intimacy, and not flee from them.

Good Boundaries　　　No Boundaries—Fusion

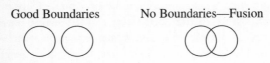

When a couple fuses and distances over and over again, they eventually triangle the relationship. Triangles are attempts to avoid conflict in the twosome and stabilize, optimal distance. But they prevent the development of personal relationships, vis à vis intimacy.

Smart Heart Skills to Break Down Your Intimacy Barriers

- Know which wounds are deepest for you and your date or partner; Abandonment or Suffocation?

- Go back home and rewrite your early script without blaming your parents or siblings. If you're disconnected from one of your parents, it will be very difficult, *if not impossible,* to connect with your partner. Acknowledge the part you played with the parent from whom you are most distant. See how this insight translates to everyday life and especially in love *and making up—or breaking up.* Bridge the connection from your parent to your partner and vice versa so you will feel safer and more secure when you closely connect. Encourage your partner to do the same (more about this in Chapter 11).
- Have fun switching roles of Pursuer and Distancer.
- Give up hope for "completing" yourself through your partner, so you can discover what you can get from yourself!

Appreciation Nurtures Intimacy; Selfishness Kills It

Women complain of being taken for granted, and yet we react to many of the things men do for us as if "that's the least they can do." If a man treats you to dinner or a movie, thank him. He doesn't owe it to you, it's a gift! A man who invests his time and money in you, whether he's your husband or your date, *wants* to please you. Make sure he knows you appreciate it. *Thanking him for the little things makes him feel more secure about giving you the bigger things—like the intimacy and secure commitment you crave.*

We're all selfish, but girls learn how to nurture in their childhood when they play with and take care of their dolls and stuffed animal toys. Boys aren't often given this chance to learn nurturing skills early on. They learn that mothers are "made to nurture them" and they associate and expect this type of treatment from their partners when they are adults.

That's why women get so angry and frustrated with men. **We feel taken for granted because most men are accustomed to having their own needs met without having to give much or anything in return.** What women don't realize is that men don't know "how" to give and feel safe at the same time. **Instead of blaming men and making them feel guilty for what they don't know, let's teach them.** Blaming them gives them an "out" and keeps them from learning the skills to develop an intimate relationship. We teach them by being firm, but loving. We don't tell them they "have to do this," or "they'd better do that." We let them know what we would love to have, start out with small requests that are easier for them to meet, and *reward them generously when they meet these requests.*

For example, if you made dinner and you want your partner to help wash the dishes, don't use anger or shame to try and force him to help.

Smart Heart Dialogue

"I really love making dinner for you because I can tell how much you appreciate it. I just wish we had more time to have fun after dinner."

Then gently suggest you do the dishes together, and show him how it will benefit *him*.

"Why don't we do these dishes together so we can get them done quickly and watch the football game together?"

According to studies conducted by John Gottman, **men who are willing to comply with their partner's needs and meet their desires are much more comfortable and content in their relationships.** The women who had success with helping their partners to comply with them used a positive, upbeat, and nonthreatening manner. *Men don't respect us when we allow them to be selfish.* They want us to call them on it, but nicely, so they can grow and be happier with themselves and with us in a relationship.

When you criticize, attack, or blame a man for being selfish, he feels suffocated. He experiences physiological changes in his body that set off alarms that warn him to withdraw, "check out," or stonewall. He puts his date or mate in the same category as he put his mother and the other women in his early life whom he felt controlled and smothered by. When this happens, his automatic response is to *disconnect* to maintain his physiological equilibrium, independence, and masculinity. Men associate being controlled by a woman with being weak and dependent and these are two of their greatest phobias.

Another aspect of selfishness is a man's feeling of guilt that he is bound to hurt his date or partner eventually—*just as he believes he hurt his mother when he separated from her in childhood.* Men also feel guilty because they give differently than women and because they want to flee from women's emotions.

Men are "allergic" to women's emotionality because it raises their physiological stress level. High emotions trigger the ancient panic buttons to "fight or flee." *Men leave relationships more because of guilt than because they're not interested in you or don't love you.* In fact, the more interested a man is in you, the more scared and guilty he's likely to feel. For example, after I had a fantastic "beach" date with a great guy, I didn't hear from him for three weeks. We both had a great time so I called him. I said, "Since we had such a great time together, I was wondering what happened. Did I offend you, or maybe we didn't have as great a time as I thought?" He apologized for not calling me and said, "I didn't call you because I could fall in love with you. I'm not ready for that."

When Men Say Yes, But Mean No

Another intimacy blocker is when men say yes but mean no. Although we associate this behavior with men, it's actually a "distancing" behavior, so it applies to 20 percent of women too! *In their defense, most Distancers don't know they mean no when they say yes. They have a delayed response* to knowing how they feel. Most of them mean yes when they say yes, then wish they had said no. Later, they are angry (mostly at themselves) for saying yes, feel beholden to you, and guilty for not wanting to give. This leads to passive-aggressive behavior. The next time you ask for something, he will refuse or "forget" to do it.

Let's say you ask your partner to stop at the grocery store and pick up a few things. He hates shopping, but says he'll go. Hours later he still hasn't budged from the recliner and you begin to fume. *If you reprimand him or badger him to go, and you succeed, he will take it out on you later.* It's smarter to let him off the hook with the smaller things so you don't end up paying more than the favor is worth! If it's a big issue, you have to hold your ground, but letting him off the hook with understanding for the little things helps him get over his self-ishness and be more willing to give!

One of the biggest reasons he has trouble giving is he doesn't want to "answer to" a woman. When you act like his mother, he goes into complete rebellion and typically does this in a passive-aggressive way. For example, the next time you ask him to call if he's going to be late, he says he will, but doesn't. He doesn't want to say no, because he doesn't want to have a conflict or incur your wrath. He doesn't think about the reper-cussions, only about his potential physiological discomfort!

As the Connection Guardian, teach your partner how to say no. **When he feels safe saying no, he'll say yes more often, and follow through.**

Smart Heart Skills to Teach Him How to Say No

- Make it safe for him to say no.
- If he says yes, ask him if he's sure. "Do you really want to do this? It's okay if you don't."
- You may have to ask him two or three times because he may have a delayed reaction.
- If you still think he's agreeing to more than he realizes, suggest that he visualize (not just think about) himself doing whatever he's said yes to before confirming it.
- Encourage him to deal with his guilt so he can be more giving when he should be, so he doesn't have to say yes to giving when he shouldn't.
- Reward him for giving and let him off the hook so he won't get back at you, disappoint you, or feel guilty when he can't or won't give.

Smart Heart Dialogue

"Taking care of the kids for a whole week while I'm away may be too much. **Why don't you take a minute to close your eyes and really imagine what it will be like for you.** If you decide it's too much, it's okay. Let me know and I'll make other arrangements. I think you're terrific either way."

He has to learn it's safe to say no to you to be able to eventually say yes, and keep his word. When you scold or shame a man for saying yes and not following through, he becomes like a little boy again and gets frustrated and angry. "Why should I have to listen to you?" he justifies to himself. "I'm a man. I'll do it if I want to do it." We get angry and blame him out of our own frustration, and we get self-righteous about it too. He sets up this negative spiral, you feed into it, and he gets mad at you for reminding him he messed up!

Smart Heart Dialogue

"If you have a chance to give me a call before you leave the office, I can have dinner on the table when you get home."

Or,

"I don't want you to have to wait for me. If you're running late and give me a quick call, I can make sure I'm ready to head out the door when you get here."

Eventually, he'll be willing to call—just to make you happy—*but not until he thinks it's his choice, not your demand.*

As a Distancer, my mother has a tendency to say yes, when she really should say no. I've had to learn how to coach her and help her to say no when I think she's biting off more than she can chew. A great example of this is the time she volunteered to make tuna salad for seventy guests who were invited to a party at my home. When she offered, I told her how much work it was going to be, but she insisted that she wanted to do it. I know Distancers sometimes "bail out" when the time to deliver arrives, so I made a back-up plan in the event my mother couldn't come through.

The night before the party she called me to say, "I'm so sorry Bonnie. I just can't make tuna salad for seventy people. I don't know what I was thinking." I asked her why she insisted on doing it when I tried to talk her out of it the first time. She said, "Because I love you and I wanted to do it for you. I thought I could do it at the time. I don't like to say no to you."

Mom was relieved to know I had already let her off the hook and made back-up plans. She brought some homemade casseroles instead, and felt good about herself. *She didn't feel guilty, because I didn't blame or shame her for not being able to come through.*

Make Friends with Fear

I know intimacy can be scary. I was scared to death numerous times during my courtship with Jeff, but *that's part of the thrill if you learn to make friends with your fears*. Running from your fears doesn't work because wherever you go, they follow like your shadow. Regardless of how much you want to believe your relationship isn't working because of your partner or choice of dates, you can't escape responsibility for the role *you* are playing. If you don't look honestly at your own fears and what they've been encouraging you to do, you will have one relationship after another—*each one stopping before it starts*. So get to know your fears and unlock the pearls of wisdom hidden inside for you.

You also need to get to know your partner's fears and this is a bit more challenging. Men are conditioned to hide their fear. They equate fear with weakness and being "less than a man." It's up to you to create a safe environment for him to *share his fears with you*. Use Smart Heart Skills to understand your date or partner's fears and help him along the various steps.

Smart Heart Skills for Befriending Fear

- Remember that you both have fears, he's just expressing them differently. He may move away from you or disconnect when he really wants to be close.
- When his fears cause him to disconnect, don't interpret it as rejection, and don't reject or smother him when you are afraid.
- Stop assuming you know his fears or that he knows yours. *Tell him directly about your fears to create safety and movement to the next level.* Tell him about

your abandonment wound and understand his suffocation wound. Encourage him to share. If he can't, ask him if you can help him. "May I have permission to mind-read?"

- Don't over-analyze. When you share time together enjoy the moments of pleasure and make them feel safe. Don't think ahead about possible rejection—that will paralyze you.

- Think the best, not the worst. There are many factors that go into all the steps from meeting someone for the first time through dating, marriage, and beyond. That's why it's important to communicate fears *early,* avoid making assumptions, and don't give up or disconnect because of *your* fearful projections or *his.*

When we're afraid, we revert back to childhood thinking. At the very moment we need to be hugged, we may push our partner away, act indifferent or cruel, or disconnect. We need to put our fears into words instead of acting them out. Part of our intimacy fear comes from our need to know we can count on our partner in a crisis or during difficult times. We want to know we can count on them, but we're afraid they won't come through for us—just as we feared our parents wouldn't come through for us as children.

For example, my patient Lori yelled, used harsh tones, and put her boyfriend Ben down just when she needed him the most. Lori had to tell Ben when she felt inadequate or helpless. She had to let him know, "I'm not angry at you, I'm afraid."

When you're afraid and blame your partner, they get angry and turn the blame back on you. In marriages, this behavior escalates into huge fights; in new relationships, it effectively pulls the plug.

Smart Heart Dialogue and Skills for Sharing Fears

Two of my patients, Frank and Janice, almost stopped their relationship because they didn't know how to share their fears and didn't think they should. Things got complicated quickly because Frank came on like a Pursuer, but when Janice responded, he got scared and ran. Janice couldn't understand why Frank had switched roles so quickly. They had been friends for years and after dating three weeks they decided to be "exclusive." Soon after that Janice found out Frank was cheating with his former girlfriend, Samantha. Frank said, "I'm afraid Janice will be too strong and I won't have any control."

When you are in love, you are somewhat out of control. You have to let go. Frank was too afraid of intimacy with Janice so he retreated back to "safer waters" by spending time with Samantha, even though he was afraid of deep intimacy with her, too.

Janice broke up with Frank and he went into a complete panic because she had become his "attachment figure." As children, our parents are our attachment figures. They are the ones we need to be able to count on. When we enter a relationship in adulthood, our partner takes on the role of our attachment figure and our expectations go up because we want to know we can rely on him or her. Frank was afraid to lose her and afraid to lose himself in her. Janice triggered his old abandonment wounds—his hurts and fears of being rejected or abandoned that he experienced in his childhood when he lost the closeness he had with his father and which he never got from his mother. The temporary break-up gave Frank a "brush with death." **A temporary break-up, like a close call with death, wakes people up and reminds them of what's truly most important in their lives.** Frank discovered his fear of losing Janice was greater than his fear of intimacy. Sometimes we need to break up to make up. Stopping a relationship temporarily—if done right—can give it a fresh start.

Janice believed the relationship was worth saving, so she agreed to use the following Smart Heart Skills.

Smart Heart Skills for Janice

- Announce when she is shifting gears or disconnecting, and use attachment skills as she announces her shift. She holds his hands, looks into his eyes, and says I'll miss you, or I love you before she leaves or disconnects.
- Ask Frank how the disconnection is going for him and how she can help make it smoother.
- Maintain her willingness to make the relationship work out and remember it isn't about control.
- Focus on making the journey peaceful and safe.
- Attend to his abandonment wound.

Smart Heart Skills for Frank

- End his cheating and say good-bye to his old relationship with Samantha.
- Give Janice the same reconnection affirmation that he needs.
- Face his fear, rather than running from it or diluting it by cheating with other women.

Janice said, "Temporary disconnections are sweet sorrow for me, not the dread of disconnection." But Frank had severe separation anxiety, due to the separation from his father he experienced when he was sent to boarding school. He saw every disconnection as the end and didn't believe there would be a reconnection.

Smart Heart Skills to Triumph Over Fears of Intimacy

- "Court Your Crucible." Take on this "trial and test" that your partner (as your crucible) is sure to bring you. Make your fear and anxiety work for you, rather than against you.
- "Act as if." When you feel afraid, act as if you're not. This "pseudo" confidence leads to genuine confidence with practice.
- Do what works—don't get caught up in what's "fair."
- Get out of your comfort zone. When you feel like you want to yell at your date or partner, hug him instead. When you want to cling to your partner to feel safe, force yourself to pull back and take some time to yourself. When you want to distance, *move toward him.*
- Acknowledge that at least part of you is scared of falling in love or getting more intimate. Watch out for your own sabotaging and his!
- Pay attention to what you're saying and doing and modify any behavior that can stop the relationship before it starts (or restarts after a temporary break-up).
- Mini-rejections, although not as upsetting as big, dramatic ones, still add up and leave scars that will affect future relationships. Don't stop your relationship before it starts, or before long you'll be stopping the next one, and the next!
- Use positive thinking and *visualize* what you want to achieve in the greatest detail you can imagine.

Intimacy brings your early, unconscious heartaches and fears to the surface because your movements with your partner trigger painful memories of moments with your parents. Your partner is the "bridge back" to your first attachment figures (Mom and Dad). These memories include fears of feeling inadequate or shamed by your parents as well as times when you felt rejected or disappointed by them. Avoiding the fears you both have is like sitting on a ticking time bomb. **Regardless of what your parents did or didn't do, you can rewrite your relationship script and co-star in a fulfilling and loving relationship.** You can also help your partner to do the same thing—even at the outset of a relationship. This is one of the best ways to nurture intimacy.

There's Magic in Touching

There's magic in touching and being present with your partner, but people avoid it because they fear it might be taken away. *Don't avoid it;* touch is essential to connect and develop an intimate partnership. Touch sets off a cascade of hormones, the most important being oxytocin—nicknamed the "cuddle hormone" because you need it for bonding, as explained by Helen Fischer in *Anatomy of Love*. Oxytocin is the hormone released during breast feeding that helps a mother bond to her baby. It increases feelings of love and safety. During power struggles the levels of oxytocin drop precipitously because cuddling and other forms of touch decrease or stop. This begins a vicious cycle; the less touch, the less oxytocin and the less partners feel like being close to each other. To get the oxytocin flowing, use the same types of skills and behaviors as mothers use with infants to nurture the bond they have with one another. These "attachment skills" include holding each other and rocking, gazing into each other's eyes, stroking each other's hair and face. *This type of interaction increases the level of cuddle hormones and consequently increases your desire for greater intimacy.*

Women often complain that their boyfriends or husbands want to have sex, but don't want to cuddle. Cuddling is considered an inappropriate behavior for men in our culture. The obvious and more acceptable alternative is sex! Making love can help your partner to feel comfortable with cuddling, but it takes time and safety for that to happen. Having sex helps it to happen sooner because sexual intimacy releases "vasopressin," the risk-taking hormone.

Smart Heart Attachment Skills to Nurture Intimacy and Increase Oxytocin

- Gaze into each other's eyes.
- Dance close.
- Touch each other's faces, arms, and shoulders.
- Feel each other's warmth and breath.
- Hold and rock each other.
- Say tender words.
- Put your arms around each other's necks.
- Stroke or brush each other's hair.
- Hold hands.
- Melt your hearts.

Dealing with Suffocating Feelings

When you or your partner feel suffocated in the relationship, you will stop the flow toward intimacy, or at least put it on hold. *Feelings of suffocation create an irrational level of fear and anxiety.* Instead of thinking through his emotions, or expressing them, most men abruptly pull back or provoke their partners to pull away. This is a wonderful way to put intimacy to death! Instead of reacting negatively, use Smart Heart Dialogue to talk it out.

Smart Heart Skills for Distancers Who Feel Suffocated

- Announce, "I can't do this, but I can do that."
- Gently announce your need for disconnection. Prepare her for the separation.
- "I want to connect, but I need to go to sleep," or "I need some quiet time."
- Balance *both* of your needs for connection.
- "How about ten minutes now and forty tomorrow," or "I can't now, but I can tomorrow."
- Balance connection and disconnection, announce reconnection.
- Reward and compliment your partner.
- Don't say yes when you mean no, and don't promise what you can't deliver.

Even if you're feeling suffocated, you still need to touch and connect with hugs and affection to minimize anger. Many people have a hard time with this. My patient George had a very hard time treating Vanessa kindly when he felt angry. He had to reverse the flow of his negative feelings by doing something positive. Vanessa had to help him reverse the flow by making it safe for him to give and receive affection, even when he was upset. If you hug your partner and he doesn't respond, don't take it personally, hug him again later or tomorrow anyway. *He can still feel your love, even if he doesn't respond.*

I learned this from my grandmother Sarah, whom I taught to love and hug. She was uncomfortable with displays of affection, so my family members didn't hug her or tell her they loved her. But as a little girl, I wanted to hug her and tell her I loved her, and so I did. She kept her body stiff, her arms straight, and didn't hug me back—but it still felt good to *hug her.* When I told my grandma I loved her she would say, "me too." But over time she began to trust me and feel safe with me. She relaxed a little more when I hugged her and sometimes gave me a quick pat on the back. She was learning how to show her love. Shortly before she died, she even said, "I love you" to me. Her behavior kept all our family members at arm's length, but she didn't scare me. Even as a little girl I knew she was frightened—not cold-hearted. So learn to hug and teach each other to hug back. Learn to say "I love you," and learn to hear it with your heart when your partner says it.

My patients Larry and Marlene were both afraid of rejection and provoked each other to make their prophecies come true. Marlene didn't feel lovable and panicked when Larry went out with friends. She felt abandoned and got angry and mean, which provoked Larry. He was repelled by her when she acted that way, thus reinforcing her belief of being "unloved." Marlene's insecurities began in her childhood but were also triggered by an affair Larry had. They blamed each other and ran away from the intimacy they both wanted.

Marlene and Larry had been married many years, but Larry was still afraid to be hers emotionally. "I don't feel safe," he told Marlene. Marlene had to work on that because in the past she didn't let Larry express his feelings without getting mad at him. She provoked him into distancing and then punished him for it. *They had to make it safe and comfortable to be scared.* They did this by coaching each other.

I told Marlene to put her wall down and announce her fear instead of hurting Larry when she was scared. Her assignment was to enlist Larry's help instead of alienating him or blaming him when she was afraid. I told Larry not to allow Marlene's fears to scare him. He needed to tell her and show her that he wouldn't allow her fear barriers to separate them. Larry was "allergic" to Marlene's upset feelings. He couldn't say no to her because he was afraid to upset her. Larry needed to learn to deal with the upset. People get upset; that's part of love.

Marlene had to accept it when Larry said "no." She had to stop trying to "sell him." When she tried to manipulate him, he stopped communicating with her and checked out. Marlene also had to learn how to control her upsets. "Don't show *your* feelings when Larry is sharing his. It interrupts the flow of his communication and deflects what he's trying to share. **When you try to fuse with a man, and want him to feel the way you do, it stops him from sharing his feelings with you,**" I explained.

Smart Heart Dialogue

Larry: "I'm not going away with you this
            weekend."
Marlene: (mirrors and responds with no judgment
            or interpretation so he can learn it's safe
            to express himself) "I heard you say
            you're not going away with me this
            weekend." ·

This was a new approach for Marlene. In the past, she refused to hear Larry's need for distance. She was learning to chill out and withhold her reaction so Larry could learn to open up and express his needs. Marlene promised, "I will hang in there when I feel like pulling away."

All couples experience each other's fears. Help each other by being willing to "coach" one another using the model dialogue throughout this book to keep each other accountable and stay on track. Coaching does not mean controlling or "talking down" to each other. It is a gentle, loving way to help your partner see his behavior, and for him to help you see yours. **Coaching means making it "safe" for each other so that both of your needs can be met, and it also means taking the initiative to suggest movements that are needed to restore balance in the relationship.** When done with love and with your emotions in check, coaching is the best way to resolve the fears and create the level of intimacy needed for real and lasting love. If you're both willing to "coach" and be coached, you can *both* win.

Smart Heart Guidelines for Intimacy

- Be present and "in the moment" when you're with your partner; don't dwell on the past or worry about the future.
- Learn to make change and the "unknown" your friends.
- Remember that insight isn't enough. *Use action and movement to shift the insight to a tangible opportunity for growth.*
- Give yourself and your date or mate more credit! Don't doubt your ability (or his) to make the relationship work. With the right skills, you can make it work *if you choose to.*
- Face your fear of being hurt to create movement in your partnership.
- "Act as if" all the fears, rejection potential, and "unknowables" are gifts that will help you discover more about yourself and your date or partner— because they are!
- To be safe and sure all the time, you will have to be lonely.

Remember that the things you want most from your partner are the most difficult for him to give. The things he wants most from you are the hardest for you to give. But the growing pains that come from stretching yourself and helping your partner to stretch are well worth the intimacy you can achieve!

part two

Smart Heart Skills
Shake Up to Make Up

"Where love reigns, there is no will to power; and where the will to power is paramount, love is lacking. The one is but the shadow of the other."

                          ⸱ C.G. JUNG

❧ 8 ❧

Why Relationships Stop Before They Start

"Love is letting go of fear."
—GERALD JAMPOLSKY

The majority of relationships (married and single) *stop before they start.* People stop relationships for many reasons but one of the biggest ones is that we're disappointed in our mates when they begin to display some of the very same traits we dislike in our own parents, or in ourselves. **When our real life relationship doesn't live up to our fantasy ideas of what a relationship is "supposed" to be, we mistakenly believe the "love is gone."** Married and single couples emotionally "check out" of the relationship (often resorting to affairs) and singles walk away before the plot thickens.

Another roadblock that we place in a relationship is the belief that it won't or can't work, or that it's too good to be true. Married couples give up on their partners and singles give up before they have a chance to really get going. *We do this because of our early scripts that say we will eventually be abandoned or suffocated.* It's this fear that permeates our hearts and propels us to predict the outcome, or the end, of a relationship before we live out the beginning and the middle. Singles are particularly notorious for this sort of self-fulfilling prophecy, but married couples do it, too, especially when they're having problems.

We're so afraid of breaking up that we stop relationships before they start. Break-ups rule our lives. We fear we will break up, we *actually* break up, or we fear the other person will break up with *us*. *Make Up, Don't Break Up* will teach you how to triumph over the fear of breaking up and stop sabotaging your own efforts.

A relationship can stop before it starts at any point—from the first date (or even before) up until you reach the Real and Lasting Love Stage. If you want your relationship to last, you must make it number one and nurture it. The most amazing stage of a relationship begins when you reach real and lasting love, *but you can't get there if you keep stopping relationships before they start*.

For example, my patients Jerry and Linda have been married for twenty years and have three children. When they met, they fell in love instantly. Linda had an affair because Jerry was a major flirt and when she told him it bothered her, he didn't change his ways. She began to feel invisible and resentful, turned to someone else to give her what she wanted, and wanted to end the marriage. Jerry had always assumed that Linda would "always be there" and he panicked when she said she wanted out. This was a big wake-up call for both of them. Linda's affair had diluted her feelings for Jerry, but I told them if they took their time and didn't push too quickly, they could thaw and restore their feelings for each other.

I explained, **"When you want to disconnect and distance, that's the time to kiss, hug, have sex, nurture, and connect with each other."**

Linda wasn't convinced. "Dr. Weil, if I kiss and hug him, maybe I'll find out that I don't really love him and should leave him."

"That's a way to avoid," I told Linda. It's not supposed to feel comfortable. If it was easy to share and show love and say I love you, it wouldn't be so precious. Don't take it for granted. You need to learn to share and connect and nurture and be nurtured. I told Linda, "You picked the person who is the opposite of you so it would force you to connect, nurture, and be nurtured. Jerry picked you because he is afraid of getting too much nurturing."

After just six weeks of phone therapy, Linda and Jerry decided to make up, instead of break up. Linda learned she had much higher expectations for Jerry as her "attachment figure"—the person we rely on the most, than she did for her temporary lover. She and Jerry recommitted to their marriage and began learning Smart Heart Skills. When Linda was taking care of their young children, Jerry lost her as his "attachment figure." Jerry's feeling of loss propelled his flirting behaviors to a new level because of his insecurities. The more Jerry flirted, the angrier Linda became, because she felt she had lost *her* attachment figure.

Married couples expect even more from each other when they didn't receive enough security and attachment as children from their parents. Because Jerry had to face the fear of losing Linda, he valued her more. He learned he has to stroke her and tell her she's the most beautiful woman in the world, instead of checking out other women and flirting. It was easy for Linda to focus all of her attention on her children because she is an emotional Distancer and Jerry was distancing with his work. Jerry saw Linda as an extension of himself, rather than making her visible. He had to allow her to have rights and feelings. He told Linda, "I need to work hard on taking you seriously."

Linda said, "My father never took me seriously either." Jerry admitted he had never taken his mother seriously.

The little steps Linda and Jerry both took began to make powerful changes in their marriage. I applauded Jerry and told him, "You made her steps possible when you stopped flirting and started telling her how beautiful she is. Now look at what you're getting back!" Jerry beamed! I told him, "You are giving her attention now in the right way for her." Most people like Jerry yearn for love and can't handle getting it.

Meanwhile, Linda, who had always been reserved, was learning to stretch to meet Jerry's needs. Jerry was stretching to understand and meet her needs to be reserved. They were learning to strike a harmonious balance. Linda had to get comfortable with Jerry's physical overtures—even though she claimed she wanted him to be more reserved. "No," I told Linda, "that's not true. You picked Jerry because he *is* so amorous." Linda said she may have unconsciously let Jerry flirt to give herself an out. She agreed it was time for her to start giving Jerry the nurturing and connection he (and she) needed through love-making.

If you want to "talk about the relationship" it means you think there's a problem, or you're trying to jump ahead and predict the outcome, rather than living and experiencing it. Frankly, many relationships that could be strong and exciting get talked to death. I say talk less and enjoy each other more. It's action, not talking about action, that makes a relationship move forward. **There is an effective way to resolve conflicts, fact-find, and learn what you need or want to know, but it requires special dialogue skills—not just dumping all your feelings on your date or partner to "get things off your chest."**

It's ironic that we can accept our friends' flaws and yet are often unwilling to accept the weaknesses of our partner. If we chose friends with the same rigid requirements we expect dates and partners to live up to, we would have very few friendships, if any. Look at your date or spouse through the same eyes you look at your close friends—with understanding, compassion, gratitude for what they bring to the friendship, and acceptance of the traits you may not be so crazy about.

Alexis and Nathaniel are another couple who almost stopped their relationship before it started. When I started counseling them they were working on the imbalance of power in their relationship. Whereas initially Nathaniel was a Pursuer and Alexis was a Distancer, now they were both distancing and the relationship was dying. Alexis picked Nathaniel because he was emotionally distant, but then she became angry with him for it. When he tried to connect with her, she punished him and pushed him away. When he disconnected, she pursued him. She had to work on her own fears, rather than sabotaging the marriage by blaming Nathaniel.

She didn't see him as an equal and didn't respect him. Alexis said, "I don't know if I love him well enough, or if I'm afraid to commit so I blame him, or if it's just not there for me anymore." She didn't want to look too closely at those questions because she was afraid she would want a divorce. She explained, "I don't want to leave, but I don't want the empty marriage my parents had either. I know Nathaniel feels like my mother did sometimes. I felt sorry for my mom when she suffered, why can't I feel for Nathaniel?"

I told Alexis, "It takes courage to love. It's a journey— you've got to stop trying to see the outcome before it happens. *Your partner reflects all of your childhood issues and pains.* Until you resolve and connect those heartaches in your family of origin and forgive your parents and yourself, you will have a hard time opening your heart to Nathaniel— or any man in a relationship."

She said, "I do love you, Nathaniel, but I guess it's been a selfish kind of love. I take responsibility for my nastiness and for trying to control you. I can see I gave you conditional love, and withheld my approval and acceptance of you."

I explained to Alexis that she couldn't really say hello to Nathaniel until she said good-bye to her former boyfriend Michael who hurt her.

She said, "I displace those feelings of rage and anger onto Nathaniel and punish him for what my dad and Michael did and didn't do. I can't stay with Nathaniel if I don't resolve this. I guess I'm ready to do the family of origin work you've been encouraging me to do." Alexis realized she was scared of connection and scared to love. Alexis's fears had led her into the affair she had, which in turn created a big shake up and wake up for Nathaniel, and also for herself.

I explained they needed to change and shift gears on the hills and valleys of love. *"Terror is part of the journey to change and love. It is your crucible. Don't let it stop you."*

Alexis was worried because she didn't feel any passion for Nathaniel. I asked her, "Are you going to let yourself feel passion when you feel guilty? You have to take this in small steps. Don't look ahead or behind, stay in the present moment of action."

Meanwhile, Nathaniel was asking, "Can Alexis ultimately change to meet my needs?" This was a typical flip-flop of roles. When Alexis began to feel some hope, Nathaniel took Alexis's pessimistic role. A couple will always bring the relationship back to the "homeostasis"—or the place where it was before one of them changed. When one partner makes a shift (in this case Alexis), the other partner goes the opposite direction. I said, "What you're doing isn't working. You have to do what works!"

Smart Heart Skills for Nathaniel

- Look at your fear of loss and use it to motivate yourself, not scare you.
- Predict changes before they happen, but don't predict the outcome or future.
- Understand that you can't always come through for each other. Predict this and announce your needs, fears, and anxieties.
- Express yourself clearly.
- Don't see her as Superwoman or project your own rejection on her.

Smart Heart Skills for Alexis

- Reach out verbally and physically when he reveals separation anxiety or if you see it coming.
- Tell him if you can't follow through. Tell him "I'm not there yet," if that's the case. Don't wait until he feels devastated.
- When you can't do something he wants or needs, do something to make up for it; replace it with something. "I can't do this, but I can do that."
- Stretch more if you know it is important to him, instead of saying "take me as I am."

We really need to change all the books that say, "Take me as I am" is the way to a fulfilling relationship. Granted, we don't marry someone to change them, but we all need to learn how to love our partner the way they want to be loved. Pursuers (in this case primarily Nathaniel) give too much. Distancers (Alexis) don't take or give enough.

Dealing with Separation Anxiety

Most Pursuers have separation anxiety and need preparation for disconnections and reconnections. *Distancers must learn to make these moves more gracefully, and by announcing them first!*

Nathaniel's signs of separation anxiety:

- He feels he's not getting enough attention then compounds this feeling by waiting for Alexis to reach out. (But she's waiting for him, as the Pursuer, to reach out.)
- Nathaniel projects his own fear-based perceptions of the relationship, then spooks himself and makes the perceptions happen.
- He provokes rejection by asking for "more" when he knows Alexis is in her "checked-out" mode. He asks for two hugs when she already rejected him before he asked for one. He hugs her twice because he felt her rejection and he responds by smothering her, which causes her to check out further.

If you are experiencing separation anxiety:

- Check in with your partner.
- Fact-find, rather than assume.
- Share your separation anxiety.
- Share your suffocation anxiety.
- Help your partner deal with their feeling that no matter what they do "it's never good enough."
- See your partner's new face and create a new positive outcome.
- *Ask for attachment skills to reverse the physiological discomfort.*

Help the Pursuer to shift his or her physiological discomfort by using "touch" and attachment skills like hugging and gazing into each other's eyes. The tactile contact reverses the flow of separation anxiety and helps the Pursuer feel more comfortable. **Male Pursuers like Nathaniel have the added physiological discomfort of abandonment wounds.**

In a partnership, both people should be coaching each other, which is the opposite of what usually happens. *To coach your partner, you need their advance approval.* Agree ahead of time that if one of you starts reverting back to your old ways, you can tell each other in a loving and supportive manner.

If He Really Cared, He Would . . .

Countless patients say these words to me: "If he really cared, he'd call." "If he valued our marriage, he'd make more time for me." "If he was interested, he would have called me back." "If I meant enough to him, he'd be willing to do what I want."

Many relationships stop before they start because we impose our own belief systems on our dates and partners. We look at their actions or inactions and "decide" what they mean. We make these assumptions without asking in a nondefensive way what is really going on, and we're usually off base or flat-out wrong. Rather than making assumptions, use Smart Heart Skills and Dialogue to determine what is really happening. Here's what you can do:

Fact-Find. Don't mind-read or assume that something is happening or not happening in your relationship. Find out by asking nonthreatening, open-ended questions.

Smart Heart Dialogue

"How would spending next weekend together be for you?"

"I was thinking it would be great to get away for a few days without the kids. How do you feel about that?"

Check Out Assumptions. If your partner isn't reacting in the manner you had hoped, don't assume you know why, ask him without making him feel guilty.

Smart Heart Dialogue

"I thought going to the movies next Friday would be a lot of fun, and it's okay if you don't want to go." (When you validate by saying it's okay if he doesn't want to go, you help him feel you are identifying with his feelings.)

For men, so she's not taken off guard, help her prepare, predict, and plan so she can reconnect and doesn't make other plans. This will also prevent her from rejecting you—which might make you disconnect or make reconnection harder.

Take a Chance. Be willing to take a risk without knowing the outcome. There is no forward movement in a relationship without risks.

Move Things Along. Don't let a relationship stop because you're not willing to be the one to keep it going.

Smart Heart Dialogue

If he says: "I'll call you sometime next week and we'll go out."

Or: "Let's make some time together next week since we've been so busy with work lately."

You Nail it: "I'm free on Thursday night and I heard about this restaurant called DeNunzio's that opened downtown. Is that good for you?"

Don't Wait Until Love Comes to You. Invite it in. Call him if you haven't heard from him.

Desensitize Yourself to Rejection; Expect It and Predict It. See rejection as a bridge to love. It helps you appreciate a great relationship when it comes along. (If I hadn't hit so many potholes on my road to love, I wouldn't appreciate Jeff the way I do now.)

Stop Assuming Your Date or Partner Isn't Interested. Don't read into behavior or try to over-analyze a relationship.

Stop Provoking or Scaring Each Other Because of Your Own Fears! If you're afraid of getting hurt or being suffocated, don't pick a fight or say mean things to slow the relationship down or get the space you want. Learn to share your fears without projecting them onto your partner or punishing your partner for what's going on inside of you.

Smart Heart Dialogue

"I really like you (or love you) but things are going too fast for me right now. I need to slow it down."

"I have fun with you and love spending time with you, but when I get home from work, I really need some 'me' time to relax and unwind."

Whenever you have a conversation that is laced with emotions, the possibility for a confrontation exists, but don't let that stop you from using Smart Heart Dialogue.

Don't Predict the Outcome

How many times have you said, "I knew he wouldn't keep his promise," or "I knew she wasn't right for me." Too many times our fears turn into self-fulfilling prophecies. If you think it's not going to work, how hard are you going to be willing to try? *Relationships stop before they start because we predict a negative outcome and then help to make it come true with thoughts and words like, "Why bother? It's not going to happen anyway."*

No matter how good a relationship is, when a couple hits difficult times, one or both of them is often tempted to give up—allowing negative thoughts and fears to wash away their hopes for the future. *One of them has to show confidence.*

This is what almost happened with my patients Vanessa and George. Vanessa called me for help because George called off their wedding and Vanessa was caught completely off guard. Neither George nor Vanessa had ever been married. They are both Distancers who had been living together for about three months. George called off the wedding because Vanessa wouldn't listen to him when he tried to talk to her about problems in their relationship. "Vanessa was too cocky. She just assumed I would stick around no matter how she treated me. She was sarcastic and didn't respect my feelings." When George told her he was unhappy, she developed "magical thinking" and told herself everything would somehow work out.

Vanessa said George changes like the weather. "When he wants to provoke me so he can get some distance, he shuts down and 'checks out' emotionally and physically instead of telling me he needs some time. He gets abrupt, nasty, and distant." George needed to disconnect from

Vanessa without hurting her so they could reconnect once he'd gotten some space.

I told George and Vanessa it's never too late to change bad habits. In many cases, I would recommend a temporary break-up at this point, but in their case, I felt George would adopt the "out of sight, out of mind" way of thinking to rationalize his fears and create too much distance from Vanessa. Instead I recommended they stay together and work it out using Smart Heart Skills and put the marriage on hold until more issues were resolved.

Vanessa complained that when she tossed out the thread of conversation to connect with George, he didn't respond. "He does not know how and needs encouragement and help. *You have to pick up the thread and gently hand it to him,*" I said.

George was stuck in limbo because he never completed his childhood stage of successfully connecting with or discon-necting from his mother. It was very difficult for him to trust getting close to Vanessa. George was disregarding the loving things Vanessa did for him because he didn't want to need her or feel dependent as he had with his mother. When Vanessa invited George's mother for a weekend visit to connect with her so she could help George to do the same, she felt hurt and angry when he didn't express appreciation. I taught Vanessa to announce it when she needs acknowledgment.

Vanessa and George were in a typical relationship of assuming and mind-reading. They weren't fact-finding and they weren't expressing what they each needed. They were both acting pseudo-independent and trying to keep their fears and needs buried. When I asked George about his reluctance to share his thoughts or the day's events with Vanessa, he asked, "How do I know what to tell her? So many things are going on in my head, how do I know what to share?"

"I'm a Pursuer," I joked with George, "What *don't* we share?" I gave George a suggestion for how to share with Vanessa that my husband Jeff thought of to share with me. During the day, he reads the paper or a magazine and circles articles he thinks I might be interested in. He also leaves little messages on my office answering machine and writes me notes. When we reconnect after work each evening he shares the articles and notes with me. I explained to George that in Jeff's first marriage he and his wife didn't communicate. He is learning how to do that now with me. "You can do it, too, George," I encouraged him.

I told George if he didn't learn to give back to Vanessa, she would turn away. "Commitment has a lot to do with connection. If we can't connect to each other, we can't commit," I said.

I reminded George to use Smart Heart Skills and *physical movements* to connect with Vanessa when he didn't feel comfortable talking. He did his homework, because he said, "I reach out and connect by looking into her eyes, touching her face, emotionally checking in, and hugging her." I acknowledged him for learning so quickly and affirmed that he could learn to share with Vanessa in time, too.

People often think they have only two choices:
1. To stay in a bad relationship.
2. To be alone.

We have many more choices than two! We can choose to learn about each other, really get to know each other's hearts and fears, and have fun in a relationship. Partners can learn how to play together and how to connect, disconnect, and reconnect without hurting each other. You've got to go beyond your comfort zone. Life is about risks and putting yourself into greater levels of closeness and intimacy so you can learn to enjoy the journey.

Don't Sabotage Your Success

Don't sabotage your relationship's success by being afraid of what life will be like if you *do* get what you want. There's a good chance that a part of you feels unworthy of having the love you desire. Rather than stopping a relationship before it starts, take a look at your past. Ask yourself why you believe this. Then look at your reasons objectively so you can see that you DO deserve to have the love you want.

Your dominant fears are probably opposite from one another's, but you can learn to understand and relate to your partner's fears.

Fears of abandonment and suffocation can manifest as fears of:

- Moving too fast or not fast enough.
- Past dramas recurring in present and future relationships.
- Setting ourselves up for disappointment.
- Not meeting our partner's expectations or him not meeting ours.
- Intimacy and exposing our vulnerable hearts.
- Inadequate sexual performance or discomfort with our bodies.
- Taking a risk and making a mistake.
- Not being good enough or not measuring up.
- Increased responsibilities or complications.
- Losing control or independence.
- Heartache and break-ups.

Even if you've been longing for more closeness or greater commitment, when things heat up, you may get scared and pull the reins in on the relationship. When this happens, *share your fear with your partner and if you need some space, announce it and take it*. It's better to have your partner be angry with you for a while for temporarily disconnecting than to sabotage your relationship by acting out your fears, instead of talking them out.

When Jeff and I got engaged, I was thrilled, but then I started to get scared about getting married again. I had to be careful not to sabotage our relationship because of my own fears. Fortunately I understood the root of my abandonment fears and was able to separate them from my love for Jeff so that I could take a risk.

Do You Sabotage Closeness?

- Do you push for closeness at times when you know your partner wants distance?
- Do you give in instead of setting limits and standing your ground?
- Do you react with anger or disappointment when he doesn't "read your mind" and do or say what you were hoping for, but didn't verbalize?
- Do you send him on guilt trips when he needs to disconnect?
- Do you avoid telling him your fears and wounds because you think you will appear "needy"?
- Do you treat him with "reactive distancing" as a way to punish him when you're upset?
- Are you too available at his beck and call?
- Do you enable his selfishness?

- Do you mind-read, make assumptions, or predict negative outcomes without fact-finding?
- Do you "act out" your fears instead of sharing them?

Does Your Partner Sabotage Closeness?

- Does he act mean or irritable, distance from you, or "punish" you after close moments?
- Is he oblivious to, or not able to acknowledge, things that you feel are important?
- Does he withdraw or check out when you tell him you need his help?
- Does he say, "come close, but move away," or "come close, but not too close"?
- Does he provoke you into pursuing him and then complain about feeling smothered?
- Does he hold grudges?
- Does he refuse to take risks?
- Is he "unforgiving"?
- Does he invalidate you or your feelings?
- Does he shrug off your problems instead of empathizing with you?

If you answered yes to more than four items on either list, your closeness is definitely being threatened!

Give Him What He Really Wants

"Do unto others as you would have them do unto you," is sound advice, but it doesn't work in a relationship if you take it too literally. The way you want your partner to treat you is probably *not* the way he wants to be treated, and vice-versa.

The acts of showing love come wrapped in many packages, so it's important to say thank you for all of the things your partner or date does for you. Don't criticize him for what he's doing wrong, praise and acknowledge him for what he's doing right. That's how you encourage him to do more of what you want.

Find out what he wants so you can give it to him (within reason). I'm not suggesting you play the role of love slave, only that you respect him and his wishes. **Don't wait for him to do this; take the initiative and do it first.** It's also up to you to let him know what you would like to have. You can't do this in a blaming way or make him feel guilty or he'll check out. Don't be negative or pushy. You have to be in the moment and ask gently and with an open heart.

Loving each other the way we want and need to be loved is a learning process. We don't come equipped with radar that tells us what to do and how to do it. We learn by opening up and letting each other in with safety. We share our desires and let our partners know it's okay if they don't fulfill them. And we realize that *it is okay!* Truly, we can meet most of our own needs. If your partner isn't meeting your needs, don't assume it's because he doesn't want to or doesn't care enough about you. It's more likely that he doesn't know how, he's afraid to try, he's afraid to get closer to you, or he truly doesn't have a clue what your needs are.

For example, my patient Darla was dating a man named Steve. She was frustrated by the relationship because they had been dating for two years and he never invited her to do anything with his family. Easter was just a few weeks away and she didn't want to spend it alone. I encouraged Darla to invite herself for Easter. "Oh no, Dr. Weil, I could never do that!" she insisted. "If I invite myself he'll think I'm pushy, and besides, if it's not his idea it won't mean anything!"

I told Darla that was simply not true. I said, "I wouldn't have gone on my first vacation with Jeff or gotten married if I stuck to the old rule that says 'women should wait for men to make the first move." I shared with her the time I invited myself to go with Jeff on his vacation. We had been dating about three months when Jeff mentioned he was taking some time off work for a vacation. "That sounds great," I said. "I understand if you want to go alone, so it's okay if you need to, but I was wondering if you wanted company." Jeff said he hadn't thought about it, but yes, he'd like it if we went some-where together. Jeff wanted to go to Cape Cod, but I had spent some time there with my first husband and didn't want to rekindle those bad memories while I was with Jeff. I suggested my good friend Brenda, who was a terrific travel agent, could give us some ideas, and Jeff agreed to look at options. But when I showed him the brochures for the Caribbean Islands, his face turned white. He told me that an "island excursion" sounded like a honeymoon to him. I asked, "What's wrong with a honeymoon?" We opted for the islands and had an unbelievable time together—so magical that we fell in love and go back there for a vacation nearly every year.

Darla agreed to invite herself to Easter and they had a wonderful holiday together. I reminded Darla of her role of Connection Guardian, and asked her to be cautious of letting her own fears stand in the way of her love for Steve, who was just learning how to connect.

I encouraged Darla and Steve to make each other "love lists." Each person lists ten ways they want the other to show them love. They exchanged lists and within days they were both feeling happier, more satisfied, and much more loved. It's best to begin with smaller requests and work your way up as the safety in your relationship increases. For example, two of the list items I gave to my husband early in our relationship were to run a bath for me and lay out my vitamin pills in the morning as he was getting out his own. Although our love list items have gotten bigger since then, he still does these for me because he knows I appreciate it and he's learned to enjoy it. Each morning when I take my vitamins I think of Jeff and smile.

Smart Heart Skills to Keep Your Relationship Moving

- Go with the flow rather than with your preconceived notions.
- Separate what you can give to yourself from what you need from your partner.
- Be consistent. Consistency is necessary for trust to be re-established.
- Say good-bye to old relationships. Loyalty is essential.
- You must set limits with your partner so he knows what you expect and what you won't tolerate.
- Announce the need for connections, disconnections, and reconnections.
- Check in with each other about how you each feel.
- Share feelings and fears to create the relationship glue that cements you together.
- Make sure there is no dismissal of your feelings.
- Be mindful of each other's wounds and what triggers them.
- Avoid abrupt shifting of gears, which causes the feelings of separation, abandonment, and loss, and interferes with attachment skills.
- Coach, and be "coachable."
- Learn not to be selfish (especially if you're a Distancer); give more and get more.

When Jeff and I were dating and one of us got scared, we held hands and talked about it. We stayed connected through our fear instead of letting fear push us apart. It is crucial not to be so in awe of love that you push it away. Fears that aren't addressed cause us to provoke and reject our partner and stop a relationship before it starts. It's easier to judge and blame instead of taking a risk because of our *own* mixed feelings.

Closing the Exits

Once a relationship is underway, make a conscious choice to close the exits. (This is a concept that Dr. Harville Hendrix's research substantiates.) In a courtship, closing the exits means stopping yourself from running or pushing your date away. It means going for it, giving it a real chance, and seeing what develops. **New relationships have no built-in safety, so people worry about being vulnerable and getting hurt.** They don't feel safe sharing their affection because they don't know how or if it will be returned. Closing the exits also means removing obstacles that interfere with your connection with each other.

Since there are so many unknowns in relationships it's hard to see the true potential. When we catch a glimmer of hope for real and lasting love, we often dash it because we can't believe our eyes—or our hearts. Instead of objectively looking at the potential for our relationship, our view is clouded by our past dating history and childhood scripts. We're afraid to hang in there because our vision for the future is based on projections from our past.

In a marriage, closing the exits means committing to hang in there through all the stages ahead, and not let interferences in. During times of trouble when you want to give up, it means agreeing to stay together and trying to work it out for at least six months. Start separating the troubles from the fun. Even when you're not getting along, go out and have fun together. You need to have *more* fun when you're struggling than when you're getting along. Leave your troubles on the doorstep and go out with open minds and open hearts to enjoy each other and remember why you're attracted to each other.

Smart Heart Skills to Remove the Stop Signs

When we're afraid, we post stop signs and build road blocks to prevent moving forward. Unfortunately that's another way to stop relationships before they start.

- Don't predict the outcome, or even think about it, in the beginning or during times of trouble. Stay in the present moment.
- Take another look at your expectations. Chances are, they're still filled with some childhood dreams and fantasies. Don't rule people out just because they don't match your image of "perfection." Look at their strengths rather than their weaknesses.
- Don't buy into the silly myth that men are always supposed to pursue you. If you're single, take a chance and make the first move. If you're married, surprise your husband by taking the initiative to invite him on an outing.
- Accept your leading role as the Connection Guardian and compassionately help your date or partner to connect with you. Reduce your own negativity by eliminating thoughts like "It can't work," or "It won't happen for me," or "It means less *if I do* the connecting"—sexually or otherwise.
- **Acquaint yourself with your partner's fears by learning more about his childhood.** When you can see

your partner as a wounded child, it's easier to handle his ambivalence and anger. Review the developmental charts in Chapter 3 with him and gently suggest he do family of origin work so he can untangle his connection with his family and let you in. For singles, *be confident about the relationship, and let him know it's "okay" if it doesn't work out.* This takes the pressure off and helps him to let down his guard. Be sensitive to his need for independence and keep the connection going.

- Don't push the envelope. Trying to manipulate, force, or guilt a man into closeness is a deadly mistake. This goes for singles and married couples. In courtship, pushing for quick closeness sends a man running, even if he was really interested in you. In a marriage, pushing for closeness when your mate needs space creates anger and bitterness on both sides. Plan fun, activity-oriented dates to reduce his stress and build the closeness. **Keep talks short and light so he can learn to enjoy them.**

- Celebrate your strengths by being the Connection Guardian. When he disconnects, give him some time and then invite or welcome him back for a reconnection. Call your boyfriend or husband at work and tell him you have tickets for a show, or send a funny or warm (but not gushing) card. Be friendly. If you're scared or angry, "act as if" you're not. *Your encouragement and positive vibes will spread and help him feel more confident.* If you act scared or negative, you give him all the reasons he needs to feel guilty or flee.

- Don't take a man's "Come close, but move away" movements personally. Keep the relationship going by pulling back and giving him space before he asks for it or picks a fight to get it.

Handling Rising Expectations

To transcend your old relationship script and handle rising expectations, take an honest look at what you expect from a partner and a relationship. This can be difficult because your emotional instinct is to "defend" your position and expectations as "right" and "fair."

Answer the following questions with complete honesty. There are no "right" or "wrong" answers. Write down your responses to help clarify your current beliefs and expectations. Keep a copy of your responses so you can gauge how your expectations shift and change.

What Expectations Do You Have of Love?
- Will love "just happen" or does it require nurturing and assistance to grow?
- Will love be everything you hope for?
- Will love obliterate your childhood wounds?
- Will you automatically be ready for love when it comes; will you know it's the real thing when you experience it?
- Is there really love at first sight?
- Will love change you?
- Are you afraid of what love may bring? If so, what is your greatest fear?
- Do you believe that love will make you feel safe and secure?
- Do you want love to "complete" you?
- Is unconditional love attainable, or only approachable?

When couples are having difficulty moving a relationship forward it's often because they're holding grudges and getting back into power struggles. My patients Paula and Steven are having this problem. Steven is not willing to meet Paula's requests *unless she can prove to him* why it's important. If he doesn't agree with her, he won't even *try* to meet her needs. If you can **both accept that if one of you thinks there's a problem—there's a problem,** you can work on resolving it instead of getting caught up in who's right and who's wrong.

I told Steven, "You have to validate Paula and do what you can to please her. When you do this, you change the climate of the relationship instead of saying 'That's your problem.' Paula should not have to prove to you that there's a problem. The fact that she feels there is one is reason enough."

Steven is very logical, as are many men, and rather than responding to Paula's emotional needs with attachment skills and by stretching to meet her halfway, he gets caught up in determining and judging whether Paula's concerns are "logical."

Paula is now saying, "I don't care why he does or doesn't do what I want. I'm tired of his reasons and I'm tired of trying to prove that my needs are valid." This is the same thing she did in her family of origin because no one took her seriously.

Paula is also having trouble with sexual intimacy. She doesn't want to have sex with Steven because she doesn't think he values her. Meanwhile, Steven doesn't want to meet Paula's emotional needs because she is not meeting his sexual needs. *I explained that they can get out of this vicious cycle by rewarding instead of punishing each other.* When Steven remembers to validate Paula and is willing to meet her emotional needs, she can reward him by meeting one of his needs and having sex with him. When Paula makes a move and is willing to have sex with Steven, he should reward her by meeting another one of her emotional needs. This give and reward system snowballs and gives you momentum. *Warning!*

Do not do this like a business deal. Do it even if your partner does not!

It's important to make a distinction between initiating sex as a reward from the practice of withholding sex because of grudges, which I never recommend doing. Sex is a form of connection and nurturing and should not be used as a bargaining chip.

Top Reasons Men Resist Meeting Their Partner's Needs
- The more I listen to my wife's needs and try to please her, the more "henpecked" I'll be.
- Why should I? No one's ever done that for me.
- She'll take advantage of me and there will be no end to it. If I give her an inch, she'll take a mile.
- If I do it once, I'll have to do it all the time. If I do what she wants, she'll walk all over me.
- She has to do what I want before I do what she wants.

If you know something is important to your partner, be willing to do it for him, and teach him—without guilt or anger—to be willing to do the same for you. When he understands that by meeting your needs he is also winning, he'll be more willing to listen, validate, and give—then you will be too. When he does meet your needs, reward him and praise him. He needs positive reinforcement to show him that pleasing you is worth his while and you won't take advantage of it. He'll also get his needs met.

How to Keep Your Relationship from Stopping Before It Starts
- Treat your relationship as if it is a rubber band. You want to test it by gently stretching it and letting it spring back. This increases the flexibility and strength.

- Act, don't analyze. You can change your feelings and your partner's by actions, not by words.

- Don't ask for something more than once. If you ask him to take out the garbage and he doesn't do it, do it yourself and don't even mention it. When he realizes you did it, he'll be grateful and probably take it out the next time without being asked. One of my patients' mothers who has been married for fifty-three years to a Distancer says when she wants something she never uses anger, because it doesn't work. Instead, she "cuddles it out of him."

- Even when you're feeling angry, keep the connection by being warm and giving him a hug to reverse the flow of emotions. Then share your feelings.

- Don't talk your relationship to death. Carefully choose the topics you must discuss. Don't get emotional. State your case or question clearly and in a loving manner, acknowledging his discomfort with these talks, and keep it short. Most men can't handle more than ten or fifteen minutes of this sort of conversation at a time because it triggers physiological discomfort reminiscent of "fight or flight caveman days." (When I first met Jeff he could handle only about thirty seconds, but now he's up to eleven minutes! Be patient.)

- You will frequently have to go backward to go forward. Let your date or partner take a few steps back without shaming him. Better yet, take a few steps back when you think he needs some space.

- Most Distancers don't believe they can change, so don't pressure him. If you want him to change, don't bring attention to this directly. You change your own pattern first. *He will automatically shift if the relationship is viable.*

- Don't cling or constantly invade their space with requests like "Come sit next to me."

- Men tend to turn their attention toward objects, movies, sports, and action-oriented activities that don't involve sharing their thoughts and feelings. Help him to strike a balance by validating his interests and sharing in his fun. When you enjoy his idea of fun, he will be more willing to share in your idea of fun.

- Don't send mixed messages. Men don't want to figure out what you're trying to say, or read between the lines of your actions.

- Remember that closeness doesn't "happen naturally." It's built over time on safe and happy moments together. It's a "sometime" thing; that's why it's so precious. Don't stop a relationship by pushing to be close all the time. Appreciate the moments of closeness and learn to like the times you're not close, and don't read anything into them.

- Don't try to "sell" your date or partner on your way of doing things. He will resist and have an excuse for every one of your arguments. Stretch your own comfort zone and learn to love him the way he is. That's the only way you give him the safety to evolve.

- **Relationships either move forward, or they end.** One tiny step forward each few weeks will equal a giant step within months. Learn to be patient but remember there is no relationship without connection, and there is no connection without movement.

- **When your husband or date takes you for granted, don't call him on it.** Without words or explanations, simply fill your appointment book with other priorities and *let him miss you.* That's the best way to help him appreciate you. Let him be the quarterback while you play the position of a "receiver." It's not a lesser position to the quarterback—it's a give-and-take relationship. You both need each other to make a touchdown.

- Don't confuse passion with intimacy. Passion develops fast, then levels off. Physical attraction is the strongest part of passion. Intimacy begins slowly and accelerates with time. Mental and emotional attraction is the strongest part of intimacy.

∼ 9 ∼

Shifting Gears

> *"A marriage is like a long trip in a tiny rowboat;*
> *if one passenger starts to rock the boat, the other*
> *has to steady it; otherwise they will both go to the*
> *bottom together."*
>
> —DAVID REUBEN

Change is the life-blood of a relationship. Without change, a relationship will grind to a halt. It's understandable that we resist and fear change because it's unpredictable and unknown. But predictability becomes boring very quickly and the unknown, while scary, is incredibly exciting!

Although we shy away from relationship changes, unconsciously we seek them. That's one reason so many people have affairs—both in marriage and courtship. They are attempting to create changes and shifts outside of their relationship that they are afraid to create within.

We have the greatest resistance to change when we need it the most! We don't want to go through change because we're afraid. **Use your relationship fears as beacons to direct you back to earlier fears of being rejected or "smothered" by your parents.** It is the imprinted memories of these early upsets that make us fear and avoid change. But once we learn to make smooth changes and transitions, we enjoy change and look forward to it because it creates movement—and without movement relationships stagnate.

If we refuse to change, the relationship eventually dies and we end up changing anyway because of a break-up or divorce.

As a relationship becomes more intimate, expectations are guaranteed to go up, so you need to predict this, prepare for it, and warn your date or partner. Many women make the mistake of remaining silent about their expectations and then become angry when their date or partner doesn't read their mind and do what they are hoping he will do. It's far better to tell your date or partner when your expectations rise. Use the following example below as a guideline for what to say.

Smart Heart Dialogue

"I know I want more from you now than I did before, and I understand if you can't give it to me. I'm just letting you know how I feel so you understand where I'm coming from. If you start to feel pressured, I want you to tell me so I can give you the time or space you need."

In addition to shifting gears through relationship stages, you need to shift gears during day-to-day life. Handling changes in a positive manner nurtures your relationship and gives you the courage to create change when your relationship needs movement.

When you embrace change it's much easier and more fun to stretch to meet each other's needs. **You both have a right to ask for change, and you can't blame your date or partner for something he doesn't know how to do.** You have to be willing to teach and coach each other, but that isn't possible until you both feel safe. In his book *Conceptions of*

Modern Psychiatry, Dr. Sullivan refers to "the quiet miracle of developing the capacity to love." He says, "The first impulse to change comes from being loved." If we feel safe, we can change and move forward toward real and lasting love.

I recommend having a ten-minute weekly dialogue session with your partner to address changes. During these scheduled meetings, you and your date or partner put on emotional bullet-proof vests and talk your way through changes, instead of acting out your fears or frustrations. Balance the negative discussions with positive talks, otherwise you will both begin to associate negative emotions with talking to each other, and you are trying to achieve the opposite! My patients Jimmy and Mary Jo credit their weekly sessions for helping them maintain their connection and stay in love. They meet each Sunday; one week they discuss problems and the following week they discuss positive topics. This is helping Jimmy to enjoy discussions and prevents him from reverting back to his "peace at any price" style of operating. They also put up a chalkboard to give each other positive and negative feedback daily.

Smart Heart Skills for Change Sessions

- Schedule a weekly meeting to discuss changes.
- Put on your bullet-proof vests.
- Assess how many changes are currently happening.
- Share with each other your predictions for changes that are upcoming.
- Discuss whether you were expecting the changes or were surprised by them.
- Tell each other what changes you feel you need right now.
- Validate each other's needs and offer options for how you can each meet them.

- Offer one or two things you are each willing to do to make the changes go more smoothly.
- End each meeting by looking into each other's eyes, thanking each other, and hugging.
- Acknowledge each other daily for the wonderful progress you're each making.
- Coach each other to make sure your weekly sessions happen and you stay on track.
- Use a chalkboard to give feedback, like Jimmy and Mary Jo.

My patient Vanessa said the following about change:
1. It's nice knowing we can change, and it's exciting.
2. It's a relief to know what I need to do, instead of feeling confused or hopeless about a situation.
3. It's reassuring to know that we won't lose our identity by changing, but actually discover another part of ourselves. It's like taking a journey into yourself.
4. It's a chance to learn to trust the parts of yourself that you didn't trust while you were growing up.
5. It's easier than avoiding change or being lonely.

My patients Jerry and Linda were having difficulty shifting gears through the day. I said, "Jerry needs to learn to shift gears from work mode to pleasure mode so he can have fun." Linda said, "When he says he'll go to the movies at noon, he doesn't even start getting ready to go until four, and then he brings his cellular phone along."

I told Jerry he had to stop making Linda wait and taking it for granted that she would wait. "You must keep your dates and appointments and honor the agreed upon times as if Linda is your most important client. *Put her in your appointment book.*"

Smart Heart Mini-Connections

- Connect each morning and *lovingly* disconnect before you go your separate ways.
- Reconnect during the day with a quick phone call. Introduce an interesting topic you'd like your partner to give some thought to during the day. This will give you both something to look forward to discussing when you reconnect.
- Create a Reconnection Ritual, like kissing and hugging each time you reconnect. If you are scheduled to reconnect at a certain time, be punctual. Shift gears from work or other responsibilities to *be present with your partner.*
- Don't discuss heavy topics when your partner first arrives home, during dinner, while relaxing or making love, or before you go to bed. (My grandma Sarah said, "Relax during dinner and nothing heavy.")
- Cuddle and connect before going to sleep each night.
- Announce disconnections and create a ritual for disconnecting.

Critical Times to Watch a Distancer

Distancers resist change and often feel threatened by the fear of change. The following list details some events that are critical times to watch a Distancer.

1   Job change.
2. Engagement.
3. First long weekend together.
4. Vacations.

5. Birth of a child.
6. Death of or divorce of a parent.
7. Meeting or visiting with each other's families (if single).
8. Going to a wedding or christening together (if single).
9. Any situation when the Distancer has to take care of responsibilities the Pursuer generally handles.
10. Discussions of any kind.
11. If you're single, making a joint purchase (it suggests "commitment" and scares a Distancer).
12. Talk of, or actually increasing the intensity of the relationship.
13. Revealing tender feelings of love.
14. Discussions of movies, plays, or other couples that bring up fears or feelings of inadequacy.
15. Talk of, or actually marrying or having children.

Remember, **the key is to shift and change gears, not partners.** If you have trouble getting through a change with your current partner, you will most likely get stuck there again with your next partner. Hang in there and learn to use changes and challenges as your building blocks for a greater commitment and deeper love.

Be prepared for changes in romance and sex and make these changes happen so those "feel-good" hormones can keep flowing on a regular basis. Use mini-crises as well as the big ones to motivate you to shift gears and change. But don't wait for the crises to make you change; do it *before* they erupt. Remember the mountain bike analogy (I shared with my patient Ziegefried) and instead of resisting or fighting the changes, let yourself go a little so you can enjoy the ride!

Making changes is easier than fighting the changes, and shifting gears takes less energy than grinding the gears. When you're standing on ceremony or refusing to make a needed change, ask yourself, "Is this behavior going to get me what I want, or do I need to shift gears to get what I want?" Make a commitment to yourself, and to each other, that you will do whatever it takes to keep the relationship moving.

❧ 10 ❧

Fighting Fair

"It takes two to speak the truth. One to speak and the other to hear."
—HENRY DAVID THOREAU

Rage! Anger! Fury! If they are not acknowledged and expressed, the hurts we feel can become covered over with anger, grudges, and defensiveness—emotional reactions that are damaging to our relationship, our well-being, *and our health.* The way to avoid negative symptoms of our hurt emotions is to express them and resolve our power struggles with our partner using Smart Heart Skills for fair fighting. You have to reach a middle ground where he doesn't stonewall and you don't rant and rave.

The fallacy is that couples who love each other don't argue and fight. The truth is that **fighting fair builds strength and understanding and is one of the most powerful tools in beating the odds.** Polite couples who rarely fight find their relationships crumbling out from underneath them before they even know there's a problem. Months or years of unresolved differences eat away at relationships silently and painfully. **That's why I call politeness in relationships the silent killer.** Stop being so polite and put more passion into your marriage.

People who don't learn how to fight fair harbor resentments. Women begin to feel invisible and become critical and contemptuous. Men withdraw and check out because they feel smothered. *Remember if one person in the relationship thinks there's a problem, there's a problem.* By fighting fair, conflicts that will either explode or drag out for days or even years can be resolved in just a few minutes.

Why Fight Fair?

Conflict is necessary for a healthy relationship. I believe that without fair fighting there can be no romantic love or true intimacy. John Gottman's groundbreaking studies on marital relationships revealed the importance of fighting: ". . . while disagreements and fights are not pleasant, and no couples except the volatile seem to enjoy them, they are necessary in some degree to all good marriages."

Polite marriages are higher in adultery and divorce. His research showed that *". . . it isn't the lack of compatibility that predicts divorce, but the way the couple handle their inevitable incompatibilities . . . the way they resolve conflicts* and the overall quality of their emotional interactions."

Fighting fair is a Smart Heart Skill that can help all couples resolve challenging conflicts. Over the course of your relationship, you will inevitably navigate difficult waters; those of you who learn to problem-solve together will draw strength from one another, which, in turn, will strengthen your bond.

Our emotional health depends on boundaries that are stable, but permeable and flexible. Just as our bodies' many little colds and infections strengthen the immune system, *weathering conflict and fighting fair immunize our relationships against break-ups.*

Fair fighting is your pathway to greater intimacy, more fun, and joy. The daily challenges of your relationship offer myriad sources from which hurt and anger can spring. You need to channel your anger in a safe and healthy way so it doesn't become a destructive force. What distinguishes *Make Up, Don't Break Up* from many other relationship guides is my perspective on handling conflict. Although below-the-belt attacks are destructive, *to stop all fighting is hazardous to your relationship.*

Fighting Unfairly Can Be Hazardous to Your Health

When two people clash—in whatever ways this happens— there's going to be some internal reaction in one or both people, generally anger or rage. If this energy is not released in an equitable way, there can be some serious health consequences.

Numerous studies over the past few years have emphasized the dangers of unresolved anger. In research directed by Murray Mittleman, M.D., hostility—a quickness to anger— was determined to be a contributing factor in aggravating heart disease. Mittleman and his colleagues found that a person's risk of suffering a heart attack was *more than two times as likely if an angry episode preceded it within two hours.*

Cardiologist Meyer Friedman, M.D., a codeveloper of the concept of Type A behavior, and Dr. Carl Thoresen, a psychologist at Stanford University, showed that counseling designed to modify Type A behavior (hurried, controlling, aggressive, and often hostile behavior) could cut the risk of recurrent heart attacks in half. Repressed anger turned inward is also a common cause of chronic depression, and has been linked to increased traffic accidents (road rage), lowered immune functioning, and many other health problems.

Fighting fair is positive because it gives you permission to let the "negative" emotions fly. But fighting fair does more than help you "get anger off your chest" and dump it on someone else. *Anger doesn't solve a problem, it gives you a bigger one.* Venting anger just to get it off your chest leads to distance and emotional divorce.

Anger stems from being hurt, but people tend to gloss over the hurt and focus on the anger. **In fighting fair, you get to the hurt beneath the anger and the love beneath the pain.** Fighting fair creates a sense of safety in us that comes from being validated. We're not asking our partners to agree with us, just to *walk in our shoes* and acknowledge our feelings. Once fighting fair becomes a habit, and you feel safe enough to release all the anger that arises in your relationship, you can keep the love from being buried by "relationship debris."

The Prehistoric Power Struggle

Power struggles are inevitable in relationships; *the way we handle them determines whether our love will grow or wither.* Most men need to learn how to listen without making their partners feel invalidated, disregarded, or invisible. Most women need to learn how to approach their partners who get defensive and feel criticized, controlled, or put down when they're given negative feedback.

But how can men listen when they feel attacked? How can women talk when men get angry, abrupt, or minimize? How can men open up when women shut them up with their hurt or angry reactions? *How can women share their needs when men feel controlled even by the simplest suggestion?* The answer to all of these questions is "fair fighting."

Anger is a reality in human relations. Our impulses to fight, flee, or freeze when in actual or perceived danger were once necessary for our survival as a species. Our prehistoric ancestors felt that surge of adrenaline and took action to protect themselves. The prehistoric male had to be even more alert to external danger than the prehistoric female. He had to quickly sense danger and physiologically respond to it by fighting or fleeing. *These same physiological reactions still happen today, but they don't work very well in modern life and relationships.* That's why when a man feels a conflict is coming on, he will often check out, instead of facing it.

Naturally more at ease when they are stalking their prey, then when their prey is stalking them, men have a very difficult time with women when we pounce on them unexpectedly—and respond to us as if we're those dangerous lions of prehistoric times.

According to Dr. John Gottman, "In modern life, this propensity to higher arousal is not nearly so adaptive; it feels terrible (to a man) and to avoid the acute distress it causes, men are likely simply to shut themselves down, refuse to respond, try, as much as possible, to turn themselves into unfeeling stone." When a man stonewalls, it increases his partner's unpleasant physiological arousal (due to abandonment wound) more than anything else he does, much more than shouting back. *Living with stonewalling and contempt can actually make a woman more susceptible to serious illness.* Gottman and his researchers were able to accurately predict the number of infectious illnesses a woman would have over the next four years simply by counting the number of her husband's facial expressions that indicated his contempt toward her. *Fighting unfairly can make women sick!*

Men don't distance because they don't care. They do it as an automatic survival response. Conflict is much more uncomfortable for them than it is for us and their discomfort lasts much longer. Some men sweat, get dizzy, or feel panicky and short of breath when a conflict reaches a level they cannot tolerate. We have to help them with this if we want to solve relationship problems together. (I finally understand why Jeff walks out of the room and can handle only ten minutes of a discussion at a time. We jokingly call these brief discussions "quickies.") Retreating is a form of protection. Disconnecting and withdrawing is a common way of self-soothing; some men retreat into the TV or sports page, others into their work or, disastrously, into extramarital relationships.

When Jeff and I discussed this concept, he said, "Since you understand this, then you accept it if I need to walk out on a fight." No, I said. *This understanding isn't meant to be used as an excuse or a cop-out.* We still have to learn to increase the safety level in the fair fight. We don't use the insight to justify behavior, *we use the insight to shift the physiological responses so men become able to stay and finish the fair fight, and feel better afterward with our help.* We also use the insight to *keep our own emotionality in check.* Ranting and raving don't solve problems, they make them worse, so we need to learn how to calm ourselves and state our needs and desires in an honest, yet sensitive manner. We also need to shorten the length and intensity of our discussion and fair fights. *We're not letting men off the hook, we're learning how to meet each other in a safe middle ground.* When men flee from a conflict, or after one, they are doing the opposite of what their body and mind really need—which is closeness and comfort.

Use Attachment Skills During a Fair Fight

Because of the physiological discomfort that men feel when confronted by a conflict, or during stressful conversations and fair fights, it's *critical* to help them through this by using attachment skills. We must use a physical approach to *reverse the flow of* emotions and soothe the physiological discomfort. **Kiss and hug before, during, and after a fair fight. Stress causes hormonal changes that require more attachment skills.** That's why women want *emotional* reconnection and men want *physical* reconnection after a fight. Learning how to soothe your partner by surprising him with affection after a fight gives him the perfect chance to ease and heal his discomfort with you, instead of looking for relief or what I call "self-medication," elsewhere.

After Jeff and I had been dating exclusively for a period of time, we began having marathon fights over commitment. It was during this time that Jeff went out with another woman and we almost broke up. He had begun to experience extreme physiological discomfort and didn't know what to do to make it better. We have since learned that the way to reverse these feelings of sickness, nausea, and feeling overwhelmed is to use physical affection. Jeff intuitively knew we should hug after our fights to reconnect and soothe each other so he wouldn't have to run out of the room, like my father used to do. *Some of my male patients tell me they feel sick for two or three days after they've had a fight.*

I believe most men (70 percent) have affairs because they can't handle the physiological discomfort from conflict in their relationship. When my father "ran" to other women for love and comfort and touch, he was looking for relief from the physiological discomfort of the conflicts and confrontations that he and my mother did not know how to resolve. He said, "the women were like drugs. I felt I needed them—like an addict needs a drug."

Men need touch and attachment skills, which are physical and emotional bonding behaviors like hugging, holding, gazing into each other's eyes, sex, and high-energy play, to release the endorphins that counteract their discomfort.

Physical play and closeness also releases oxytocin, the "cuddle hormone." When oxytocin is flowing freely, men feel better and don't need to seek solace from other women, or use alcohol, drugs, or other self-destructive methods to soothe themselves. Sex also releases vasopressin, the risk-taking hormone, which helps men to regain their emotional balance and sense of control and safety.

When my father and many of my patients sought out affairs, they were looking for a way to *balance their hormones and "self-medicate."* **However, most men end up going back to their wives because when their mistresses begin to "expect" things from them, a new power struggle begins. Once again, the physiological discomfort is triggered and sends the man running.**

Obviously this "distancing" response in men creates extreme physiological discomfort for the woman because of her early rejection and abandonment wounds. In time, this destructive pattern leads to breaking up, instead of making up. I believe adultery is a by-product of hormonal changes from the physiological discomfort of conflict, which is made stronger when women don't know how to reconnect with safety and soothing to bring men back. Don't give him the need to seek comfort elsewhere. Give him the attachment skills he needs before he leaves.

Most men are stuck in the "separate and return" stage of childhood development because of the guilt they felt when they separated from their mothers (see Chapter 3). If their mothers were ambivalent or hurt when they pulled away, they *did not receive a warm welcome* when they returned. Their guilt transfers onto us when men disconnect after a fight. Many men have trouble reconnecting because they fear they are facing more discomfort. It triggers their terror and when women misunderstand this and get angry, we *make it* *worse.* **It's no wonder that men hate discussions and say yes when they mean no; they are trying to avoid physiological pain.** It's up to us to change this pattern, by showing them they *can* leave (without cheating) and return to our open and welcoming arms. There is something to be said about making up by **making love.** We can learn something from men because this physical encounter soothes both of our fears and discomforts.

Remember that when men distance, *they are not trying to punish us,* they are hurting emotionally and physiologically. They are seeking to heal a wound and soothe the stress that goes along with it. What's so fantastic about having this new information on the physiological component of anger is that it helps us prepare ourselves and anticipate so we don't take it personally when our men distance, retreat, or get angry because they can't fix it or solve it. Since *healing a physiological wound requires a physiological solution,* instead of getting angry, touch! Kiss, hug, cuddle, massage each other, and have high-energy play together. Then say, "Now that you feel better, let's come up with a solution."

Share Your Scripts

To help avoid a fight and to ensure clear communication in a fair fight, you must announce your "script" so your partner isn't surprised and understands exactly what you want and are asking from him or her. When I say that everyone has a "script," I mean that everyone has different thoughts, beliefs, and feelings concerning how they want things to go, and think they should go. No one's script is the same, but often in relationships we get angry at our partner for having a *different* script. We don't share our scripts because we think our partner already knows what we want, we fear the repercussions of asking for what we want, or we assume that we won't get it anyway, so why bother. *What makes this even more complicated is that in addition to your own script, you also have a script of what you think your partner's script is.* This leads to assumptions, which can eventually create conflicts or grudge-holding. **A very important part of learning how to solve problems, get your needs met, compromise, and fight fair is for partners to share their individual scripts with each other—and also to share their scripts of each other's scripts.**

For example, when I was writing this book, I often asked my husband Jeff to read chapters and give me feedback. I didn't just hand him the chapter and ask, "What do you think?" I gave him my script when I asked him to read a chapter so he knew what type of feedback I was seeking. I might say, "I'd like you to read this and tell me only the good comments for now." I would tell him, "I'm looking for strokes and I feel vulnerable about any other feedback right now." I also asked him how he felt about my script and whether he was able to respond in the manner I was requesting. This is a form of the Three P's: preparing, predicting, and preventing. You set the stage to ensure that you resolve something together. It really works!

I knew he often had constructive criticism to offer me and I would ask him to please wait until the following day to give me this sort of feedback. Jeff would ask permission to share ideas and suggestions with me *before* he told me, and if I was not ready to hear this feedback, I would tell him when I would be ready. I also acknowledged Jeff for being willing to follow my script even when it was hard for him, since it's not *his* script, and I thanked him. **Sharing your script with your partner is one of the best and easiest ways to let each other know what you need to be loved the way you need to be loved!**

You have to tell your partner, "I'm going to make it *safe* for you to tell me what you're thinking and feeling." You also have to agree to hear each other's words "safely" *without getting angry or hurt by each other's scripts.* Jeff says, "Give me your script." **To ensure that we don't get hurt, we use attachment skills before, during, and after we share our scripts, instead of disconnecting from each other and trying to find comfort outside of our relationship.**

Think of it as if you are both actors in a play. If you know only your own script and you don't know each other's, the play would be chaos and pandemonium, rather than an organized and harmonious flow of actions between each other. Role-play your script to your partner and then ask him to role-play his script for you. We don't give out our "scripts" because we're afraid of disconnection, but that leads to more disconnection.

Challenges for Men and Women in Fair Fighting

The advice in this chapter applies equally to men and women, yet each sex has its own special set of needs. Men may have had more "permission" to fight when they were boys, but the practice didn't necessarily give them tools to fight fair in marriage and other relationships.

Men have to learn to listen, validate, and take women seriously. Dr. Howard Markman, a psychologist at the University of Denver, echoed my own observations when he said, "Men have more trouble expressing and hearing negative emotions, and are more reactive to them. But our *studies show that the critical skill in making up, not breaking up, is being able to listen to a wife's concerns and complaints about the relationship.*" We're in a double-bind here.

Overcoming this "allergy" to women's emotionality—as Dr. Thomas Fogarty described it—is a skill that can be learned. Men—especially those of you who are Distancers—as you learn your partners' scripts, depersonalize your partner's frustrations, listen, and validate, your partners' needs will seem less overwhelming, and your own need for space will be less of an issue.

Women—as the Connection Guardian, you need to be strong enough to weather the inevitable storms and struggles, *and re-establish connection after each disconnection.* Your partner will feel safer, more relaxed, and more passionate with you and you will feel more at ease and sure of the relationship.

Both men and women need to change the ways they respond in a fight, and both need to help the other break unhealthy patterns before they destroy the relationship. In my sessions with couples I teach them how to coach each other and be coachable. Couples therapy is successful only if you can take your new-found knowledge and apply it regularly at home *without a therapist.* I tell my patients I want them to get rid of me as soon as possible and I teach them how to do it without me.

Jeff and I take golf and tennis lessons together so we can coach each other to improve our game and strengthen our skills away from our teacher. *Coaching is my term for the way you will assist each other—respectfully, patiently, with permission, and without judgment—reminding one another of your goals and dreams, keeping each other on track with the changes you want to make, and helping one another* to *announce it and reconnect after each disconnection.* It takes two to tangle, but it takes only one to begin the process of untangling. If you begin to fight the old way again, remind each other and start over the right way, with permission.

You also have to help a man with the guilt he feels when he flees after a fight. *He gets angry when he feels guilty.* The key is to surprise him **with the unexpected by giving him attachment skills to alleviate the guilt.** Hug him to show him the fight is over (or put on hold) and welcome him back for a fun reconnection. *If you are angry with him when he disconnects, he will be afraid to come back or be defensive when he returns.* Unexpected actions create passion and excitement and release your powerful hormones. They also help both of you to avoid affairs.

Here are some key ground rules that form the basis for fighting fair.

Smart Heart Ground Rules for Fighting Fair

- Don't criticize or blame; suggest instead. Ask and give permission to do so.
- No sarcasm, abruptness, or negative tones.
- Say what you mean and validate what you hear.
- One issue at a time. Don't throw everything in at once.
- Don't play therapist—coaching is different.
- Fact-find. No mind-reading unless you ask permission.
- Take responsibility for your part; no excuses.
- Say whatever you need to say once.
- Respect, hug, show affection; use attachment skills, and give compliments.
- Men, don't run away. During a fight, if you feel you need a break, ask for a time-out. Don't leave the room without an announcement for disconnection!!! (And reconnect without her begging within twenty-four hours.) Use exercise or attachment skills to release your discomfort.

- Women, if he leaves the room during a fight, don't follow him. Give him time to cool down!
- Women, **limit the intensity and frequency of fights.** Don't resume the fight until the appointed time—have fun and play during your reconnection.

How to Fight Fair

Only one person talks at a time. The one who has a frustration to work through speaks first. The other partner listens for the content of the message being communicated and blocks all his own thoughts out. The listening partner *simply holds a safe space* for the upset partner to say it all, and offers encouraging phrases such as "tell me more about that" or "is there more?"

One of the key skills in fighting fair, and communicating in general, is to learn how to "check in" with your partner. The purpose of checking in is to find out what your partner needs to feel loved, rather than relying on the assumed script you have for him. While checking in sounds simple, most couples have difficulty with this step. They complain that when one of them checks in, the other doesn't respond or doesn't share his or her script in its entirety. For this reason, particularly when dealing with a Distancer, you need to check in *three times*.

Check in with your partner (especially if he's a Distancer) three times because:

- He may give you a "polite" rather than accurate response.
- He may simply say what he thinks you want to hear to keep the peace.

- He may be trying to "be more flexible" even though he's not feeling that way.
- He may not know how he feels. Remember that Distancers *have a delayed reaction.* Give him a chance to think about what you've asked, and then ask him again. After his second response, **ask him to visualize what he has just shared,** asked for, or promised so he has a very clear picture. **Then ask him if he is "certain" this is what he wants.**

Fighting fair is about committing to a new way to feel safe to communicate and to validate. **A core skill is announcing to each other, directly, honestly, and respectfully, your scripts and your changing needs and requirements for closeness and space.** You agree to listen without debating, shaming, distorting, defending, criticizing, or trying to "fix the problem." In order to do this, practice using the *visualization of placing a big, clear bubble around yourself.* Actually see it in your mind. This is to remind yourself that you and your partner are two **individuals with separate boundaries and different scripts.** (Couples often "prick" each other when they believe they should both have the same script, such as wanting the same things or sharing opinions.) You also visualize putting **on an invisible bullet-proof vest.** This step is to remind yourself *that "bullets" and "verbal darts" spoken by your partner cannot penetrate you.* You practice feeling safe from his words, listening to the content but not feeling emotional in response. I added the visual technique of putting on big, invisible, **very soft and fluffy gloves so that you would both remember to "cushion your words,"** rather than just blurting out whatever comes to mind. All of these visualizations will help you to learn and reinforce the fighting fair skills.

The goal is to get the anger out, get to the hurt and emptiness beneath the anger, and have these feelings validated without hurting or alienating your partner so you can find a resolution. All fair fights start with validation. This ensures that you empathize with each other and fosters closure and connection. Simply validating each other's experience—walking in each other's shoes—and acknowledging that it "makes sense" can bring about a whole new way of relating. When I say "walk in each other's shoes," I mean that you must make a true effort to imagine what your partner is feeling—from his or her perspective—without letting your own defensiveness get in the way. The expression "walk in his shoes" is akin to a Native American prayer that says you should "Walk a Moon [a month] in someone's moccasins before you judge him." The more couples walk in each other's shoes, the more they understand each other and the easier it is to validate each other.

Smart Heart Steps to Fighting Fair

Initially, you need to practice these skills with small and less volatile issues to get the hang of them. Think of it as "on-the-relationship training."

- Ask permission; set a time-limited (ten minutes to start), mutually agreeable appointment and keep it.
- Enclose yourselves in your bubbles and put on your bullet-proof vests and fluffy boxing gloves.
- Raise your right hands and pledge: "I will make it safe for you and I will not be hurt by your script, words, or emotions."
- Block out your own thoughts and feelings and listen to your partner.
- Don't say "What about me?"

- Echo what your partner said back to him or her to make sure you understood. (These simple skills can eliminate countless misunderstandings.)

- Walk in your partner's shoes. Make him or her feel safe—no criticism or zingers.

- Stretch! Go beyond your comfort zone. Agree to give your partner three changes in behavior that are not easy for you.

- Do not "give to get." Do not ask your partner to make any changes when it's your turn to offer your own.

- When your partner relates an experience with a particularly charged emotion, ask when she or he felt this way before, such as from childhood or with an ex-spouse **(do not throw this vulnerability up later in the dialogue or at any time).**

- Before, during, and after each fair fight, give each other attachment skills such as hugging, kissing, stroking each other's hair, and gazing into each other's eyes. Also engage in "high-energy play" like pillow fighting (à la Dr. Hendrix), wrestling, exercising together, or having sex to create endorphins and reverse the flow of negative emotions.

Questions and Answers on Fighting Fair

1. *What's the best way to ask permission?* Start by saying, "May I have an appointment to have a 'smart heart-to-heart' with you?" This simple request can make a big difference in the way either of you responds to a forthcoming expression of frustration, angry outburst, or touchy discussion. Asking for permission makes your partner feel safe and prepares you both. If one of you forgets to ask for permission, remind each other to do so.

2. *Why is it so important to set a time limit?* Keeping it time-limited gives you both a sense of comfort. It is particularly helpful for men since they are allergic to women's emotions and can only physiologically handle conflict in small doses.

3. *When is the best time to have a fair fight?* When you and your partner are emotionally and physically ready. **If you are recovering from an affair or crisis the appointment should be set as soon as possible—immediately, if time permits.** *Get back to each other within twenty-four hours of asking if you can't do it immediately. It's important for men to be coached with this, because they will often forget.* (Don't ever fight when when one or both of you have been drinking alcohol!)

4. *Why should I block out my own thoughts and emotions when my partner is talking?* It will be easier to hear the content of your partner's message, and keep you from making your own interpretations and being defensive. Otherwise there can be no resolution and you will stay in the power struggle and not reach real and lasting love.

5. *Why must I walk in my partner's shoes?* In order to make up, not break up, partners must validate each other. You can disagree, but you must respect each other's opinions. Empathy is a prerequisite for intimacy. It is one of the hardest things for many men to learn, since they are prone to being rational and logical.

    Sometimes my husband is impatient because he thinks I should know something is logical, or he gets angry when he thinks he knows why I'm upset and is frustrated because he feels helpless that he can't fix it.

(That's his script.) I say, "Just validate and walk in my shoes" (that's my script), and I give him the details.

6. *How can I keep myself from becoming defensive and closing off?* Enclose yourself in your "protective" bubble and put on your bullet-proof vest (perfect for stopping verbal darts!) as a reminder that *no one's words can hurt you unless you allow it to happen.* Becoming defensive closes off your heart and mind to creative solutions and resolutions. Defensiveness prevents you from making a change, and without making the changes that are necessary for the relationship to grow, it will be more likely to break up. *The relationship has to change as the people in it change.*

7. *Why do I have to give my partner three changes that are not easy for me?* Remember that you pick a partner who will give you the most trouble. Mother Nature wants *you* to change for the better; it is a gift to your partner and to yourself. Recall how you've felt when your partner has honored one of your suggestions for a change on his or her part, whether it was to do something in a different way or to stop an annoying habit. Chances are you felt heard, respected, and loved. Making requested or desired changes shifts the climate of the relationship, and creates a win-win relationship. **(Often the changes our partner wants us to make are the same ones we need to make for ourselves!)**

8. *How do I know which are the three most important changes to make?* Ask your partner to write a list of his or her top three criticisms of you pertaining to the issue you are fighting fairly about. Then, work with your partner to identify the specific change on

your part that will handle that conflict. This is ideally a reciprocal process. The two of you can make your lists and change agendas together. Here are two examples:

> My partner's frustration with me: Not letting him know when I'll be late.
> One change that would please my partner: I will call ahead if I know I'll be late.

> My partner's frustration with me: Interrupting and finishing his (or her) sentences for him (fusion).
> One change that would please my partner: I will let my partner finish expressing his thoughts before responding. If I forget, he'll coach me and I'll be coachable.

All fighting is really a roundabout way of getting our earlier needs met and our frustrations resolved.

Smart Heart Skills That Make Fighting Fair Work

- Appreciate change.
- Coach each other and reward each other for changes that are sustained.
- Take time-outs when either of you begins to feel overwhelmed, emotionally flooded, or overloaded with information. Time-outs are not punishments! Use them to regroup and appreciate each other.
- Do not minimize or "but" your partner's feelings. Minimizing and saying "but" are forms of invalidation.

- Accentuate the positive; think positive thoughts about your partner three times daily, especially after a fight.
- Make specific complaints in a positive way (women especially). Do not attack. Ask permission to give a criticism and validate your partner before you state the complaint.
- Stay focused on the topic and coach your partner to do so if he or she strays.
- Soothe your partner. If your partner is upset, don't say how upset *you* are.
- Use humor and affection.
- Don't compete or counter-attack, just walk in your partner's shoes—you will get your turn, but wait for at least one hour (preferably one day) so it's not seen as a contest but rather listening to your partner without just waiting your turn.
- Don't shake your head "no" or smile or laugh inappropriately while your partner is talking; do not call him or her a liar or roll your eyes. That's invalidation.
- **Don't worry if the new way of communicating feels mechanical or artificial;** it will for a while. Resist the temptation to recreate the old homeostasis and go back to your old and ineffective ways of fighting.

Even after my patients Vanessa and George had been in therapy for some time, they still had trouble communicating and bridging reconnections after their disconnections. Both are Distancers who take turns rejecting, pulling away, and then reaching out again. Each expected the other to be the one to reach out and became furious when this didn't happen.

Their assignment: **Don't punish your partner for not knowing how to connect, disconnect, and reconnect.** And don't think of it as being rejected. We need to have realistic expectations and remember there's a *learning curve*. You will both learn in time if you have the desire and use the skills.

But George was angry about having to change "for the sake of the relationship." He wanted to put the burden on Vanessa because, for him, change represented his mother saying "You have to do this!" He wasn't comfortable with being accountable. "Life is more complicated with a partner who is conscious," he said. (Funny, these were my husband Jeff's words to me exactly. It's no coincidence that Jeff ended up marrying a therapist after a first marriage in which there was no communication!) When George verbally attacked Vanessa or told her to "shut up," she went straight for his jugular.

Vanessa felt unlovable and didn't know if George would hang in with her if she made mistakes. She was afraid to bring up difficult issues and wanted to learn how to get George to take her seriously. After their temporary break-up, Vanessa and George switched roles; a typical response to bring the relationship back to homeostasis. I taught Vanessa to reward George when he remembered to initiate a conversation with her, checked in, or expressed concern. I told George, "Unless you learn how to announce your disconnections, reconnect, and acknowledge Vanessa's needs for announcements, you'll be living alone."

George is learning he can get more space for himself and can disconnect when he needs to if he controls the movements by announcing his needs for closeness and for space.

Both Vanessa and George are very sensitive and easily hurt by each other. I gave them each a game plan to follow to help them resolve conflicts with less pain. In addition to their individual instructions, I also gave them my special instructions for the *very sensitive*. Learn how to do it by seeing what I shared with them.

Vanessa's Game Plan

- Announce your trigger—a sensitivity from a wound that happened before you met George. Give George permission to coach you. See it as giving you some relief finally, not more pressure.
- Let him know you can see he is changing, and reward him for it.
- Trust yourself; if you think there's a problem, there's a problem.
- Ask permission to mind-read and fact-find. Unless you're a therapist (or a psychic), you have to ask permission.
- Take the risk of bringing up difficult topics and be willing to speak your mind without censoring—if it's safe and *only* if your partner makes it safe.
- Receive each communication as a *gift,* not as a criticism to be taken personally.
- Appreciate George and feel gratitude for him and the relationship rather than taking him for granted.
- Approach learning about George as an exploration and as an adventure—like taking a journey to another country.
- Keep embracing and liberating the positive parts of yourself and stepping away from the negative.
- Appreciate your ability to change.

George's Game Plan

- Give Vanessa instructions and information, instead of trying to control her with hostility or rage.
- Shift gears to problem-solve, compromise, give, and walk in her shoes.
- Continue to work on avoiding laying blame or dumping your anger.

- Make it safe for Vanessa to express her feelings, anger, and a differing opinion.
- **Be mindful of your tone of voice.** Practice speaking nicely and with respect.
- Watch for your tendency to become reactive.
- *Don't punish or use Vanessa's wounds against her.*
- Listen to the content of the message, don't get lost in its form.

For the Very Sensitive
(like Vanessa and George, who have deeper childhood wounds and whose sensitivity makes them defensive)

- Make specific complaints in a positive way, even when your partner has his or her vest on.
- Disconnect in loving, supportive ways.
- Announce when you're going to be giving and connecting, and when you are going to be disconnecting.
- Give a time for reconnection.

Fighting fair has helped Vanessa to channel her angry energy more positively and helped Vanessa's illness to go into remission. It's helped George to feel more comfortable and safe because he knows Vanessa is not going to suddenly lash out at him or catch him off guard. Both partners are feeling safer, more lovable, and more passionate toward each other.

Ultimately, fighting fair is about making a commitment to your relationship, yourself, *and your physical and mental well-being.* To intentionally engage in a process of helping one another discharge anger and rage in order to get to the hurt hidden **beneath them is an act of love and devotion.** You will be creating a safe space for healing, and letting each other know you will both be heard and validated without feeling inadequate, judged, or shamed.

Fighting fair gets the energy moving in your relationship, ending the politeness and avoidance of difficult issues that damage and inevitably end many relationships. When partners commit to this new way of resolving conflict—or even use the process to discuss "touchy" topics—they are telling each other, "I love you and I am in this relationship with you for the long haul. Your needs and desires matter to me. I want you to feel safe, loved, nurtured, and heard by me unconditionally." This is a powerful message.

～ 11 ～

Reconnecting with Your Family: Going Home Again

"To love is to return to a home we never left to remember who we are."

—SAM KEEN

Understanding and forgiving your parents is essential to finding and keeping love in your life. You *can* go home again. In fact, you *must,* if you are going to love fully—with all your mind, heart, body, and soul.

Going home again means taking *one* step back into your family of origin so you can take *two* steps forward in your adult relationships. **It's the key to getting past the third date, creating intimacy, making commitments, and sustaining love.** Doing family of origin work is very valuable throughout your adult life, **but it is imperative during the break-up stage and the make-up stage of a relationship.**

In order to be in an intimate relationship without excessive distancing or pursuing, you need to have a one-on-one relationship with each of your parents separately.

You may have a great relationship with one of them, but people rarely have the same level of closeness with *both* of them. If you're reading this and thinking, "My parents are impossible to get close to; they hurt me; I don't want to go back home; they'll never work on this with me; it's probably not worth it; or, it won't work," you are just afraid and trying to avoid it.

Don't let the pessimistic side (the wounded parts of you) make this decision. *The more you don't want to do it, the more you need to do it.* It takes courage, but it's easier than ending up alone. When we stop blaming our parents for their shortcomings and take responsibility for how we also *may have hurt them,* based on their wounds, we can open up our hearts to them, and therefore to our partner. (This is particularly true for a Pursuer who wants to open his or her heart to a Distancer.) **We pick a partner who is most similar to the parent we were most distant from as children.** If our adult relationship style is to Pursue, we pick a partner who is most like our Distancing parent—usually our father. Distancers pick partners who are most like their Pursuing parent—usually their mother.

The disconnection with your parents keeps you distant from your partner or potential partner. **For singles, if you're cut off from your family of origin, you will be cut off from the person you're trying to form a relationship with and will have a difficult time getting past the third date or getting committed. For married couples, you will not be able to reach real and lasting love without completing your early stages of development.**

There's a big difference between *disconnecting* with your parents so you can reconnect, and cutting them off. Do not cut them off. Cutting off your parents is like cutting out a piece of your own heart in an attempt to punish them.

When you "go home again" to connect with your parents they can take you through the parts of your **developmental stages that you missed. Not only that, but you can take them through the childhood development stages they missed!** You are healing them, as they are healing you. By looking at the developmental stages charts in Chapter 3, you can determine where you, your parents, and your mate got stuck, so you can do something about it. Going home is akin to throwing a pebble into your family pond. You begin with one parent, but the ripples of love and connection spread throughout the entire family and beyond into all of your relationships and your family members' relationships. That's what makes family therapy so incredibly powerful.

The Rewards of Going Home Again

Connecting with your parents not only heals your heart; it also heals your mind, body, and soul. *Many experts agree that our emotional pains show up in our minds and bodies and cause sickness and disease.* That can be avoided if you are willing to heal those pains. To think of yourself as an isolated "I" stops you from reaching out for your families who can help you by connecting and strengthening the "we" of your family.

Paul Pearsall, Ph.D., in his book *Making Miracles* states, "I promise you that at times of severe crisis (such as terminal illness), when you need a miracle the most, the fact of your oneness with the universe will be driven home with force. You will feel the power of prayer even if those persons praying for you are miles away. You will feel the need for the loving care of others, and you will sense, as I did, that when you are most afraid, your inner need for connection with others is the strongest."

Pearsall also says, "The path to miracles is made by being open to our oneness (with our loved ones, family members, and the universe) even when we feel the most isolated and confused."

One of the most striking examples of how connecting to your family can create healing is the story of a man named Tim. When Tim became my patient he was on a variety of prescription drugs for psychosis following a series of nervous breakdowns. He was almost completely dysfunctional. He could barely speak, couldn't read or write (although he was somewhat of a scholar before the breakdown), and was on the verge of giving up entirely. His behaviors were like those of a three-year-old; his means of communicating was drawing pictures.

I knew his emotional pain started in his early childhood and I asked his wife to tell me about his parents. Tim was completely cut off from his parents and his siblings whom he loved and missed. He felt alone in the world and didn't think connecting with his family would help. But I knew differently and I was committed to helping Tim through his difficulties. I flew his family members in to New York from all over the country. We sat together in my office and I helped them to heal their wounds and create a strong connection based on respect, caring, and love.

Within weeks Tim was off his medication and shortly thereafter his reading and writing skills returned. He made a complete recovery, decided to move to be closer to his parents and rejoin the family business. He has been off medication now for several years and he is still happily married. If Tim had not connected with his family, I really believe his physical and mental health would have continued to deteriorate and that he might not even be alive today. He agrees with me and each year sends me a wonderful card and photos to show me how well he and his family are doing.

Doing family of origin work is essential because you really can't develop an intimate or more intimate relationship with your partner until you have healed the buried wounds that still run your life. **In addition, you can help your parents to heal, which will help your relationship with them and the relationship between your parents!** After my mom and I bridged a stronger connection and learned to love *each other as we each needed to be loved,* she told me I healed her wounds. My mother felt invisible and needed my love and understanding. She said, "You helped me to heal my own childhood wounds and you also healed the wounds I felt from you when you hurt me."

Going Back Home Can Help You Get Past the Third Date

Relationships start with hello! *But the script for your relationship was written long ago.* In fact, the script you follow in relationships is the same one you drafted before you reached the ripe old age of seven. Your fears of being abandoned or rejected and conversely, the fears of being suffocated or smothered are written in these yellowing pages of your early life. Your relationships and marriage can help you to review these old scripts, so you can rewrite them in a way that works! *The wonderful part is that you and your partner can do this together.* In doing so you create the power and magic that transforms relationships into real life love.

My patient Karen had a pattern of being attracted to very elusive men and extreme Distancers. That relationship script was written when she was a child because she had no emotional connection with her father. She thought it was better for a man to reject her right away, than to wait until they were emotionally intimate. She created pseudo-intimacy, instead of the real thing because that was less frightening for her.

In Karen's eyes, her father never valued her, and consequently she didn't value herself. I encouraged Karen to connect with her father so she could connect to other men, particularly a man named Jason whom she had recently started dating. He was afraid of intimacy and closeness and one night after intense lovemaking, he said, "I'm falling for you and I'm scared." Karen and Jason broke up three times because of Jason's fear. Each time I urged Karen to connect with her father, but when she pulled back from Jason she was in so much pain and emptiness, instead of connecting back home with her father and mother, she moved toward *him*. **She dealt with her emptiness by "fixing" his;** it was another way to avoid dealing with her own wounds. Consequently, he did not have a chance to deal with his emptiness or experience it for a prolonged period of time.

I explained to Karen that she must: (1) Help Jason to be alone so he can find his direction and see that he misses you, and (2) Help him get in touch with his emptiness because he was numb.

Karen couldn't find it within herself to do this, and she and Jason eventually broke up permanently. **It was the pain of this permanent break-up that compelled her to "go back home."** This process allowed her to enter relationships with less fear. She learned to ask for what she needed and she was quickly able to get *past the third date and begin developing a real relationship.*

Karen will always be attracted to Distancers, but "going home" shifted her attraction away from the elusive types of men from her past. She found herself attracted to and attracting men who were much more "connectable." The man she is involved with now is a Distancer, but he is

not extreme; he is definitely "connectable by instruction"
and Karen can avoid repeating the old mistakes she used
to make.

My patient Donna also reaped rewards from "going
home." She had huge abandonment issues with her father and
she also was angry with her mother. She said, "I hate my
mother. She really screwed me up." I told her that instead of
hating her mother, she should look at her mother's pain and
see her mother as a wounded child. I shared with her the story
of my mother facing her fear of flying so she could be with
me at one of my television appearances and at my book party.
I said, "Your mother probably wanted better for you than she
had for herself, and probably wanted to protect you from the
pain and heartache she had experienced in her own life."

"That's funny that you would say that, Dr. Weil," said
Donna. "My mother always said she wanted to spare me from
pain and tried to shield and protect me. She wanted me to have
it better than she did." When Donna was a child, she saw her
mother's actions to protect her as being stifling, overbearing,
and critical. During the last fight she had with her mother, as
Donna was blaming her for not treating her the way she
wanted to be treated, her mother said, "You always talk about
how much I hurt you, but you don't seem to realize how much
you've hurt *me*."

Mothers and daughters have a challenging relationship
because they are constantly shifting and changing roles with
each other. It can literally take decades for them to reconnect
and balance their relationship. Whether the daughter admires
her mother or dislikes her, she is guaranteed to share many of
her mother's traits. The message I once read on a wall hanging
said it all: "Mirror Mirror on the wall, I am my mother after all."

Donna was using her grudge to avoid getting close to her
mother. I explained, "That's how you behave in relationships.

You cut off from your father and your mother and you cut off from relationships *and stop them before they start*. The way you behave with your parents is the same way you behave with your dates and unless **you go back home and do what I've told you to do, you may never get past the third date."**

Two days later Donna called me crying. She said, "I can't do it, I have something invested in hating my mother."

I asked Donna, "What would happen if you stopped hating your mother?"

"I guess I would have to get past the third date and deal with my fear of being loved by a man who doesn't vanish," Donna replied.

"What would that feel like?" I asked her.

"That would be really scary," she said. "I'm afraid to let a man see who I really am because I'm afraid I won't be good enough. What if I can't measure up?"

"You have the same fears as your mother," I told her. "When you work on this with your mother, you will both be rewarded. **Your mother loved you, she just didn't have the skills to show you."**

Going Back Home Prepares You for Marriage

"We would like to thank all of our friends and family for joining us to celebrate the exchanging of our wedding vows.

A special thanks to our parents who, through their strong love for one another, have taught us how to love each other. Without their support, encouragement and love, *we would not be who we are today."*

Love, Kim and Steve
wedding program

Kim and Steve, whom you read about in Chapter 4, are among the 2 percent of people who do not have painful childhood wounds to heal, since they both came from families that were securely attached. I'm including this family because I want you to see how powerful the family of origin is, and how much it affects your life, and generations to come. People like Kim and Steve are rare, but by going home again, you can join their elite circle.

One of my most convincing personal experiences in the power of going home is that I met Jeff just a few weeks after I reconnected with my father. This is precisely what Dr. Fogarty had predicted.

When Jeff and I began dating, I still had a few wounds from my father's adultery that I hadn't healed, but I was much more ready to let Jeff in, instead of keeping him at a distance as I had done with the men I met after my divorce from my first husband. (I also sought out ambivalent men whom I could hide behind.) Even though I trusted Jeff, in the back of my mind I was concerned that he would be unfaithful. Shortly after I met his mother and shared a holiday dinner with his entire family, Jeff began to get scared. While I was at his childhood home I saw a portrait of his mother, Helen, hanging over the mantel. It was painted when she was about my age.

The resemblance was remarkable and it played a big head trick on Jeff. He began acting more distant. A few days later I answered the phone at his house and one of my tennis partners was on the other end. "How did you know I was here?" I asked her. She said she didn't know, she was returning a call to Jeff. He had answered her personal ad.

I was confused and felt humiliated. When I asked Jeff about her he said after the family dinner he began to feel smothered and decided to answer the ad just *to see who else was out there*. He apologized and said he wasn't really interested in her; he just *wanted to be sure about me*. But it still triggered some of my deepest wounds. I told him our relationship was over. He assured me his relationship with Sherry was not sexual, but since we were in a committed relationship I still viewed his actions as infidelity.

Jeff pleaded with me to stay. He said, "It's not like me to do something like this. I just feel very strange inside. I wasn't trying to hurt you. I don't know why I did it, but I can't lose you. I think I'm falling in love with you. I love you," he said.

I was too upset to listen. I wanted to run from the fear. I wanted to blame Jeff and be the blameless victim, even though I knew we were both acting out similar deep-seated fears.

Not sure what to do next, I called my father and asked for his advice. "Bonnie," he said, "no one should know better than *you* that relationships are hard work. Before you leave Jeff, find out if he was scared. *Was Jeff's action a cry for help, as it was for me?*"

Yes, it turned out that it *was* a cry for help. I learned that Jeff was afraid of closeness. His father had died suddenly when Jeff was only twenty-two, before he had finished dental school. In addition, his first marriage had broken up, leaving him with more wounds and more fear. He was afraid to get married again for fear of making another mistake. He was also terrified that I would leave suddenly, as his father had. **Jeff distanced himself to reduce his involvement and protect his wounds.** I agreed to continue to see Jeff only if he would go to therapy with Dr. Fogarty and heal his wounds and mine.

Even though Jeff isn't the "cheating kind," *the combination of his fears and mine had taken us to this point*. Jeff didn't think he had any wounds, but he now realizes that his father's death deeply affected him. He thought he had all the time in the world to get to know his father later, after college, so the news of his death came as a shattering blow. He had never had the chance to say good-bye. Jeff was certainly living up to my "Imago," and I knew we both still had some work to finish with our families of origin. (You never really finish the work. It's a journey, just like love. But the more you do, the better your relationships will be.)

Even though I was very hurt, I knew it was only a matter of time before my adultery wound would resurface. I felt fortunate because it was a **second chance** for us to rewrite critical parts of our relationship scripts. I really believe the phone call from Sherry was a *gift,* although it didn't feel like a gift at the time. If Jeff hadn't called her, he wouldn't have had a chance to resolve his wounds with his father. **If he couldn't disconnect from his father and reconnect with his mother, he wouldn't have been able to truly connect with me.** This was also a chance for me to work through my issues with adultery. If I hadn't, it would have reared its ugly head again.

In therapy, Jeff told Dr. Fogarty that he wanted to be sure about wanting to marry me. He said he was afraid I would complicate his life. Jeff said he answered Sherry's personal because he wasn't sure how he felt about me. He thought he would just wake up one day and suddenly know beyond a shadow of a doubt that he wanted to marry me. Dr. Fogarty said, "No, that won't happen. You have to take a risk and she *will* complicate your life. **But you'll never feel really ready to marry her and the alternative is loneliness."**

Dr. Fogarty suggested Jeff ask himself if he wanted to be alone, and Jeff had a chance to experience his emptiness because I kept a distance throughout this process. He also suggested that Jeff go back to his family of origin by visiting his father's grave.

He was reluctant to do this and put it off for a year, refusing to let me go with him and help him. **Our relationship and movement toward commitment was at a standstill.**

What happened next truly transformed our relationship and our relationships with our parents. My father told Jeff and me that he wanted to help. He wanted to go with Jeff to his father's grave and help him do the work he needed to do. It was the first time Jeff agreed to go. He needed my dad to go with him, which was wonderful of my dad and very brave of Jeff.

When they arrived at the grave, my father spoke first. "Your son here loves you so and is distraught that you're not here to help him at another important crossroads in his life. I know you would be proud of him today. He wants to marry Bonnie but he is having difficulty showing his deeper feelings. Part of it is your death, part of it is that he married his first wife to avoid the emptiness of your death. Instead he felt even emptier and had to leave her.

"Jeff needs to talk to you and I will take your place and help him if it's okay with you. I know he loves Bonnie like I loved my wife, **but I too had trouble showing it until I almost lost her. He could lose Bonnie if he doesn't come to terms with his fears associated with your death."**

Then Dad hugged Jeff, who was now shaking, and Jeff spoke: "Dad, I have a deep hole, a deep void, something stops me from committing myself all the way to Bonnie. I love you. I need you and your blessings so I won't make the same mistake again. Saying I love you and miss you and crying with my 'new dad' holding me, helps me." **(Jeff had never cried for his father; now he cried for him with mine.)**

"I need to forgive Mom. She did her best. She never told me you were dying, but she was in her own pain. She was protecting me so I would finish dental school. She was afraid if I got too depressed, I would quit."

This moment in time changed many things for all of us. With my father's support, Jeff forgave his own father for leaving, and he forgave himself for not saying good-bye. He also forgave his mother for trying to protect him, and therefore she was able to help Jeff grieve the loss by reminding him how special he was to his father, even though he was not affectionate with Jeff. **She encouraged him to trust again so that he could finally let himself commit to me. This experience that my father shared with Jeff was also Dad's way of reaching out to me. He made up for lost time when he wasn't there for me by being there for me at one of the most important junctures of my life and Jeff's.**

A few months later Jeff called my dad and said, "Dad, I love you. Is it all right for me to be in the family as a son? I love your daughter. I feel passion and friendship. I know we'll be happy and she will help me to learn how to communicate and ask for what I need." My father, crying open-hearted tears, said, "I now have not one son, but two."

Today, Jeff and I turn to each other for healing and we make it a priority to connect with our parents and continue to learn about them and ourselves. Just the other day, for example, I found out something from my childhood that I never knew and it made an emotional difference for me. When I was a child, my brother broke one of my favorite games called "Beat the Clock." I thought my mother didn't care because she didn't buy me a new one. As it turned out, she went to *eleven* different stores to try to buy it for me because she knew how much it meant, but it was out of stock everywhere. I didn't remember my mother's efforts, I only remembered my own sense of loss.

Meanwhile, Jeff and his mother continue to grow closer and she is a very important person in both of our lives. Jeff recently wrote a note in his mother's birthday card that thanked her for the skills she taught him and helping him to learn to take failures in stride. He thanked her for loving him and nurturing him, which shows the connection and bridge he's made back to his mother.

Going Back Home Can Help You Make Up and Stay in Love

I strongly encourage the committed and married couples I counsel to do family of origin work to strengthen their relationship. *Most of them kick and scream about it when I first mention it, but when they understand the benefits and how it will forever change their lives for the better, they are usually willing to do it.* In every case, going back to their childhood wounds, or what I sometimes call "returning to the scene of the crime" helps them to understand themselves and each other much better and opens the door for more meaningful and fulfilling connection between them and with their parents.

For my patients Alexis and Nathaniel, going back to their families of origin was a *requirement for them to be able to move on to the next stage of love*. Alexis was having a hard time emotionally committing to Nathaniel. I said, "You must connect with your parents because you are unconsciously acting out in your relationship what your parents didn't resolve in theirs."

When Alexis "went home" she learned her mother had a huge fear of commitment. When Alexis's father proposed to her, she said, "Okay, we'll get married for one year. If it doesn't work, we'll get an annulment." Alexis was basically saying the same thing to Nathaniel even though they had been married for ten years.

If you are in a relationship and your partner is projecting wounds from his or her parents onto you, gently coach him or her by saying something similar to the following dialogue.

Smart Heart Dialogue

"Perhaps you're seeing me differently than I really am because of your childhood wounds and sensitivity. Teach me how to relate to you so I can help you and so I don't wound you further, but help you heal instead."

Don't ever use your partner's wound as a way to attack him or her. Do it lovingly so he or she can "see you with a new face." When you "go home again," don't get stuck in the analysis stage. Some patients glean a few insights and say, "I'm done." **Insight isn't enough because it doesn't necessarily bring movement or change.** You need to take action. If you stop at the point where you've discovered some things but don't do anything with your new insights, you will not accomplish your goal of healing those old wounds. In addition, you may be tempted to use these wounds as an excuse or rationalization for why you can't find the love you want. If you want to get along with your parents, which will help you get along with your partner, you need to spend time with them alone, *instead* of distancing from them.

How to Reconnect with Your Family

Rather than dwelling on what your parents didn't do for you, or how they hurt or ignored you, *ask yourself what you did or are doing for them to heal the relationship.*

For example, Dr. Fogarty showed me the part *I played* when my father was being unfaithful. I was close to my mom but I helped to keep my father distant, lonely, and cut off from me, by being distant from him. I wasn't there for Dad and my actions made him feel alone and abandoned too. When I looked at the part I played in our relationship I saw a correlation with the way I kept a distance from other men. Either they would distance from me, or I would distance from them. **I picked unavailable men because my dad was emotionally unavailable when I was a child.** I wanted Dad to reach out for me and he wanted me to reach out to him. I did the same thing with the other men in my life, and this is what most of my female patients do, particularly those whose biological clocks are ticking. I remember Dr. Lieberman, one of my graduate school professors, asking, "You're not dating are you Bonnie?" I said, "How do you know that?" She said, "Because I give the class twenty books to read and you're the only one who reads them."

Influence of Your Opposite Sex Parent

By examining your feelings toward your parents and the opposite sex, you gain many helpful insights that you can use to make changes.

- Do you really like men (or women) or are you afraid, angry, or intimidated by them?
- Do you respect men (or women)?
- Who are you more comfortable with, men or women? (When I was beginning my family of origin work, Dr. Fogarty helped me to see that both my mother and I were more comfortable with women than men. My father and brother were more comfortable with men. Initially we worked on that.)

- How did your father treat your mother?
- How did your mother treat your father?
- How did *you* treat your father and mother?
- How did your father and mother treat you?
- How do you treat your dates or partner?
- How do your dates or partner treat you?

If you're honest with yourself, you will be able to see many similarities between your adult relationships, the relationship you had with your parents as a child, and the relationship your parents had with each other and their parents.

When I was working on my advanced certificate in family therapy, instead of doing a genogram (family tree), I brought my parents into class with me, and Dr. Fogarty led us through a family session. He took my father into the "emptiness" he had felt as a child. Miraculously, my anger began to melt. Mom and I saw our part in his loneliness and began to understand his pain, which helped our love for him grow stronger. Dr. Fogarty helped Mom and me to connect with Dad and he to us. **I realized then how magical and necessary it was to develop a personal relationship with my father.**

Dr. Fogarty instructed me to have a one-on-one relationship with my dad, instead of connecting with him through my mom, which was my life-long pattern. "You are too focused on your work, which makes you a great therapist, but why are you not in a relationship?" I said I honestly didn't know. Dr. Fogarty asserted, **"Until you connect and do the work with your father, you will not be able to connect to a man."**

The first time I called my dad to make a connection, he thought something was wrong or that I needed something. "Do you need money, Bon?" he asked me, and was willing to send it to me. "No," I explained. "I just want to get to know you so

I can get to know myself better." I worked hard to connect with him and make him feel loved. For a long time, he still felt my anger and the pain of some of the things I had said to him earlier in our relationship. Unfortunately, after an individual therapy session I actually said, "I hate you," and it *took me years to undo the hurt and trauma.*

Family therapy taught me that each member of the family affects all the other members. **It works like a mobile; when you move one part, they all move.** It was this understanding that propelled me to tell Dad I loved him and apologize for wounding him.

Doing family of origin work completely changed the way I saw my father and myself in relation to him. **When I saw my father as a wounded child it was truly a magical moment for both of us. My heart—which had been partially frozen—began to melt and I felt a tenderness for my father that I had never felt before. We both experienced the magic of connection.** Our hurt and pain was transformed into deep tenderness and real love. It was just before that time that Dr. Fogarty told me, "You can take your patients only as far as you have gone yourself."

Dad and I worked on this as a team. After dragging him through several museums—something I like to do—I remembered to love him the way *he* wanted to be loved and I suggested we go bowling together. It's important when you connect with your parents to choose something they will enjoy. (Remember that you are healing *them,* as they are healing *you.*) Dad helped me because he wanted me to be happy and have a good relationship. Once we reconnected through having fun together, I asked my father for forgiveness for being so distant from him. He apologized for hurting me and said he'd make it up to me, and he has—probably more than he knows.

I also realized how important it was for me to strengthen my relationship with my mother by initiating more connection myself. I had to disconnect to reconnect.

My mother always worked very hard to connect with me, but she didn't always know how. Mom made many sacrifices on my behalf because she wanted me to have the opportunities she didn't have. (She even sold tupperware to pay for my college.) I was named after my paternal great grandmother who was a social worker and my mother always wanted to support my childhood dream to become a therapist. Up until this time, I did not pick up the clues from my mother that she needed me to connect with *her*. Mom had wounds from her own childhood, and she needed healing from me.

I learned that I didn't know how to love my mother the way she wanted to be loved. When she hurt her wrist I wanted to bring her chicken soup (a typical Pursuer response), but my mother said she wanted to be alone to heal. My mother, I learned, was a "closet Distancer." Later, since I felt hurt and rejected that it had been six weeks before she would allow me to visit, we talked about it together. She told me how much she loved me and explained that she needs space when she's healing and was protecting me from seeing her that way.

Shortly thereafter when *I* was sick my mother called and said, "Well I won't come over because you probably need to be alone." I told her, "No, I don't want to be alone. I want some company." This sequence of events showed me **how differently my mother and I both wanted to be loved.** It also taught me that it is important to respect and validate *her* choices, rather than *feeling rejected by them*. This was an important lesson and helped me to learn how to give Jeff the distance he needs when he's healing. When he's sick or hurt, he wants to be alone, but he also wants some nurturing. I learned to ask for his permission to nurture him and ask how he would like me to do it.

Working on this book together with Jeff helped him to get in touch with some of his past memories and wounds that still needed to be healed. One day when I was working on the differences between Pursuers and Distancers, Jeff told me, "Please don't say, 'be careful' when I leave for my office in the morning." He said it made him feel like I was an over-protective mother and reminded him of the sometimes smothering love he received from his grandmother. (It's not surprising that he married me—a therapist—because he really needed someone who could help him to help himself, and he needed a wife who was willing to nurture him the way he needed to be nurtured—which sometimes means giving him *less* nurturing!)

I had been saying "Be careful" every morning for eight years, but it wasn't until we talked about this topic for the book that Jeff finally told me he didn't like it. I agreed to stop saying it to him because I want to love him the way he wants to be loved, but it bothered me not to say it. It was my way of sending him off with a blessing. Now after I kiss him good-bye in the morning, I wait until he rounds the corner to go to the elevator, and then I whisper "Be careful" to the air.

Some of my best work with patients comes from understanding my wonderful mother and father; understanding how Distancers operate and what they need and don't need. **I learned how to disconnect, so I could connect, which is exactly what I'm teaching you to do.** What practice I've had with Distancers my entire life! My dad, my mom, my brother, my grandmother and grandfather were all Distancers to one extreme or another. (I think one of the reasons I was Grandma's "favorite" was because I was a Pursuer and reached out to show my love even when she didn't respond.)

At the same time that you must reach for your parents to connect and reconnect, they also need to reach for *you*. When I was having a party to celebrate the success of my first book, *Adultery, The Forgivable Sin*, my mother didn't want to come because she was afraid to fly. I really wanted her and Dad to be with me to celebrate because it was their triumph in **"making up instead of breaking up"** that spurred the book and showed adultery really is a forgivable sin. My mother felt that as a therapist I should understand her fear, but I said I wanted her to face her fear. "You have to choose between your love for me and your fear of flying," I told her. When Mom walked into my book party I knew how much she wanted to love me the way I wanted to be loved.

When I saw her I burst into tears, but she didn't understand why I was so moved. "Mom," I said, "you'll never know how much this means to me."

She said, "I thought as a therapist you would understand that I am afraid to fly."

I told her I understood intellectually, "but I always felt you didn't love me because when I needed your connection, support, and love you didn't hear."

She said, "I am so glad that I could do this for you," and I told her, "You wiped away every single one of my childhood wounds."

She smiled at me and said, "And you wiped away mine."

I asked her, "What do you mean?"

She said, "You wounded me too."

I was really surprised. "I did?" I responded.

Just like many of my patients, I saw only half of the picture—the way my mother wounded me. I didn't realize that I wounded her too. In addition, Mom had wounds from her own family of origin and also from her relationship with Dad that went back to a time before I was born. *She was looking for acceptance and unconditional love from me.* She wanted me to love her as she was, with her faults and her fears. When Mom faced her fear and flew out to support me, we helped each other heal wounds. My ultimatum forced her to stretch her comfort zone and work on her fear of flying.

This was a second turning point in my relationship with my mom, and also with Jeff. It really helped me understand my husband. I learned and accepted that people are human (even our parents) and just because they can't do something for us, doesn't mean they don't care about us.

I learned a lot from my parents by their example, but I didn't realize how profound it was until I did my family of origin work. **For example, my mother understood my father's need for disconnection and she supported him.** When Dad arrived home from work, my brother and I were not permitted to bother him. We kissed him and said "hello" *and then Mom announced his disconnection.* After he relaxed for a while and read the paper, Mom would announce we could see Dad now and we'd jump on his lap and laugh and he'd throw us up in the air.

Making Conscious Links

Going back home helps you make conscious links between your behavior and that of your parents. Whatever you think you were missing in childhood, you will unconsciously seek to find in an adult relationship. For example, my first husband looked identical to my childhood friend Barbara's father, who was very trustworthy and faithful to his wife. I was unconsciously looking for a man who wouldn't cheat.

My husband Jeff—even though he is a periodontist— loves to eat candy and carries it around with him, just like my father, and I bear a striking resemblance to Jeff's mother. In addition, his parents and mine met on blind dates, and Jeff and I met through a personal ad in *New York Magazine*. Jeff's dad saw a photograph of his prospective blind date (Jeff's mom) and that's what convinced him to give it a try. It was also the photograph I sent to Jeff that motivated him to call me. I sent the photograph after I didn't receive a response from the letter I wrote to answer Jeff's personal ad. It's a good thing I sent the photo, too, since he never received my letter!

Smart Heart Insights

- List all the positive and negative qualities of your parents and caregivers.
- List all the positive and negative qualities of your partner, previous partners, and dates.
- Compare your lists and find the similarities.

Dealing with Ghosts

The ghosts of our ex-lovers, including boyfriends and husbands, may appear to get in the way of getting past the third date, *stopping a relationship before it starts,* or impeding the progress toward making a commitment. Those ghosts—*"Blasts from the Past"*—are really re-enactments of our hurts, disappointments, and expectations of *our parents.* This is why they hurt even more. It's like a double-whammy. This is also why getting rid of a person (your exes included) doesn't get rid of your problem and why reconnecting with your family is crucial for connection and intimacy with your partner.

When my patient Mary Lou began her therapy with me, she wouldn't share her feelings or fears with her partners. She wouldn't move forward and she wouldn't move back.

She wanted to believe all the promises her dates made her, and at the same time she was clinging to the promise she made to be loyal to her fiancé who died of cancer. She was also "Daddy's little girl," and had never completed the developmental stage of leaving her father. No one could measure up to Dad in her eyes and she couldn't cut her ties with her dead fiancé as evidenced by her frequent visits to his grave and the close connection she maintained with his mother.

I told Mary Lou, "You must deal with all the ghosts in your closet; not only your fiancé who died, but also all of your other ex-boyfriends and your father. **Reconnect to people you let go as a bridge to new connections. You may even have to see some of them to disconnect.**

Smart Heart Skills to Put Ghosts to Rest

- Say good-bye to the old and create closure with past relationships. (You may have to say hello again to the old, before you can say good-bye.)
- Live in the moment, not in the past, and help your date to do the same.
- Be grateful for the past, even the painful relationships, because they all add up to make you who you are today.

It is essential to have closure on past relationships to bridge the gap from the old to the new. You may have to help your date to sever old ties at the same time that you gently encourage him to help you do the same. A great example of this is my patient Marcia who had to help her date to work through his relationship with his ex-fiancée before he could move on to the third date with her. She could have said "forget it," and she thought about doing so, but I helped her to see that this man was "connectable."

I told her, "If he could walk away from an engagement and jump right into a new relationship, he would be the type of man who is avoiding connection and intimacy. This man is showing you he's connectable because it is taking some time for him to disconnect and have closure from his previous relationship." I encouraged her to be patient and use Smart Heart Skills and Dialogue. She hung in there and they are married to each other today.

Our Reality Is Limited to Our Experiences

Our reality is limited to our experiences, and how we interpret those events and circumstances. We all tend to forget that our friends', partner's, or dates' realities are very different from our own. I remember when my friend Barbara slept overnight at my house when we were in seventh grade. When it was time for breakfast the following morning, Dad got out the lox, bagels, capers, and all the "fixings," and I began enthusiastically crunching away on a pickle.

Barbara was shocked. She asked, "Why are you eating pickles for breakfast?" I paused for a second and then asked, **"Doesn't everyone eat pickles for breakfast?"** This was my first conscious experience with fusion—thinking that the way *my* family did things was the way every family did them. Barbara invited me the following week for Sunday brunch at her home—which was always lasagna. We spent a great deal of time together and had the chance to see how each other's families did things and how they related to each other. Her parents had a solid marriage, and consequently Barbara, her siblings, and all of their children are among the 2 percent of people who grow up without significant childhood wounds. (You read about Barbara's daughter Kim and her husband Steve in Chapter 4.)

When you heal your wounds you don't pass them on to your children. You're not only doing this work for yourself, you're doing it for future generations. **If you want to see how well you are doing, take a look at your children!**

Smart Heart Steps to Reconnect with Your Family

Begin with the parent you feel most distant from now, or the one you felt most distant from as a child. Once you connect with this parent (separately), begin your work with the other parent. (It's important to mention that in some cases one or both of your parents may not be physically or emotionally able to do this work with you. In those cases, do as much as you can on your own and as much as is possible with your parent or parents or use a surrogate.)

Let both of your parents know what your plan is, so one of them doesn't feel excluded. It is not necessary for your parents to be alive for you to do this work. You can communicate with your deceased parent through a surrogate friend or family member (by going to the grave, like Jeff did with my father), or your partner can serve as the surrogate.

1. Write a heartfelt letter to each of your parents telling them what you wish could have been different in your childhood, *without anger or blame.* In this letter, validate why they were not the way you wished they were. Also keep your parents' wounds in mind to help you understand why they acted as they did.

   When you list the things that hurt you, be sure to look **a little deeper** and discover how these wounds also *helped* you in some way. Did they make you stronger? Did they help to shape your purpose in life? (As my parents' problems helped to shape my purpose as a therapist and my calling to write books and share what I've learned.) What did you learn that you would have missed if things had been the way you say you wished they had been?

2. Count your blessings. Write about the positive things they did, the things you're grateful for, and thank them for what they did "right."

3. Examine the role you played in the family dynamic and in being distant or keeping them distant, and ask for their forgiveness. (If you are ready to forgive them, do so. If not, don't push it.) **Remember forgiveness is a gift you give yourself.** It takes time and it is a journey of small steps.

4. You do not have to send these letters if you do not feel ready yet, but you *must* read them to your partner. If you are not in a relationship, share them with a friend you trust and feel safe with. If it is not a "blaming" letter, **consider reading it aloud to your parents when you are with them.** If you do this, make sure you **validate them and give them attachment skills to buffer your words—before, during, and after.**

5. Write yourself a letter from each parent that you would like them to write to you. In this letter, they ask for *your* forgiveness. Share these letters with your partner.

6. Write a letter to your parents detailing the changes you would like them to make and the changes *you are* willing to make, and send it to them.

7. Write a letter to express your anger and hurt feelings to your parents—but **don't** send this one. Share this one with your partner or a close friend and then burn it in a fireplace or destroy it as a symbolic ritual of letting go of your blame and anger.

8. Plan some outings with the parent you feel most distant from or are the most angry with today. Pick something you know your parent likes. If you don't know what they like, ask them. Do not confront your parent or try to get close, **just connect with them. Keep these get-togethers light, brief, and activity-oriented.** No heavy discussions at this point. **Be sure to let the parent you are closest with know your intentions and ask for his or her permission.** Stay in touch with this parent and let them know how things are going.

9. If you feel that both you and your parent can handle it, gently tell him or her that you are having trouble with your dates or partner. Don't blame your parent, but gently let him or her know that you **believe part of your struggle is because of some unfinished business from your childhood.**

Open your heart to your parent and ask for help with your problems. Be sure to let your parent know you understand he or she did the best that was possible under the circumstances. **Once a connection is formed with your parent, bring your partner along on visits sometimes so your partner and parents can share in the healing and forgiveness process.**

10. Create a family history chart—a genogram—with your parents. Ask your parents to tell you about the family background, including broken engagements, divorces, adultery or other betrayals, abandonment, or grudge-holding. Stress that you are doing this to help heal your wounds and theirs—**not to shame or blame them.**

11.   If your parent has died, visit the cemetery or a favorite quiet place of yours and meditate on this subject. Put your feelings in a letter and read it out loud. **Tell your parent that you are having trouble because of emotional wounds you developed growing up and ask for help. Forgive your parent and ask for forgiveness from him or her. (If this is too difficult for you to do alone, take someone along for support.)**

12.   **Share your letter with your partner and with the parent who is still living.** If both of your parents are deceased, share the letter with one of your partner's parents.

After you have completed these Twelve Steps for Reconnection, invite your parent to do the *Embraceable You* exercise with you.

The Embraceable You Exercise

Do this exercise with the parent you are most distant from. Bring your partner along occasionally for this exercise, too.

For this exercise you will be using attachment skills such as hugging, touching, stroking hair, gazing into each other's eyes, and other bonding behaviors.

Here's what to do:

One at a time, after you and your parent have vented your feelings (wearing emotional bullet-proof vests, cotton gloves, and bubbles), the listener must comfort the one who has shared by using attachment skills such as saying yes, nodding your head, and looking into his or her eyes. (The listener must remember not to get hurt by the words.) Hold, snuggle as a baby, and rock the person for fifteen minutes.

Cry together. Talk about childhood hurts that influenced your adult behavior and about the wounds that still haunt you. Come up with behavior changes and do them together. Your parent changes, then you do. Hug afterward and do something fun and energetic to get the endorphins flowing. (Remember, NO BLAME!)

Teach your parents to announce connections, disconnections, and reconnections, and you do the same.

The more uncomfortable, unimaginable, or scary this exercise sounds to you, the more you need to do it.

Accept the fact that you cannot intimately connect with your partner or potential partner until you have connected with your parents. Praise yourself for doing this exercise, because it takes courage.

There is no denying the power of forging a love-filled connection with your family of origin. **The patients I've worked with who refused to do family of origin work make up the 2 percent of the married couples in my therapy practice who break up instead of make up, and the 2 percent of singles who still are not in committed relationships.** I'm convinced that couples like Paul and Rhonda could have saved their relationships and gotten married instead of breaking up if they had been willing to do this work. My single patients Karen, Nancy, Judy, and Donna could have avoided a lot of pain in their relationships if they had agreed to do the work when I first assigned it to them, but at least they were eventually willing to take the necessary steps and are now reaping the rich rewards of making these family connections.

Every one of my patients (in over twenty-two years in practice) who has gone back home to heal his or her wounds and helped his or her parents heal has gone further in his or her relationships, whether that meant getting past the third date, keeping a relationship growing, entering a committed relationship, getting married, or saving the marriage he or she has and making it better.

Those who did not go back home are still stuck in their developmental stages, still feel wounded and frightened by relationships and intimacy, and still want to blame their parents instead of accepting their part of the responsibility. The singles can't connect with anyone; the married couples either divorce or end up in an emotional divorce.

Remember that your family of origin work is never really finished; there's always more to do and more to learn. We want to think we're done, but we're not. After my first semester in professional family therapy school I proudly proclaimed to one of my teachers, "I'm done with my family of origin work!" Dr. Guerin smiled at me and said, **"You haven't even begun."** He was right. Don't stop with reconnecting to your parents. Keep going and discover how amazing your relationship with each other can become.

Taking the journey back home gives us courage and opens our hearts to greater joy, happiness, and love. **We experience the magic of connection and have less emptiness and more success in our relationships as well as in other areas of our lives**. Healing old heartaches is the most powerful, effective, and fulfilling route to reaching real and lasting love in our adult relationships.

I urge you to go back home. Heal your heart. Help your parents heal their hearts, and rewrite your relationship scripts so you can enjoy all the wonder, magic, and bliss of a "connected" love-filled relationship with your dates or your partner.

part three

Getting Past the Third Date
Shake It, Don't Break It

"What we are aiming at when we fall in love is a very strange Paradox. The paradox consists of the fact that when we fall in love we are seeking to re-find all or some of the people to whom we were attached as children. On the other hand, we ask our beloved to correct all the wrongs that these early parents or siblings inflicted on us. So that love contains in it the contradiction, the attempt to return to the past and attempt to undo the past."

☙ WOODY ALLEN AS PROFESSOR LEVY
CRIMES & MISDEMEANORS

❦ 12 ❧

Potholes on the Road to Love

"If you can find a path with no obstacles, it probably doesn't lead anywhere."

—FRANK A. CLARK

There's no doubt that the road to love can be filled with potholes, but if you maintain your sense of humor, it's much easier to keep things in perspective while you traverse this road. It's also essential to keep your sights on your goal, which is to reach real and lasting love.

Many of my patients feel discouraged by the dating game, and often after a string of bad dates, they're tempted to give up and join the ranks of the "jaded, walking wounded." **My message to you is don't give up.** As my mother repeatedly reminded me while I was dating, "It only takes one." To support you and encourage you to hang in and keep trying, I'm sharing some of my own stories. Hopefully, you can laugh along with me and see that you're not the only one who has experienced potholes on the road to love.

During the years between the end of my first marriage, which lasted less than four years, and the time I met Jeff, I had hundreds of dates. In the two years when I was really determined to create a relationship I chalked up seventy-six coffee dates, which is a sign of my persistence. Persistence and a sense of humor are definitely two of the most important traits for any endeavor in life.

I married my first husband two years after I graduated from college. We met my senior year, but I wanted to live on my own for a while before making a marriage commitment. When I reached the point where I could "want" a man without "needing" one, I got married. While that marriage created some new wounds, it also opened my eyes to some valuable truths. In many ways it was my first baby step toward a successful relationship. I call it a baby step because I married a man who reminded me of the father of one of my childhood friends. I saw him through the clouded vision of the child who hid under the covers at night, trying to block out the angry words my mom and dad shared when they were struggling with my dad's infidelity.

At that time I was not consciously aware that my parents were fighting about adultery, but children have an uncanny sixth sense about what's going on between their parents. On an unconscious level I sensed my father's fears and frustrations and my mother's pain and heartache. I chose my first husband because he seemed like a man who would be faithful. I thought I knew what I wanted and needed, but I unconsciously chose him based on an "overcorrection" of what I knew I didn't want since I hadn't yet dealt with the issues I had with my father.

It's important when choosing a mate for life that you keep in mind what you don't want and what you do want. The ending of the marriage with my first husband also helped me to learn firsthand **that getting rid of the person doesn't get rid of the problem.** The separation and divorce was very painful for me because I loved him very much. It took several years for me to heal. Perhaps that's why I can relate so well to the couples who come to me with hopes of rebuilding their marriages that have crumbled into pieces. I understand and feel their pain, which helps them to trust me and be willing to learn the skills they need to trust themselves and each other. First, I make them hang in and work smarter instead of running away from each other. If I had known during my first marriage what I know now, and had he reconsidered getting help together, we would probably still be married. But, of course, I have no regrets, because if I'd stayed with my first husband I would never have met Jeff, who truly is my best friend and soul mate.

It's helpful to remember that every relationship you have—*even the ones that are over before the end of the first date*—is valuable because it offers you a chance to learn more about yourself, create more realistic expectations, and refine your criteria for the type of person you will someday marry.

Every man I dated, even those I spent only thirty minutes with, helped to prepare me and make me ready for and appreciate the day I met Jeff. So rather than thinking of dates that don't turn into relationships as failures, I encourage you to view them as important stepping stones to love.

Unfortunately, patching up the potholes in our hearts is not as easily done as patching up the potholes on the pavement, but with persistence, perseverance, optimism, and a sense of humor, you can do it! Remember, too, that "All roads lead to Rome," As my mom says. It takes smooth roads and potholes to get to love, but eventually you will get there if you keep in mind *that love is a journey of small steps.*

For years, even though I was dating, I told myself that I was fine on my own. I had a successful career as a family therapist, a loving family, and many wonderful friends. But when I was really honest with myself, I knew something vital was missing—*an intimate, loving, and committed relationship with just one very special man.*

I had thrown myself mind, body, heart, and soul into my work, but I wasn't actively dating. I had become a workaholic in an unconscious attempt to avoid courtship since my divorce.

I shifted gears and began taking dating more seriously. It became a mission and a priority. While there *are* men and women who prefer to remain single, I was not one of them. For me, a full life meant having my "soul mate" by my side to share with and connect with in good times and in bad, in sickness and in health. I wanted to get married and I decided that by the time I was forty I would. **I began to visualize myself in a white dress standing next to my beau as the rabbi pronounced us husband and wife,** and each time I hit another pothole on the road to love I focused on my vision of marriage until it became a firm reality in my mind and heart.

Whether you are single or married, visualizing the love you want is one of the most powerful tools to creating that love, but you must be careful that your expectations are based on adult realities, rather than childhood fantasies.

Bachelor Number 1

I began my quest for love by perusing the personal ads in *New York Magazine*. My first official dinner date of my new quest for love was with a man I met through the personals. He wanted to take me to dinner at a very exclusive four-star restaurant in Manhattan that was within walking distance from my apartment. **I was impressed that he was willing to invest so much in a first date. I thought it was a good sign, but boy was I wrong!** Before the appetizers were served, he said, "Can I share something tragic and personal with you? Being a therapist, I'm sure you've heard this kind of thing before. My father is in jail for killing my mother."

Now, I believe in honesty and sharing, but this tidbit of information, dropped so abruptly on the table before the shrimp cocktail had even arrived, made my stomach ball up into a tight knot. He became more eerie as the night went on, justifying his father's actions and empathizing with him. I couldn't get out of there fast enough. As soon as the two-and-a-half-hour ordeal was over, I told him I was taking a cab home to Queens so he wouldn't try to take me home. He said, "That's funny, your area code isn't for Queens." I feigned surprise and said, "Well, I guess I am different."

As soon as I could slip away from him I practically ran back to my apartment, looking over my shoulder the entire way! Of course he called me back the very next day. It's akin to Murphy's Law I guess. The ones you never want to see again *and wish you hadn't seen the first time,* always call back. He called me early in the morning and when I picked up the phone, all I heard was heavy breathing. I was about to hang up, thinking it was a crank call, when he said my name in what I guess was supposed to be a sexy voice.

He sounded more like a rasping smoker. This guy wanted to take me on a five thousand dollar shopping spree at Saks Fifth Avenue for our second date. He said, "How would you like to shop 'til you drop?" He even had the nerve to say, "Just think how many sexy teddies and fishnet stockings five grand can buy." The feelings of nausea from the night before washed over me again. As much as I love to shop, there was no way I was going anywhere with Mr. Eerie again!

It was from that experience that I decided the coffee date was a much safer alternative for a first date. I also decided not to give my phone number or address out until after I met someone and decided whether or not it was safe to do so! **I already had rules about not letting a man into** my apartment or riding in his car until I got to know him, thanks to the cautions of my mother when I was growing up, but it was clear I needed more guidelines for my personal safety now that I was a New Yorker.

Bachelor Number 23

But alas, I broke my own rule about not letting a man into my apartment when I went out with a man who was a psychologist. He lived quite a distance from me and when he dropped me off after our sixth date, he asked if he could come in and use my bathroom before making the trip home. I was hesitant, but he assured me that he would simply use the bathroom and leave. He didn't want to use the restroom in the subway station and he played on my sense of guilt. How could I be so cruel? He seemed to be in pain and I fell for it and let him in.

After about fifteen minutes had gone by, I started to wonder what he was doing in there, so I walked down the hall to see if he was okay. He was okay alright. In fact, he was perfectly comfortable sprawled out *spread-eagle* on my bed, naked, which I suppose he thought looked sexy. I screamed at him to put his clothes on and get out!

I ran into this guy again a few years later in the produce department of a market in the Hamptons. He looked familiar, but at first I couldn't place him. Then I saw him pick up a cucumber and the memory came rushing back. I left immediately, deciding that we could have dinner without a salad that day!

These experiences were disheartening, **but I was determined not to give up!** I had a number of dates with nice men, but none of them were at all interested in creating relationships. They were dating for fun or sex alone.

Bachelor Number 37

When I said good night to this date, who had driven to Manhattan from Philadelphia—a four-hour drive—he asked, "Aren't you going to make my tolls worthwhile?" I asked "What do you mean by that?" Famous last words of a therapist! Boy was I sorry I asked that question. He said, "If you're not up for intercourse, how about a blow job?" My mouth fell open and I said, "Are you kidding?" He said, "With all the money I spent coming to see you and the gas and tolls, the least you could do is give me a hand job."

When I called my mother I told her, "I did not pass go," and I questioned whether I should enter a convent, even though it would require changing religions. I was trying to be light-hearted and make a joke, but my mother knew I was really upset. She said reassuringly, "Bonnie, your day will come." I said, "I think it's already come and gone!" She reminded me to be patient and keep trying. It was also after this date that one of my friends gave me a little stuffed toad that turned into a prince when you turned it inside out. I didn't date for a month after that, but everyone was cheering me on and I'm not a quitter, so I kept trying.

Bachelor Number 49

Eventually I met another man who seemed to have potential. He was kind and he was funny and we went on three dates together without him pressuring me for sex. Again, I took this as a good sign. But by the end of our third date, he professed his love for me and in the same breath asked me for a $10,000 loan so he could buy a car. I was taken aback, but I didn't want to hurt his feelings, so I validated him and told him I didn't believe in loaning money to people unless they were family members or close friends.

He got up and left—but not before snatching my Rolex watch off the counter on his way out. I didn't realize he'd taken it until he was gone, and when I reported the crime to the police, the detective sided with the thief. He said, "Oh, this happens all the time with women trying to harangue men. This man is a pillar of the community, so there's really nothing I can do." I was shocked, but I refused to let these bad apples spoil the whole barrel of men, so I pulled myself up by the bootstraps and tried again.

Bachelor Number 57

After a coffee date with this man, I decided I liked him enough for a second date and felt safe enough that he could pick me up at my apartment for our next date. He arrived with flowers, and I was thrilled. I said, "Thank you, they're beautiful." He said, "Oh, sorry, they're not for you, they're for my mother." I wasn't quite sure what to say, but I managed something like, "Isn't the second date kind of soon to meet your mother?" He said, "Oh, it's nothing like that. We'll be passing by her on the way to the restaurant, so I thought I'd just pop in for a minute and drop these off." I have to admit I was disappointed that the flowers weren't for me, and I wasn't looking forward to meeting his mother yet, but I reasoned, "Well, at least he's thoughtful and cares about his mother; that's a good sign." **Men who treat their mothers well treat their wives well.**

When we pulled up in front of a large mansion, I thought it was his mother's house. The door was unlocked and we walked into a large marble entryway. It didn't feel like a house at all, and I was starting to wonder where we were when I saw the big star on the floor with Judy Garland's name on it. I thought either his mother was a huge fan of Judy Garland, or maybe they were related, but either way it seemed odd to have a memorial star devoted to her in your house.

"Are you related to Judy Garland?" I asked. He looked at me like he didn't understand the question. "No," he said. "She's just one of the people who are here." "But, she's dead, isn't she?" I asked. He said, "Yes, she is," and then took my hand and walked me into a room that had name plaques all over the walls. "Where are we?" I wanted to know, realizing finally that this was certainly not his mother's house. "We're in a mausoleum," he replied as if I should have known that. Being Jewish, I had never been in a mausoleum and I had no idea what one looked like.

He proceeded to introduce me to his mother as a candidate for marriage, gave her the flowers—by putting them in a vase near her vault—and asked her if she would mind if he gave one to me. I guess she said okay because he pulled a carnation out of the bunch and handed it to me. If I'd had a cell phone back then, I would have called for a cab, but I was at his mercy, so we went on to dinner together. He was feeling wonderful, but once again I found myself sitting in a restaurant with no appetite.

Bachelor Number 68

I had great anticipation when I answered a personal ad to a man who described himself as "the John Wayne Rugged Type." I loved watching cowboy movies with my grandpa when I was growing up and was a huge fan of John Wayne, so I was really anxious to meet this mystery man. We agreed to meet for a drink at a club in the Hamptons and told each other what we would be wearing.

When I arrived, I didn't see anyone who fit the description, so I walked around the club introducing myself to all the men who might have passed as "rugged" types. I met sixteen different men in just over an hour and exchanged cards with all of them, but none of them were "John Wayne." After nearly two hours of "acorn gathering"—as if all of us singles were squirrels preparing for a long winter—I was relieved to be heading home.

Maybe John Wayne was out chasing bad guys, I joked to myself as I walked toward the door. But when I pushed open the door, there before me stood a man who was wearing exactly what John Wayne said he'd have on. He said, "Bonnie?" and I said "John?" He apologized for being late and asked me if I would be willing to stay a little longer to have dinner with him.

As you know, I had sworn off having dinner with men on the first date after Mr. Eerie, and I was still taken aback a little because "John" didn't look at all like John Wayne. He was severely hunched over and had an uncanny resemblance to the Hunchback of Notre Dame. "You probably won't want to have dinner with me," he said. "You're so pretty." My heart went out to him. I was brought up to be kind and as a therapist I know how the pain of a single moment can last a lifetime, so I broke my no-dinner rule and sat down with him.

He was a nice man, but very timid and withdrawn and not at all the type of man I was looking for. We were seated right next to the door and as we had dinner, each one of the sixteen men I'd exchanged cards with earlier walked by and either ignored me or did a "double-take." One guy's mouth actually fell open as he nudged his buddy and pointed over to our table. I was once again shocked at how insensitive and cruel people can be. Not one of those sixteen men ever called me, and even though I would have generally taken a chance and called most of them, I decided that if they were going to judge me based on who I was having dinner with, they were too superficial and shallow for me to waste my time.

Bachelor Number 72

The next time I made it to the third date, it was with an *animal lover.* We had a lot of fun on the first two dates, so I *really primped* for this one. I wore a beautiful angora sweater with a sexy skirt and very expensive stockings. He picked me up for this date and when I started to get into the front seat of the car, I was usurped by a seventy-five-pound dog. I shrieked because when I was only two, I was knocked down and had my little angora sweater ripped off by a big Boxer dog. I've been afraid of big dogs ever since. I suggested maybe the dog could ride in the back seat. "Oh no," he said, "Floozy rides with me."

I said, "Well, it's gotta be her or me because she has already ripped my stockings and is on her way to shredding my sweater." I wasn't disappointed when he opened the door and let me out. Maybe I should skip the personal ads for awhile, I thought to myself as I walked back to my apartment looking more like a bag lady than someone on her way to a date. That's when I decided to try a dating service.

The service had a money-back guarantee so I felt I had nothing to lose. The woman I spoke with said they had a very high success rate and *she guaranteed me that I would meet the man of my dreams.* One of the things I indicated to her was that I wanted to meet men who were looking for a relationship, not just a good time. She said, "No problem. **We have lots of men who want relationships.**"

Bachelor Number 76

After dating six or seven men who wanted everything and anything *but* commitment, I called the dating service and said I wanted my money back. One of their representatives asked me to give it one more try, saying she had *the perfect man* for me. She gave me his name and told me he was a famous journalist. She assured me he was looking for a woman who wanted to have a relationship. I thought, great! I'll give him a try.

The next day I attended a sexuality seminar with some of my colleagues and one of my male friends asked, "Hey, are you getting past the third date these days?" I said, "No, but I'm looking forward to a date tomorrow with a man who is supposedly the man of my dreams." When I told him the man's name, he said, "He's not just a journalist, Bonnie, *he's a sex guru!* He writes porn." I was sure we were talking about two different men.

Since this new date had been so highly recommended I agreed that he could pick me up at my apartment for a breakfast date, even though I hadn't met him yet. I was impressed when a limo pulled up, and curious, too. Then out stepped a cherubic-faced man with no shoes, a huge medallion hanging around his neck, wearing a kaftan. Hmmm. I reminded myself not to make a hasty judgment and we went to The Brasserie for breakfast. I thought I should at least give him a chance if he was supposed to be the man of my dreams, but I choked on my bagel when he said, "How would you like to be a *Playboy* bunny and float around in a hot tub with me, Hugh Hefner, and some of the other bunnies?"

I got up, thanked him for the bagel, and in between choking and coughing informed him I had my own jacuzzi in my country home. He said, "That's too bad, you would make a great bunny." I decided it would be fun to scare him, so I said, "And you would make a fantastic husband!" With that, he asked for the check and instructed his limo driver to drop me off wherever I wanted to go, without coming along for the ride, of course. When I got into the limo the driver winked at me and I knew he was somewhat familiar with this routine.

I dropped the dating service and decided to give the personal ads one last try. And thank God I did! **It was through a personal ad in *New York Magazine* that I met Jeff, my seventy-seventh coffee date and thankfully my last!**

Remember, it only takes one. In the meantime, try to keep a sense of humor. While the dating stories I've shared with you didn't seem funny at the time, they're very funny to me now.

Success rarely comes easily, but it does come if you don't lose hope. The most successful people credit their mistakes and failures for taking them to the top—not only in relationships but in all areas of life. Einstein failed math, Edison's first inventions were scoffed at, and Walt Disney was told early in his career that he should give up cartooning and try something different.

So be persistent and don't let anyone tell you that you can't have the relationship or the love you want. You can and you will, if you use Smart Heart Skills and refuse to give up!

❧ 13 ❧

Connecting on the First Date

"Relationships always involve this kind of fluctuation between bonding with another and maintaining our integrity as individuals, yielding to our partner and asserting ourselves, reaching out and going deep within."

—JOHN WELWOOD

From across a crowded room your attention is magnetically drawn to one of two types of men. The first is Mr. Wow! He elicits an almost irresistible attraction. **Put on your seat belt because while this man is the one designed to bring you the most joy, he is also the one who will cause you the most trouble.**

The other type of man who might catch your eye is Mr. Nice Guy. He's pleasant, caring, and polite. He reflects your parents' positive traits, but this makes him less exciting. He's a little too easy, not enough of a challenge. Unless you shift your relationship style by getting in touch with your own wounds and healing them, you probably won't pick Mr. Nice Guy, even though he might be the better choice. You generally will pick

Mr. Wow *because you need some element of challenge to mimic the childhood struggles you are still trying to work out. You can have a great relationship with Mr. Nice Guy if you build some challenge into the relationship dynamic. Either way, don't trust your first response.*

Smart Heart Skills to Set Up the First Date

- Give him your card or number or ask for or accept his.
- Show him with friendliness that if he asks you out, you'll go.
- If he seems interested but shy, ask *him* out.
- Be willing to make the phone call, or respond to his call with Smart Heart Skills to set up a time, date, and place. As I tell my patients: Nail it!
- Don't be passive. **Be quietly aggressive.**

These same skills apply in cyberspace. There's a new trend to meet and court one another via e-mail and chat rooms; this must be handled carefully. It's easy for someone to look good and come across well "in writing." A cyberspace date or lover can share what he wants you to know and hide the rest. Having a long, ongoing Internet relationship can be as destructive as spending too much time on the phone with each other. *It's action, not talking, that moves a relationship forward.*

If a man tells you in an e-mail message that he'd like to get together some time, Nail it! Suggest a time, a safe public place, and a date. If you don't get a positive response, move on! If your biological clock is ticking, don't waste time on men who want only to "toy" with you. Be honest about what you want, **but don't scare him.**

Smart Heart Dialogue

He asks: "What are you looking for?"

You give him an honest response. For example: "There was a time that I wanted only my career. I'm ready now to have a relationship. I know I want to get married some day so I'm looking for a man who is interested in taking a risk to see where a relationship can go."

What If You're Having Trouble Meeting Men You Want to Date?

We encounter new people all the time—at the bus stop, at work, in the grocery store, standing in line for concert tickets, at the library, in the video store, and the list goes on and on. Since the ways we meet are often in passing, it can be difficult to strike up a conversation and get something going, but it can be done. My friend Brenda met her husband at a bus stop. She was attracted to him, so she smiled, looked into his eyes, and gave him her card. **Her encouragement gave him the confidence to call her.**

Smart Heart Steps to Meet Men

Step One:

Make it a priority and treat it seriously, as you would any important goal you have in life. Tell your friends and family you're very interested in meeting a nice man and having a relationship. Ask them if they know a man you might like.

Don't be embarrassed to ask for help. We all need help and our loved ones are happy to help us.

Step Two:
Don't be ashamed that you're not in a relationship. Get over the stigma! For some reason the words, "I'm lonely," carry a lot of shame, but there's no reason for that! The first time I said it, I felt better. So throw away *the shame and guilt you have about not being intimately involved or a vicious cycle will ensue.*

At the same time, don't make excuses. Promise yourself to do something about it and come up with a game plan. Unfortunately, the more you have to give, the more intelligent and attractive you are, the harder it is to meet men. They're threatened because they think you'll say no if they ask you out. I stopped dressing in hats and high heels because my male friends said I looked like a model. They said if they didn't know how down to earth I am, they would look at me and assume I wouldn't give them the time of day. So look at how you dress, how you behave with men, and *how welcoming or rejecting you are.* Be willing to adjust some things to be more approachable.

Step Three:
Don't get discouraged or predetermine you'll never meet anyone, get past the third date, or get married. *These negative thoughts can turn into self-fulfilling prophecies if you start to believe them.*

Step Four:
Visualize and meditate on that white dress, picket fence, station wagon with three kids and a dog, or whatever your

dream is. Seeing it in your mind will help you to create it in your life.

When I was working on my Ph.D., I visualized my diploma on the wall of my office and bought myself a pen engraved Dr. Bonnie Eaker Weil. This method of bringing dreams into reality is very powerful. *If you can't visualize yourself having what you claim to want, ask yourself how badly you really want it.*

My patient Tara lamented about not being able to get past the third date, and although her biological clock was ticking and she really wanted children, she couldn't even visualize herself in a wedding gown. When I asked her how badly she really wanted to get married, she said, "Not badly enough I guess." Her fear of losing herself in a relationship was overriding her desire.

Step Five:

Consider a dating service, the personal ads, or checking out the available men in cyberspace. Many people have had great success with this route, including my husband and me. We are proud to have both been wise enough to use this method of meeting that works so well for busy people.

If I Can Do it, You Can Do it!

The day I opened the *New York Magazine* and one personal ad practically popped off the page, I actually thought, "This is the man I want to marry." *It was a feeling of intuition that came over me like a big wave.*

The ad read: Be my Guinevere—A truly romantic, handsome dentist, 37, seeks a *caring* relationship with an attractive, professional woman 25–33. I enjoy photography, movies, skiing, racquetball, tennis, traveling, candlelight dinners, and holding hands. How about you? Please send bio/photo.

It was the part about candlelight dinners and holding hands that really got me, and I sat down to write a response. (I was actually thirty-nine at that time.) But two weeks later, I hadn't heard a thing. When I shared this with my friend Brenda, she asked me if I had sent a photo. I hadn't and she accused me of being ambivalent. "What? *Me? Ambivalent?* My patients are ambivalent, but I don't think I am!" I protested. Brenda reminded me that when I wrote the letter I told her I really thought this guy was "the one." My old abandonment wounds had risen to the surface when he didn't respond to my letter.

Brenda was right, I was feeling ambivalent—which is one of the biggest reasons women have trouble getting past the third date. She urged me to send my photo, since I hadn't sent one with the letter. I mailed off a photograph of myself taken on my recent vacation in the Caribbean. I was wearing a sarong, standing barefoot in the sand while the tropical winds blew back my long hair and gently bent the palm trees behind me.

A few days later the phone rang and it was **him!!** As it turned out he never received my letter. We had a great conversation, started dating, and have now been married more than ten years. It hasn't always been easy, but it's definitely been worth it!

Today, Jeff and I teach a class together on how to meet through the personals and many of the people in the class call us to let us know how much fun they're having and how many great people they're meeting. (We've been invited to lots of weddings!) Use all of the resources out there and treat meeting a man like a job search. Give it energy, attention, and time. Don't sit at home and wait for someone to magically show up at your door.

As Dr. Fogarty urges, "Take risks, desensitize yourself to rejection, and learn the skills that will ensure your happiness, minimize your loneliness and **meet your only need in life— which is connectedness."** Remember that men seek closeness too, but like you, they're afraid of it. You help the ambivalent man realize he is lonely by enticing him and then pulling away when he misses you most so he gets in touch with his loneliness. It takes getting in touch with loneliness to do the most difficult thing in the world—to risk, give up control, and love.

If you meet someone ambivalent, ride it out with him. Don't panic with him and don't make him feel guilty—that prevents both of you from moving forward. Work with his ambivalence. *Allow it, don't fight it.* Accept that you are going to feel restless and insecure and *that hurt is part of relationships and love.* If you're using all your energy trying to make sure you don't get hurt, you will either sabotage a new relationship or you will avoid all the men who could potentially get close to you. **Be quietly aggressive,** like I was.

Most women want to be more aggressive but behave in a passive way because they've been misled to believe it works. I'm not suggesting you chase a man (remember you really can't pursue a Distancer!), but you have to take action to let him know you're interested in spending time with him. Put out positive vibes and energy. Smile, let down your walls, and put out the welcome mat so men feel comfortable approaching you and responding to your approach.

Please stop ruling men out because they don't immediately match your idea of "the one for you." You can't judge a book by its cover! You have to take the time to open it up. It takes time for a man to feel comfortable enough to open up so you can really get to know him. All of the men you meet and date help you to practice and prepare for the day when you do meet "the one," or the day you realize the man you've been dating—whom you may not have been so crazy about at first—*is* "the one"!

Five of the Biggest Reasons Women Have Trouble Meeting Men
1. They're too picky.
2. They stereotype and judge men on superficial qualities.
3. They're ambivalent or scared.
4. They're afraid to make the first move; they think if they do it won't last, or see this as disinterest of men or neediness of women.
5. They misinterpret men's lack of movement as lack of interest.

Single people put up walls. If you're extremely defensive or picky, you're probably afraid and secretly want to push people away. *Extreme defensiveness or pickiness is a sign that you're rejecting yourself.* If you stereotype men and write them off for trivial or superficial reasons, you are ambivalent. From now on, when a man asks you out, if you think you can have fun, learn something, or be friends, say yes. So what if it doesn't turn into anything.

Many women can't meet a man they like because they want it to happen romantically by chance, by serendipity, or by clairvoyance. People do meet by chance, but why wait? Remember most men are waiting for *you* to make the first move, so make it!

If you're afraid to lose control, *you can be more in control by taking quiet, aggressive steps and pulling back before the man has a chance to feel frightened or overwhelmed.* You're never completely in control when you're in a relationship because there's someone with you. That's why some of you are avoiding it; you have control only when you're alone. *The more out of control you feel, the more you try to be in control and the more out of control you end up being.* Try to relax and have fun with dating. Think less about "finding a husband," and more about being connected!

Whatever you do, don't buy it if someone (even your therapist) tells you you're not ready for a relationship! You'll never feel really ready. Just plunge in and go for it. *You learn by doing, not by talking or thinking about it.* The more you date, the more you learn about yourself and the more you discover what you want and don't want in a partner.

Smart Heart Dating

Dating stretches you to see how far you can go inside yourself. You get an opportunity to get in touch with parts of yourself you're not aware you have. Jerry Seinfeld jokingly says, "A date is like a job interview that lasts all night." But a first date should be anything **but** an interview. The idea that you're supposed to find out in the first twenty minutes if he's interested in marriage and children and what he wants out of life is terrible advice. You can't take the measure of a person in one date, let alone twenty minutes—unless he's an obvious psychopath and gives it away. Enjoy each other and get to know each other a little before you start asking questions or lay your expectations on the table. It's understandable that dating can be both exciting and stressful, because all of our issues come out.

If you're leery of dating, I understand. When you go on a date you are being judged and evaluated and you are doing the same. *It makes both of you vulnerable and uncomfortable— especially on a first date.* Don't fall into the trap of thinking that good relationships and lasting marriages begin with a "perfect" first date. If you turn down a second date with a man because he spilled wine on your dress, wore a loud tie, or didn't laugh at your jokes, you *might be stopping a great relationship before it starts.* Don't trust your first impression of a man being "wonderful" or "terrible." On first dates, we often idealize a man's positives, or we exaggerate his negatives. It takes at least three dates to gain a real perspective of who he is and where he's coming from.

My parents went to Coney Island Amusement Park on their first date. They ended up on a violently circling ride, and got a free second spin cycle when the ride attendant mistakenly started it up again before they could get off. Dad was holding on to Mom for dear life, and they threw up all over each other. After they had their balance back, my dad asked, "You don't like rides?" She told him she didn't. He laughed and said, "I don't like them either. Why didn't we tell each other?" Not very romantic, but they've been married for more than fifty years. They began learning the value of telling each other how they felt about things from their first date "ride trauma." **They learned that truth was smarter than "being polite."**

After Jeff and I met for coffee, I knew I liked him and felt safe enough to have a date with him. For my first date with Jeff, I invited him to my country home in the Poconos for a day of swimming, hiking, and boating.

After watching a gorgeous sunset, we decided to slip into the jacuzzi, where we spent hours talking, laughing, and kissing. Jeff shyly asked if he could stay the night, since he wasn't sure he'd find his way back out of the mountains. I let him stay, but told him he couldn't sleep in the same room with me. I did end up letting him sleep in my room, but we didn't make love.

In trying to reassure me he said, "sex isn't important anyway," which made me worry he wasn't interested in sex. I was afraid he would be like my ex-husband. *At that point, I could have put up the walls with Jeff, but I decided to take a risk and ask him what he meant.*

He said, "I meant to say that sex is important, but it's more important right now for us to get to know each other." We slept chastely side by side and the next morning I got up and put on a white summer dress that he said, in a horrified voice, "looked like a wedding dress." When he dropped me off at a family gathering on his way home, he suddenly found himself surrounded by the smiling and inquisitive faces of my relatives. Jeff couldn't drive away fast enough from that scene—me in a white dress surrounded by family. He didn't call for two weeks, but he *did* call. If I hadn't heard from him, I would have called *him*. Our first date was far from perfect. **We both had one or two moments when we could have run away, but we didn't.**

Men and women come to a first date with different expectations, but they're both seeking a connection on some level or they wouldn't be there at all. Each wants to be liked for who he or she is, not for his or her money, looks, sexual appeal, or ability, and not for "giving" or "withholding sex." Nobody wants to be rejected, which is why insecurity is part of dating. *If you were completely secure on an early date, there would be no excitement, chemistry, movement, or growth.*

Smart Heart Dating Skills

What Works:

- Evaluating men on their ability to teach you something or broaden your horizons, or be your friend, rather than whether they're "husband" material.
- Keeping it light and having fun!

- Being yourself, but being willing to stretch, temper, and modify your style of behavior in a relationship.
- **Clarifying** anything that will make either of you run. If you don't understand something he (or she) says, ask.
- Staying in the moment and being present!
- Savoring the mystery and all the unknowns.
- Being discriminating about *when* and *how* you reveal yourself. Exposing yourself too much or immediately connecting is as risky as sleeping with him too soon. Just serve the appetizer for now; there will be plenty of time for dinner and dessert later.
- Using Smart Heart Dialogue to share your issues and fears *with humor*. It's not too early to begin doing this early on. If you don't begin sharing on the first and second date, there may not be a third date.
- Showing him how to have fun so he looks forward to the next time.
- Giving him space, but staying connected.
- Understanding his fear of vulnerability and his fear of dependency.
- Letting him know other men are asking you out; it's good for him to know you're not going to wait around for him forever, but you don't want to make him too jealous or his insecurity may make him walk away.
- Talking softly, without anger, for short periods of time. Teach him to enjoy talking to you by mixing the talking in between lots of fun and activities.
- Offering to pay sometimes to show him *he* can be taken care of, and you don't always expect him to take care of you.
- Letting him be in charge. Most men feel like they need to take the lead, so let him set the pace, but you firm

up the dates and plans by suggesting times, days, and places, so there will be a next time. Nail it!

- Validating him. Everyone needs and wants to be accepted and understood.
- Knowing when to nurture and when to give him space.
- Doing whatever it takes to elevate your own self-worth so that you can *want* a man, but not *need* one.
- Using your dating experiences to make you more resilient and seeing them as a chance to *develop* your Smart Heart!

What Doesn't Work:

- Being picky, stereotyping, analyzing, or criticizing (out loud or in your mind).
- Sitting at home, waiting for a phone call from a man, mind-reading, and getting angrier by the minute.
- Confronting him about his disconnection. **Don't give him any attention for his disconnecting.** *If he doesn't call you, don't even mention it.* Engage his interest again by having a good time together.
- Playing the part of "the bitch," which most Distancers unconsciously provoke. Don't let his actions or lack of actions provoke you into this behavior. If you do, he will blame *you* for his own behavior and won't see into himself.
- Pointing out his fears or issues; let him discover them for himself, or help him by gently guiding him so he can see them.
- Letting him take you for granted.
- Talking too much. Talk less and play more.
- Provoking him. (It will scare him.)

- Overreacting or assuming you know what he's thinking.
- Buying into his excuses. Make him accountable, but do it in a very gentle but firm manner, with no anger.
- Standing on ceremony for trivial things that really don't matter one way or the other.
- Scolding him. Don't give him the satisfaction of treating him as his mother did. Don't criticize, judge, blame, or punish him. None of these things will work. If you want to help him and help yourself, teach him by your actions and your words.
- Letting your friends make your decisions for you. Don't let your friends or associates talk you out of a relationship. If they don't understand the dynamics between the two of you, they won't understand your desire to hang in.
- Paying too much attention to his words or taking him literally. *Instead, look at the movement.* Particularly on first dates, people say what they think their date wants to hear, or, alternatively, what they think their date doesn't want to hear to keep them at arm's length.
- Coming on too sexy. You can scare men away or give them the wrong idea.
- Overextending yourself or trying too hard to please him right away by making his "favorite dinner" or buying him an expensive gift. It could scare him—or set a pattern that will make him take you for granted. It could also "guilt" him since he doesn't know if he can return the "feeling."
- Expecting to hear bells and see angels the first time your lips meet. This first kiss is almost always more awkward and tentative than it is romantic. Give it some time.

Seven Points to Remember

1. The Porcupine Analogy. Get close enough for connection, but not so close that you prick.
2. **Moments of closeness will be followed by distance.** Anticipate this and do not see it as rejection; this is a man's way of maintaining his boundaries.
3. Expect the relationship to shift from the Euphoria feelings of the first and second date to the Power Struggle Stage. This is natural and unavoidable. *Use Smart Heart Skills and Dialogue to work through this stage, so you can get past the third date.*
4. There's a part of you that is afraid of being vulnerable, inadequate, disappointed, rejected, or suffocated. Keep that part in check so you don't talk yourself out of a potentially great relationship.
5. **Just because you have sex with a man doesn't mean you have to do it again the next time you go out.**
6. Men don't like being told what to do. They don't want a woman to have power at their expense.
7. When you begin dating a man, you are not only dating him, you are also dating his past—family, girlfriends, ex-wives, etc.—because they all contributed to who he is today.

Don't put heavy expectations on a first date. View it as a mystery, a chance to explore unknown regions of yourself and your date. If it's not the "date of your dreams" so what? It's better than ordering pizza and watching reruns! (At least most of the time!)

The First Date Between the Most Likely Couple

Since most women are Pursuers and most men are Distancers, this pair-up accounts for the greatest number of couples. If you're a Pursuer, on a first date, you look across the table and want to replace the expression of ambivalence on your date's face with one of love and devotion. You want something to happen, something like love at first sight, instant chemistry, a meeting of souls. On the dance floor, or sitting next to him in the theater, you *expect* to feel a thrill when your bodies first touch; and *so you probably will.* Leaning forward, you anticipate movement and want to control it.

Learn how to keep your desire for control in check so you don't intimidate or scare a man away. Project availability, not neediness. (A man who is a Pursuer must learn how to make a woman feel desired and appreciated, not come on so strong that his date begins to wonder if she's being stalked.)

Smart Heart Skills for a Woman Pursuer on Her First Date with a Man Distancer

- Ask open-ended questions like, "I read in the paper that the city council is thinking of making a new bike path. What have you heard about that?" Don't ask questions that can be answered with a simple "yes," "no," or "I don't know."
- Smile, be warm and friendly but not overpowering.
- Refrain from asking, or even hinting, about future dates. Don't tell him you have tickets for a game or invite him to your best friend's wedding.

- Keep it light. Don't talk about your mother's depression, your fear of being down-sized, your friend's divorce, or your therapy. If he takes the conversation in that direction, gently guide it back into safer waters.
- Don't have more than one drink. You will be more inclined to have sex before you're ready. You may get emotional or too close too fast, and you'll probably talk too much about the wrong things.
- *Don't use the word "relationship."* Some women (the extreme Pursuers) ask "What happened in your previous relationship?" before the appetizer arrives.

Smart Heart Skills for a Male Distancer on His First Date with a Female Pursuer

- Move toward her. Then she won't feel like she has to lean too far toward you.
- Do something spontaneous. You've made dinner reservations, bought tickets for a movie or play, now it's time to think on your feet. Do something you didn't plan to do—like buying a flower for her from a street vendor, or exploring a new route home after the date. It will make you feel less controlled and confined by the structure of the date.
- Don't flirt with other women, and don't talk about them either. You'll make her feel insecure and she'll withdraw, pull away, or move too closely toward you.
- Ask her personal questions, but not the kind that lead to relationship discussions. Ask about her work, hobbies, and interests so she knows you want to get to know her.
- Don't end the date by saying, "I'll talk to you later," or "I'll see you soon," unless you are really going to call her.

The Second Most Likely Couple: Female Distancer with Male Pursuer

The Pursuer/Distancer coupling is more common with a male Distancer and a female Pursuer, but in the reverse the relationship has many of the same dynamics. The difference is that the 20 percent of women who are Distancers and the 20 percent of men who are Pursuers often feel like a square peg trying to fit into a round hole.

If you're a female Distancer, learn how to modify your behavior or dating will seem like a losing battle for you. Most of my female patients who can't get a relationship going or keep it going are female Distancers. **If you're in this boat, you have an underlying intimacy problem, but you probably don't see yourself as the issue.** You say you want a good relationship, but the thought of being vulnerable and intimate with a man probably scares you. Come to terms with this or you will continue to judge men for their weaknesses, and completely miss their strengths.

Everyone has some strengths and if you can't see any, it's because your own fear isn't letting you. **Chances are, you're not attracted to Pursuers who come on so strongly they scare or repel you, or you're attracted to Extreme Distancers because unconsciously you don't really want to be close.** If you pick one elusive man after another, stop blaming them and start looking honestly at yourself. I know this is hard-hitting information, but you must accept the truth of who you are if you want to make some changes and have a good relationship.

The magnetism factor in relationships means that as a female Distancer, a Pursuer will be more attracted to you, and you will not know how to handle his affection and attention. Remember, behind every Pursuer, there's a Distancer, and vice versa, so the two of you are more alike than you may think. *Teach a Pursuer how to slow things down so you won't be afraid or become ambivalent.* Take it one day at a time and ask him not to bring you flowers or call you at work if that makes you feel smothered. Say it with kindness and explain you are afraid of being overwhelmed.

Smart Heart Skills for a Woman Distancer on Her First Date with a Man Pursuer

- Have that glass of wine or two; it will help you relax.
- Move physically toward him when you feel like pulling away. Uncross your arms and legs. Lean slightly forward. Open up when your instincts tell you to be closed.
- Spark the chemistry. Before you say "no chemistry," *try to make some happen.* Touch his hand. Return his gaze.
- Don't say, "Take me home" the minute he does or says something "wrong." **The urge to run might mean the chemistry you think isn't there, really is, and you're scared.**

Smart Heart Skills for a Man Pursuer on His First Date with a Woman Distancer

- Avoid talking too much about your feelings or emotional goals. Don't say, "I want to get married," or "I've never been so attracted to a woman on a first date before."
- Refrain from asking for a second date before the first date comes to a close. Women Distancers are very vague, unpredictable, and ambiguous. They don't like to be pinned down to specific plans in advance.

- Stop yourself from talking about the future in any form. Distancers are spontaneous.

- Don't introduce heavy topics. Don't tell her how other women, your boss, your kids, or the IRS have done you wrong. Don't tell her you're a recovering alcoholic or that you come from a dysfunctional family. And unless you're filming a Woody Allen movie together, don't introduce the subject of death.

- Don't drink alcohol. If you do, you may introduce those heavy topics I just advised you to avoid. If you have too much to drink, you could end up telling her she reminds you of your dear, departed, sainted mother—and you'll never see her again.

- Don't suggest "going back to her place." If you're a male Pursuer, you may not be doing this to push for sex (as a Distancer will do)—you may just want to be invited into her home as a way of getting close to her. You can go in, if she invites you, but it's her call.

Should I or Shouldn't I?

The question of whether or not to have sex is often looming in your mind as the date progresses—or possibly from the moment the date was set up. **Even though most men are emotional Distancers, they're usually sexual Pursuers.** The standard advice for women is: "Don't give him sex too soon, or he won't call back." The truth is that making the next call may be difficult for him whether you have sex or not. *But if you sleep with someone too soon, you may regret your decision, especially if he doesn't call you again.*

You can push someone away by sleeping with him, and by not sleeping with him. Speak up and set your own pace.

Get to know a man before you sleep with him, because sex can complicate a relationship, or complement it, depending on why and when it happens.

I don't tell women to hold back sexually to manipulate a man into making a post-date phone call, *but I do suggest they wait until they know the man better so they won't feel so abandoned when he pulls away.*

The 20 percent of women who are Distancers tend to have sex early in a relationship. Sex is an expression of caring, nurturing, and connecting. Don't use sex to determine if you like a man, use it as a way to show a man how much you like him, when you're really ready to do that.

One of my patients, Randy, said, "I do need space after sex. Like most men, I want to roll over and go to sleep, and she wants to talk and cuddle. I do feel close to her, which I admit scares me, but I need some space—not to run to another woman—to be alone." Many men need some space after sex. **The trouble is that the longer he waits to call you the more guilty he feels.** He thinks you're going to be mad at him (based on his previous experience), so he talks himself out of calling you altogether.

If two or three weeks go by and you haven't heard from a man you had a great time with, call him. If you call him and invite him to join you for a movie or something you know he will enjoy, and you don't mention anything about his not calling you, he will begin to relax. He'll see that you're not going to suffocate him or be overbearing and he'll look forward to spending time with you again.

If he calls after a week or more and you berate him for not calling or make him feel guilty, you're playing right into his hand. You're fulfilling his belief that women want too much and he (once again) didn't live up to expectations. He will revert back to his childish behavior, pout, and say, "I didn't like her anyway!" Since he's afraid of relationships and commitments, he's looking for a reason to run away and *I guarantee you that guilt and anger are two sure-fire ways to make him run.*

What to Do If You've Already Had Sex on the First Date:

- Give him some room. Don't expect him to call right away, and don't panic if you haven't heard from him in two weeks.
- Do NOT call, fax, or e-mail him the next morning to say, "I had a lovely time." (Wait at least a week or two to reconnect.)
- When you do hear from him, don't chastise him for not calling sooner. He'll feel pressured, guilty, and suffocated and distance again, instead of wanting to get together.
- Don't chastise yourself for making a tactical error in dating, and don't feel guilty. If you had sex because you wanted to have sex it's not the end of the world. (I hope you were using condoms and practicing safe sex.)

Smart Heart Dialogue

"I was carried away because you're so attractive, but I really want to get to know you better before we become sexually intimate again."

When you do begin having sex, don't be too critical of your partner's skills or expect doves to fly overhead when you're skin to skin. The first few sexual experiences between a couple are similar to the first few kisses. It's hard for strangers to gratify each other sexually. You need to take the time to get to know each other and make an emotional connection so that sex feels safe. Talk to him about your decision to wait a while.

Smart Heart Dialogue

"You are very attractive and it will be hard for me to wait to have sex with you, but just think how great it will be when we do."

This lets him know that you're not just leading him on or teasing him. **Be very complimentary and reassuring when you tell him you want to wait, because he will feel a sense of rejection.** I once explained this to a very handsome man after our third date and he said, "Oh, I thought it was because you didn't think I was attractive. I'm glad you told me that because I wasn't going to ask you out again." (We ended up together for four years.)

You Need at Least Three Dates!

When the relationship dance begins you're unfamiliar with each other's timing and steps. *You need to stay on the dance floor long enough to learn how to give each other enough space and avoid stepping on each other's toes. If you run away or disappear before the music ends, you'll never know what might have happened.*

In the next chapter, you will learn how to handle a man's vulnerability and reconnect for a second date.

~ 14 ~

How to Reconnect for the Second Date

"Only in a relationship can you know yourself, not in abstraction, and certainly not in isolation."
—J. KRISHNAMURTI

The first date was incredible and you're walking on air. Days pass and the phone rings, but it isn't *him*. You begin to wonder if you misinterpreted his behavior and worry that he won't call. You may feel rejected or get angry with him. Meanwhile, he's trying to minimize his feelings for you. Yes, he *did* have a great time—*maybe too great!* **The more he likes you, the more he needs to keep a distance for awhile.** He may wait a week or more to call as a way of asserting his independence. He may wait to call because he is ambivalent and wants to provoke you so you'll reject him and he can be free and clear again. Or, he may write off the first date as "too good to be true."

Countless relationships stop before they start at this point. With Smart Heart Skills and Dialogue you can make sure that doesn't happen to you! Most men feel very vulnerable after a first date—especially if they are strongly attracted to you. He's fighting the connection. He's happy and yet he's lost. He wants you, *but he doesn't want to need you.* If you don't take this personally, you're way ahead of the game! Rather than reacting negatively to his mixed emotions, express your vitality and "aliveness," which are two of the traits he finds most attractive in you. "Act as if" you're confident and reconnect with him, instead of running or pushing him away.

It's not uncommon to enter a power struggle of some sort before the second date. The conflict may have been triggered during the first date, or it may occur between the first and second date. For example, if he doesn't call you soon enough after the first date, or if he doesn't say what you want to hear when he does call, you may get angry or upset. **Remember, he doesn't know your script!** (When you catch yourself doing this, your "sabotage red flag" should go up! Put up the white flag instead, and validate him!) If he doesn't call after a few weeks, **reach out and reconnect with him.** If he doesn't say what you want to hear, or says something that scares you, "act as if" you're not upset and validate him.

Sometimes it takes two dates for a man's vulnerability to take over, and it may not happen for a month or longer. But eventually, these feelings will come up. **The more prepared you are, the easier it will be for you to handle them with kid gloves!** One of my patients had two blissful dates with a man, but when he called and canceled the third date, she was livid. Renee said she wanted to either call him and rake him over the coals, or never speak to him again. I told Renee to think of him as a very vulnerable man who needed stroking. "Call him and use Smart Heart Dialogue to invite him for dinner."

She did, and when they met for dinner and she looked into his eyes, she saw his vulnerability. He tried to keep the walls up, but in sneaked the tender feelings they had experienced on the first and second dates. **Remember that a scared man sometimes acts the opposite of how he really feels.** Much to

Renee's surprise, when she asked why he canceled their third date, he told her he had such a great time on the first two dates that "this is as good as it gets." She said, "That's so sad because you stopped in the middle." He said he felt disconnected from her when he called to cancel. She gently pointed out that **he** was the one who disconnected. She was helping him to be account-able for his actions. He was using his "this is as good as it gets" belief to avoid getting into a relationship.

For Distancers, the "out of sight, out of mind" cliche holds true between dates. *You* need to bring them back to connection. They're stuck at the *separate and return stage* in their developmental process. **Don't mistake their "laissez faire" for indifference or disinterest.**

Smart Heart Skills

- If the man disconnects, stay connected.
- He may get scared and put a wall up, but if you have already shared some good memories—even just a date or two—there's a good chance to reconnect. (**Smart Heart Dialogue helps you create the "glue" to keep you together.**)
- Look at his actions and movements; don't listen too much to his words.
- Watch him closely. Regardless of what he's saying, what is he doing?

Smart Heart Dialogue

(Here's how to correct a mistake of getting angry at your date if he cancels or doesn't call.)

"I wanted to call and apologize for getting so angry the other day. You have every right to your space and if things are getting too intense for you I understand. But I want you to know I care about you and really have fun with you. You're a terrific, handsome guy. I'm just curious—what happened on your end?"

Don't be surprised if his response is similar to Renee's date's response, "This is as good as it gets," or "I don't know."

By being understanding and unemotional, you give him the safety to open up. If he feels safe, he can share his mixed feelings with you. **Tell him it's okay if he doesn't know how he feels or what he wants to do.** If he worries about hurting you, let him know you can take care of yourself. Many men feel torn between being free and being in a relationship. **They use disconnection as a way to stop the relationship so they won't have to face the fears that are being triggered by the closeness.**

In my patient Renee's case, she wanted to help her date get in touch with his fears. She also realized he was struggling with the loss of his mother the year before and the dissolution of a relationship. I was able to help her see that he set up the abandonment scenario—not to reject her, but to gain control in case she left *him*. She wanted to be patient, but she also wanted to make him *accountable*.

Smart Heart Dialogue

"We can move forward and see what happens, we can stop seeing each other, or you can call me back when you feel you are more ready."

This will make him feel secure, rather than pushed. He'll also realize that his ploy to provoke you didn't work. Your role is to remain loving, but firm, and let him know you're leaving the door open, but you're *not* waiting.

Why Men Say They'll Call—But Don't

Most men don't like risk-taking when it comes to their emotions. They fear rejection—more than women do—but they act like they don't care. The pace of the Distancer is very slow as he's moving toward you. He and his date both mistake his emotional reaction toward disconnection as a sign that he's not really interested, but the emotional reaction is actually based on many other unconscious factors. **This "misread sign" is one of the biggest reasons relationships stop before they start and marriages fail.**

Here's what men in my seminars say about why they don't call when they say they will:

The Number One Answer:

"The day after the date or when you first meet is too soon. The next day still feels too aggressive and desperate. The third day is the turning point. If four days go by, I start thinking she might bitch at me by now, since it's been four days. By the fifth day, **I feel too guilty**. I know she'll be mad, so why call?"

Other Answers:

"She was so intense, I told her I'd call so she'd leave me alone."

"I need time to think."

"I might just want to be friends."

"It seems like she's looking for a husband."

"I want her to like me for who I am and she seemed more interested in what I do."

"She wants to have kids. I'm not even ready to be a husband, let alone a dad!"

"I wanted to see if she'd call *me*."

"I don't want her to think she's got me wrapped around her little finger."

"What if she says no?"

"I like her too much."

"I was just being polite."

How People Decide Whether They Want a Third Date

Chemistry and magnetism play important roles in developing a relationship, but many singles can't get to the third date because they misunderstand these mysterious forces. Some singles bail out before the third date because "There's no chemistry." Others set themselves up for possible disappointment because "There's so *much* chemistry between us. He must be the one!"

If someone turns you on, it doesn't mean it's going to last and if someone doesn't turn you on, it doesn't mean that it won't eventually happen. Give someone a chance even if you don't think he's "your type." **In many cases the "type" you've been consistently attracted to is actually the type you won't get very far with.** Dating men who are "not your type" helps you to modify your relationship behavior and you can do this with less fear when you're less attracted to a man and not so worried about the way things turn out. **Go out with men you're not the most attracted to so you can shift your patterns.** I tell my patients, "Don't let the chemistry make your decisions; it's up to you to make the chemistry."

What About Magnetism?

Magnetism is the attraction of opposites and that's why Pursuers and Distancers are usually attracted to each other. The trouble is that you try to change each other to be more like yourself. But, if you were both the same, much of the magnetism would disappear. *This magnetic attraction between opposites can help to keep the relationship moving.* If the Pursuer starts to pull back, the Distancer will be pulled forward. If the Pursuer pushes forward, the Distancer will pull back.

If you want to test the viability of your relationship, pull back (if you're a Pursuer) and see what happens. If you're a Distancer, move forward. This tests the rubber band of the relationship. **If Distancers are left entirely to their own devices they get more distant, so experiment, make a move.** If that doesn't work, pull back. The key is to initiate movement forward or backward. You observe his responses and shift gears to make the movement that will help him to reconnect to you.

Don't let him scare you or make you angry. *Remember you are being quietly aggressive.* If you let his fears get to you, you will be tempted to distance from him. It's called "reactive distancing." People do it for all the wrong reasons, and it never helps. When you move back from him, you want to do it on *purpose, with sensitivity for his wound*—**not** out of reaction. That's why you should pull back *before* he takes you for granted. Pull back with a smile and give him space so he can miss you. When you pull back, do it with kindness **and don't tell him what you're doing.** Actions, not words, are what work. *Let him experience it.*

The mistake many singles make is to think a close relationship is dependent on instantaneous chemistry and magnetism. While both of these forces play a part in moving couples forward, they cannot do the work for you. Sexual intimacy and emotional intimacy are horses of a different color. It's the emotional intimacy that turns great sex into ecstasy. It's what moves you beyond the physical pleasure into an out-of-body sense of spiritual connection; your hearts and minds make this link—not your groins.

Patients like Dawn have a tendency to jump into bed with men very quickly in an attempt to force intimacy. This generally leads to hurt and disappointment because the physical closeness can actually push you apart if it happens before you're both ready to deal with the emotional consequences. Dawn was so afraid of being rejected, she "played the sex card" to force chemistry and hurry the process along. This way, when the man didn't call her back, she could accuse him of wanting only sex and blame him instead of looking more deeply at herself. **While she told herself she was using sex to connect, she was unconsciously using it to disconnect.**

To get to the third date, give relationships a fair chance by not going too fast or too slow. Face and share your ambivalence and keep your emotions in check when your date shares his. You're working on not freaking each other out and not feeding off each other's fears. Sharing your fears and wounds in a light-hearted way is much different from telling a man your expectations. Do not confuse the two, because sharing expectations early on does much more harm than good.

The moderate Distancer is willing to stretch a little, but if he can't, remember that it's often his issues, not yours. If you're patient and understanding of his ambivalence and don't make him feel shamed, guilty, or inadequate, he may be able to work out his issues with you and help you work out your own.

Ambivalence is the coat of armor many singles wear to avoid rejection and therefore avoid intimacy. We all have fears, but we don't have to let them run our lives or ruin our relationships.

Patients say, "I'm not going to date anymore. It hurts too much. I'm better off alone." These men and women are on the verge of joining the ranks of the "walking wounded." I show them they have more than two choices—being alone or being in pain. They can choose to learn the skills and desensitize themselves to rejection so that it doesn't hurt so much. The pain of life alone is far greater than the temporary pain of rejection. If you need more incentive, read the health statistics. **Single people have more depression, weaker immune systems, and shorter life spans than those who are in committed relationships or married.** We need love. It heals us and it frees us. It's worth the pain.

Remember that men want to keep the ball in their court, so they play hard to get. They need a signal of encouragement from women to move forward. It's important to look into his eyes, smile, and mesmerize him on the first few dates. He's looking for love and approval. He wants you to make a fuss over him, but not too much. **Men don't mind listening while you talk, because they often don't know what to say.** Keep the conversation light. By modifying your own behavior, you help a man to modify his. If you demand change, or criticize him for being the way he is, you stop the relationship. *When you have an urge to push too hard or too fast for closeness, visualize those two porcupines in an igloo. To get change, delicately guide and suggest, praise and reward.*

Smart Heart Savvy for Women Only!

Men:
- Don't want to face that they need women.
- Want to be liked and acknowledged for who they are.
- Are just as afraid (if not more) of rejection as we are.

- Like it when women initiate conversations and dates.
- Are attracted to women who have a zest for life.
- Like a sense of humor as much as good looks.

Handling Emptiness

If you're "in your emptiness"—*and you are* if you can't get to or past the third date—use it to your advantage to learn more about yourself. "Emptiness," a term coined by Dr. Fogarty, is a dawning realization that those closest to you are not really close. When you date, you may feel lonely because it's a superficial relationship and it reminds you of what you never had with your family, or what you had and lost.

When power struggles begin, you feel unsure and insecure. This is where you might be tempted to "discard" your date. You're comparing your old insecurities from childhood with your new insecurities in your developing relationship. You associate the insecurity you feel with your date with these same feelings of your early childhood. That's why it's so hard to let the barriers down. The first step is to lower your expectations. **After you have given up hope of getting from your date what you can get from yourself, your expectations become much more realistic.**

Smart Heart Skills for Handling Emptiness
- Accept that emptiness is inside everyone.
- Trust the emotional bonding and test it through your movements.
- Give your date a chance by lowering your expectations of him, yourself, and your family.
- Redefine what you can get from yourself and what comes from and works between you and your date.

- Instead of carrying anger for your date or parents, see them as wounded children to help melt your pain and theirs.

Your power comes from lowering your expectations so you can blend with your date, instead of struggling or fusing. **For a Pursuer, loneliness arises because she is seeking from a relationship what she should be seeking from herself. For a Distancer, loneliness arises from the confusion of seeking from himself what he should seek from others.** When you realize that each date can give you only what he has, you can keep the relationship moving!

Feelings of emptiness should be shared between the first and third date. If you don't share them, you're going to run away. Share your emptiness in *small pieces,* when and where it's appropriate. If you see your date in his emptiness, you won't be afraid if he doesn't call you. You can reach out to him.

The third date gate will not open if:
- You want to be sure you won't be hurt.
- You predetermine what "should" be and have trouble re-evaluating. This is a sign that your mind is closed.
- You won't give up trying to get from others what you can get only from yourself.
- Your ambivalence makes you picky.

A few weeks after Jeff and I began dating, he announced he was going on a ski trip with his friends. I asked him if he would mind staying connected with me via the phone. I said I could understand if he didn't want to, but since I had a childhood wound of abandonment (because of my father's adultery), it would be easier for me if he kept contact, but if he didn't it was okay.

Jeff called me from a ski lodge and I could hear the music and all the people in the background having fun. I said, "I hear all the people; I'm glad you're having a good time. Thanks for calling." I kept the conversation very short (about thirty seconds) and said, "Well why don't you get back to your fun!" Jeff said, "Are you sure?" He was so cute and very thoughtful. He felt like we were hanging up too soon. I said, "Yes, I don't want to take you away from your fun! I'm just happy to hear from you." Before he hung up, he said something very sensitive to my wounds. "There are no women here." I thanked him for letting me know and we hung up. He was happy with me for being so understanding and for not keeping him on the phone since his friends were all waiting for him. When he came home he brought me a beautiful pair of earrings. How's that for a reconnection with a Distancer!

Men will never get as much distance (freedom and space) as they want, and women will never get as much closeness as they want. This built-in dynamic keeps the relationship moving, with each partner stepping forward and alternately pulling back at various times. Your opposites actually help you to maintain a balance. Let the Distancer feel like he's in control, but be willing to ask for what you need and tell him it's okay if he can't do it.

My patient Tammy went out twice with a Distancer named Mike and they had a great time. When she didn't hear from him for a week after the second date, she called me and was furious. She said, "I can't believe he hasn't called me!" I told Tammy, "He wants you to get angry; he's testing you. Don't fall for it! Give him a few more days and if he doesn't call you, call him. If he does call you, don't let him know he got to you."

Mike called a few days later, and when he did, he asked, "Is anything wrong?" She asked, "Why would anything be wrong?"

He said, "You know why I like you? I told my mother how wonderful you are. You seem so patient and so forgiving." She laughed to herself because she was on the verge of ripping his head off when she called me for advice! Tammy passed the test and showed Mike she wasn't going to fall for his attempts to push her away.

One of the reasons so many Distancers are workaholics is because they feel confident they can succeed at work, but they fear failing at relationships. It's understandable because there's no real preparation for a relationship, most people don't know the skills to make it work, and there is very little accurate information for people to rely on. The myth is that relationships develop naturally, and that's another reason so many relationships *stop before* they start.

Distancers, Elusive Men, and Vanishing Men

Men who are Distancers are not all alike. They can't all be lumped into one category any more than women who are Pursuers can be treated alike. There are degrees of distancing and pursuing and since we all have both sides within us, we have to be careful not to use these labels as another way of stereotyping.

On the other hand, you have to determine if a man is "connectable" or not. Many women waste time hanging in there with men who will probably never be emotionally available to them. These men aren't willing to learn new skills or make a firm commitment to the relationship. **If you want to get to the third date and beyond to get married, you have to learn how to tell the difference between men who are**

open to connection and those who "act like" they want connection, but run from it.

The men who are Distancers cover a wide range:
- Those who know they want a relationship some day and are "connectable by instruction."
- Those who are Elusive and aren't really sure what they want, who *might* be *connectable with instruction.*
- Those who are Vanishing Men, who are so freaked out by relationships they may never move into true intimacy with anyone, no matter how much they like a woman.

The difference between the Elusive Man and the Vanishing Man is that Mr. Elusive, while a bit more afraid than the moderate Distancer, can often be coached or taught to connect. Mr. Vanisher, on the other hand, comes on strong and then disappears into thin air, leaving nary a trace.

An Elusive Man who is still "connectable" becomes more distant when heavily pursued, but you can connect with him if you make him feel safe. Be subtle and don't overtly chase him. Be available and accessible, encourage him to come to you and validate him.

The Vanishing Man comes on strong with flair and romance. He sweeps you off your feet with charm, charisma, and lines that sound like they're right out of a movie script. (They just might be!) He hooks you in with all of his great qualities, but he's not there for you when you need him, and he doesn't want to do anything but what *he* wants to do. You hope he'll change, or you think you can change him. There are Vanishing Men who can change, but only if *they* want to.

It's crucial for women to know when to give up on Mr. Vanisher. **If he says he has no desire to act differently,**

please believe him. Don't be one of the women who refuse to heed the warning signs.

My patient Cecelia's husband, who had an affair when she was pregnant, was definitely a Vanishing Man. He never emotionally connected with her and was always very selfish. The night she had a miscarriage, she found out he was seeing another woman. She may have been able to forgive him if he had showed any remorse, but he said, "I am what I am. You knew I wasn't perfect when I married you."

The Vanishing Man suffers from an extreme fear of intimacy. He's so scared, he digs in his heels and actually works his way back to square one. *He compartmentalizes his feelings, and in his mind, people are replaceable.* Most of these men don't set out to drive women crazy; they're selfish and they rationalize all of their behavior. If the woman a Vanishing Man is dating isn't happy, he figures "that's her problem." Some of these men really are mean and think it's great fun to keep a woman dangling, so watch out for the Vanishing Man! **One of the biggest mistakes a single woman can make is to hang on to one of these guys in the hope that he'll eventually change or agree to get married if you love him enough.** Even if he does marry, putting a wedding ring on his finger is not going to change his ways. *Married or single, the Vanishing Man will always be unpredictable and emotionally unavailable most of the time.*

How to Spot a Vanishing Man

- He tries to make you feel guilty or silly for wanting to have a commitment or get married.
- He expects you to be cheerful, even when he sleeps with another woman or doesn't call you for weeks or months.

- He disconnects and expects to pick up and reconnect where he left off, with no explanation.
- When you have sex, he makes you feel like no one measures up to you—then forgets you exist for two months. For the Vanishing Man, sex is another way to keep emotional distance. He uses it as pseudo-intimacy to avoid the real thing.
- He talks the talk, but doesn't walk the walk.
- He cannot, under any circumstances, empathize about hurting you. Instead, he accuses you of overreaction. He blames you when things aren't working out, saying you're too demanding, too needy, and want too much.
- He also projects his feelings and shortcomings onto you. (Beware! He *provokes* your neediness and pursuit because he gets off on it, but he loathes it at the same time.)
- He's allergic to your emotions and discussions.
- He forgets you on your birthday, and calls you a week or two later to celebrate.
- He doesn't respond to kindness, patience, and understanding and interprets these actions as "crowding."
- You can't make him jealous.
- Just when you've forgotten him or gotten over him, he pops up again like a Jack-in-the-box.
- When someone else is interested in you, he can almost smell it, and he calls you up to pull his hook again.
- He wants to date others, but still see you—and either doesn't want you to date anyone else, or doesn't care if you date anyone else.

If you're attracted to Distancers, don't waste your time on the Vanishing Man. Focus your efforts on moderate Distancers, or even on Mr. Elusive.

A moderate Distancer, like my husband, needs to *know* he can have his space more than he *actually needs or wants it*. A Distancer will fight, provoke, and test you just to get his space. The secret is to let him have it, even before he requests it or tries to push your buttons. Give him space even if he says he doesn't want it! Show him you have no desire to run his life by having an active life of your own.

Mr. Elusive represents what you wanted but couldn't have as a child. Chances are if you're attracted to Elusive men, **you're somewhat elusive as well.** If you're not attracted to men who fall all over you, but thrill in the heart-pounding excitement of the chase, you'll have all kinds of chemistry with Mr. Elusive. If you are elusive, you feel like you don't deserve the men who want you or you're afraid you can't sustain a relationship. Your own ambivalence about risking, falling in love, or getting hurt is **masked behind Mr. Elusive. He allows you to avoid facing your own fears, shifting gears, or changing.** There is no danger in closeness with Mr. Elusive because there isn't enough closeness for the porcupines to prick. He is charming, charismatic, and appealing, but *if you get too close or pursue him, he will sprint away.* Women who are attracted to Elusive men often have issues with their fathers. It's likely that one of the following scenarios fits you:

- Your mother was suffocating so you identified with your father and fear engulfment.
- You were Daddy's little girl and no one can measure up to him (in your little-girl memory).
- Your father was very controlling and you are trying to avoid being controlled.
- You didn't get enough attention from your father, so you're recreating that scenario again, with hopes of getting the attention you desire.

My patient Judy dated one Elusive Man after another. They called her when they wanted to connect and distanced from her when she wanted to connect. It was very painful for her because the relationships were always on the men's terms. She could not reconnect because she didn't want to appear needy. One of Judy's boyfriends wanted her to allow him to sleep with other women. He would push Judy away with one hand and hang on to her skirt with the other. His actions were reflective of the ambivalent mothering he got.

The Elusive Man is very much like a five-year-old. He wants what he wants, when he wants it. If he's not at all jealous, and wouldn't mind if you were seeing someone else, it's a sure sign he's elusive. With an Elusive Man, your control comes in knowing that you're *not* in control; he's maintaining the safe distance you need. It's easy and there is no fear of commitment. You resign yourself to the idea that you are going to be disappointed and you tell yourself that you're not going to let him hurt you—but he does.

If you're not sure if you're elusive, go out with a Pursuer. If you think he's too much, or his intensity scares you, **you know you are a Distancer, and an elusive one at that!**

Beware! Don't mistake a man who is recovering from another relationship as an Elusive Man. There are circumstances that can cause a man to behave elusively, but that doesn't mean it's his normal mode of operating. My patient Lisa went out twice with a man named Robert who was in the process of breaking off his previous relationship. Once Robert's relationship was over, he bounced in and out of Lisa's life like a rubber ball. Lisa was very frustrated but I helped her to understand he was grieving. I said, "That shows he can attach and connect to someone." She took my advice and when he didn't call for a week or more at a time, she didn't get angry with him. She knew he was testing and provoking her. When he called, she just picked up where they left off. When she invited him to stay over one night and he said he couldn't, she used the dialogue skills she'd been learning.

Smart Heart Dialogue

She said: "I understand you're still healing and that's okay. I want you to set the pace so you feel comfortable. It feels so right between us and I understand if you're not sure at this point."

He said: "It feels right to me, too, but I'm still not sure what I'm feeling. I want to make sure it's not just rebound feelings. I do have feelings for you and I wanted to talk to you about it but I didn't think you'd understand and I didn't want to hurt you."

She said: "I do understand and I want you to talk to me about it because it will help you get through it. You need time to grieve and I'm not going to be selfish about it."

He said: "But I feel so guilty because I'm coming to you with only half a heart."

She said: "Whatever shape you're in is okay and our feelings don't have to equal each other right now. Half a heart is a lot to be coming to me with. I'm happy to have what you can give and if you feel like you want to give more later, that's great, but if you don't, I understand. Let's just take this one day at a time and see what happens. We have such a great time together. You don't have to feel guilty about how you feel."

He said: "What do you want me to do?"

She said: "Just do what you're doing. I'm secure enough to handle it."

The truth is that Lisa cried after he left but she knew she had to "act as if" she felt confident when she spoke with him **because he needed her confidence so he could feel more**

secure. If she had acted hurt, angry, or worried, he probably would have stopped dating her.

Robert was ambivalent for *situational* reasons. After several months of dating, he healed his old heartache and was ready to open up and let her in. After dating another year, they got married and are still having a great relationship.

How to Recognize Someone Who Cannot Connect

- He won't acknowledge he has fears of intimacy; insists he has no fear.
- He is not capable of validating you.
- He doesn't miss you when you're apart.
- He disconnects when you connect.
- He never lets you "nail him down" on times and places for get-togethers.
- He does the opposite of what you say you want or need.
- He "comes close and moves away."
- He hooks you in and keeps you dangling.
- He provokes ultimatums and limit-setting, then blames you for his distancing.
- He leaves long times between contact.
- You always have to be the one to make the connection.
- Reconnection is impossible unless he wants it. It's his way or no way.
- He tells you, but doesn't show you, how great you are.
- He feels pricked before closeness is even attempted.
- "He gives great phone," but doesn't see you.

How to Recognize Someone Who Is Connectable (by coaching and instruction)

- He responds once you teach him how.
- He validates you, even if only by instruction.
- He listens to your needs and makes some attempt to fill them with *instruction and guidance.*
- He sometimes reaches out to connect with you, even if it's awkwardly.
- He lets you nurture him and wants to learn how to nurture you.
- He welcomes reconnections and is happy to hear from you when you call.
- He makes time for you.
- He lets you set firm dates and he keeps them, although he may need some prompting and encouragement.
- He misses you during disconnections.
- He tells you—AND shows you—that you are valuable and important to him.
- He's like a butterfly. You can't catch him by chasing him, but if you stand still, he will come and sit next to you.
- He values you.

Most Distancers are connectable if you take the time and patience to teach them how to do it. In the next chapter you will learn how to get past the third date!

⌁ 15 ⌁

Getting Past the Third Date

"Driven by the force of love, the fragments of the world seek each other that the world may come into being."

—TEILHARD DE CHARDIN

One of the most common complaints I hear from single women is, "I meet some great guys, but I can't seem to get past the third date." Having experienced seventy-six one-hour coffee dates of my own, I can really relate to your frustrations. **The vexing and sometimes funny thing is that sometimes we don't even know if we're in a relationship.** When I ask the people in my singles seminars to raise their hand if they're in a relationship, many of them say they don't know.

Another factor that adds pressure to this hurdle is the biological clock. If a relationship doesn't seem to be going smoothly, or if you're having trouble starting one, the stakes go up. Both women and men can begin to worry that their time frame to have children is ticking away.

More often than not, we throw away what could be a fantastic relationship because we mistakenly believe "people can't change." The idea that we can't change is so pervasive that we seldom even try. I've lost count of the number of times patients have told me, "I didn't think I could change, but you were so sure I could that I tried it and found out it was true!"

On the first date, the masks are on. During the second date, the masks slip. Before the end of the third date, the masks are off and the power struggles begin.

While many singles dread the moment the masks come off, it's actually a moment to await with anticipation. *It's on the third date, the same time the power struggles are beginning, that you receive the gift of seeing a little deeper into your date, and therefore into yourself.* But beware: The third date often sets off alarms for men and they may start backing away. **He may say something like, "I don't know if I can feel the way about you that you feel about me," or "I'm afraid I'm going to hurt you."** Put your protective bubble around yourself as a reminder that nothing can get inside you to hurt or rattle you unless you allow it.

Smart Heart Dialogue

Smile at him and say, "That's okay." Validate his feelings. "It's okay that you don't know if you're going to feel more later on. I can handle it. We're having fun, so let's just see where this is going without worrying about what happens later."

When my husband, Jeff, and I were dating, he said, "I'm afraid I'm going to hurt you because you like me more than I like you." If I had taken his words at face value, I may have felt crushed and stopped the relationship before it started. But I understood his fears because I understood his childhood wounds. I knew actions meant more than words with Distancers, so I didn't react negatively to his statement.

I said: "You know what, that's the breaks of life. I may get hurt, and you may not like me as much as I like you, but I'm willing to take that chance and take it easy and go slow. I'm not worried about whether or not you fall in love with me. If you do, you do; if you don't, you don't. I'm having a great time with you, so let's just enjoy it and see what happens. I don't know where this is going, but I'm willing to see where it's going and take a chance."

That reassured Jeff and took the pressure off him so he could continue in the relationship. If I hadn't said these things to him, *his guilt of* feeling less for me than I felt for him could have driven him away. Distancers **want** to "feel" some of the emotions that Pursuers express, but it doesn't come easily for them because of all of their fear.

Many women are afraid to share their anxieties with their dates because they think they will come off as weak and needy. Use the Smart Heart skills and model dialogue given throughout the book so you'll trust yourself more. Using these skills helps not only your own growth, it also helps your date to become a *more conscious person.* This leads to an aware relationship that you can both work on together. *But you must hang in there through the Power Struggle Stage, or you will end up back at square one with someone else.*

The depth of your childhood wounds from your early developmental stages will determine how long the Euphoria Stage of courtship will last. If you find yourself suddenly losing interest, look a little deeper at what's really going on. Are you losing interest, or are you talking yourself out of it because you don't have the skills to take it further, or you assume your feelings aren't being returned? You have to *fact-find* to determine his level of interest and get to know how he thinks. What's going on in his head is rarely what's going on in yours, and vice versa. **In addition, your own feelings of ambivalence keep you from thinking clearly.**

Acknowledge and begin to understand your own fears so you can help your date to share his and feel safe doing it. **This is a chance to gain insight into how your issues dovetail;** how you play out your needs and how your date's frustrations and unmet needs from childhood play into yours. When you both avoid sharing fears, you end up acting them out. You may judge, criticize, or find fault with each other. This is one of the worst things you can do.

My patient Patty said she couldn't get past the third date, so I suggested she bring her date along to a therapy session so they could learn a little bit about how they both behave in a courtship. Although Robert had gone out with Patty only twice, he was willing to come in because he also had trouble getting past the third date, and he saw it as an opportunity to shift his behavior. It didn't take long to determine what they were doing wrong. They were both criticizing. They were stopping short, putting all kinds of projections on each other, and making assumptions. They weren't fact-finding or discussing their fears, they were running away from them.

Don't add to your date's wound by pointing out his weaknesses or the things you don't like. Help him to heal. *Even if things don't work out, he will be a little less wounded and have a better chance in his next courtship and so will you.* Let's stop treating each other as "the enemy." Men and women both want closeness, so we need to make it safer for each other and work together for everyone's sake. Whether you like or dislike your date's opinion, choice of clothing, life dream, or ambition, you must validate him. He has a right to his thoughts and opinions. Validation builds mutual respect and friendship, the building blocks on which the temple of love is built.

If you make it to the second date, by the time it's over you're often in a power struggle. This happens less because of real issues and more because of your combined fears. If he's worried about you gaining too much control, and you're worried about not having enough, you both trigger each other's deepest anxieties. **It's best to expect and predict the power struggle,** rather than running from it or going into magical thinking. If you tell yourself "everything's fine" when you know it's not, you may miss the chance to shift gears and keep things going. To avoid running from your fear, or sabotaging, you need to put your fear into words. It's better to tell your date that things are moving too fast for you than to act out your fear by sending mixed messages or leaving.

Observe your strengths and weaknesses and learn what you need to develop and what behaviors to modify. **Relationships serve as a magic mirror.** When you look closely at your date, you also see the reflections of yourself and your parents that you like and dislike. That's why relationships are the best way to work out your issues and grow in your capacity to love and be loved.

The students who attend my "Getting Past the Third Date" seminars are often relieved to finally understand how to jump this courtship hurdle. *They're surprised to know there are dynamics at work besides what they are consciously thinking about on a date.* One woman said, "We're really not that different, it's just that we act different because of our childhoods. I finally understand what works."

The men in the class are often even more excited about learning Smart Heart Skills than the women. Many of them want a relationship and haven't been able to stop themselves from running or pushing their dates away. One man said, "I can't believe I've never heard any of this before! I really thought I was just screwed up. I was really starting to think I didn't deserve to be in a relationship. All the women I went out with acted so upset and hurt, and

I never understood why. Now I can really start watching my own movements and know when I'm talking myself out of something that might be the best thing that ever happened to me!"

Questionnaire for Singles

Answering the following questions will give you insight so you can shift and modify your relationship style.

1. What is the barrier that I put up; What am I hiding behind?
2. Where am I stuck? How do I get "unstuck"?
3. What am I kidding myself about? How do I stop kidding myself?
4. Do I know the skills to connect?
5. Do I resent that I do all the work?
6. What is my long-term goal for love and what's in the way of my goal?
7. Do I unconsciously pick men who are not connectable?
8. Am I pushing away the men I could really connect with?

One of my patients, Lillian, is in her fifties, has never been married, and had never really gotten past the first date. She took care of her elderly mother for years and she said, "It's hard to shift gears from being a caretaker to learning to take and receive." The thought of having a relationship scared her, even though she wanted one. She didn't want to give up her independence and saw marriage as a twenty-four-hour, 'round-the-clock job. She said, "Being single, I don't have to be accountable to anyone, I'm my own person, and no one is telling me what to do." But she was unhappy because she wanted someone to care about her.

I showed her that she was projecting her fears of her domineering parents onto her dates and helped her to view going on a date like taking a mini-vacation. "Don't worry about what tomorrow might bring, or not bring," I told her. "Just stay in the moment and have fun." She is now in a relationship with a noncontrolling man and they are talking about getting married.

Smart Heart Keys to Unlock the Third Date Gate

Some singles talk about the third date as if there is some imaginary force field keeping them from entering that stage. They are frustrated and bewildered that time after time a relationship stops before they even had a chance to get to know each other. What these same singles don't realize is that it's their own ambivalence that makes the Third Date Gate impenetrable.

It's crucial to teach your date to respect you right from the start. One of the ways you do this is to **coach him** out of his selfishness. Instead of blaming him, **teach him.** Be firm, but loving. I remember the first time I cooked dinner for Jeff. We had been dating for about a month and I invited him over for a pasta dinner, complete with candles and romantic music. We had a wonderful dinner, and when I started to clear the table and take the dishes to the kitchen, he went into the living room and turned on the TV. (Exactly what my dad always did after dinner.) This wasn't a precedent I wanted to set, so I knew I couldn't let it slide.

Smart Heart Dialogue

I said with a smile, "Oh, so you're a Prince." He was a bit taken back, but since I was smiling, he smiled back.

He said, "What do you mean?"

I said, "I loved making dinner for you and I don't mind washing the dishes, but if we do it together it would make me very happy. Then we can cuddle up and watch TV together."

He said, "Oh, I guess I should have offered to help you."

I said, "I'll tell you what, I'll treat you like a Prince, if you'll treat me like a Princess," and I gave him a quick kiss.

We did the dishes together, and he felt good about himself instead of feeling guilty for being selfish. I felt good about myself and good about him. If I hadn't handled this with Smart Heart Dialogue, I would have felt resentful and we could have gotten into a power struggle.

Don't expect a man to be head over heels about giving up his selfishness. He may pout or sigh, but ignore those childlike behaviors and give him attention for the positive behaviors he's demonstrating. Don't allow him to use anger or bullying as a way to talk you out of what you want from him. When he does this, validate don't escalate. If he's angry and you get angry, then the anger is doubled. **Let him be upset, and don't get sucked into his vortex.**

Tell him, "I understand you don't enjoy doing this and I can appreciate that." But don't let him off the hook, and don't get caught up in the notion that "If he really cared about me, he'd help without sighing." Pursuers, in particular, take all of their dates' responses, sighs, and shrugs personally. When you do this, he gets **to feel guilty and go on being selfish while claiming that you just can't be pleased.** Don't feel sorry for him because that perpetuates his selfishness. **He needs to have "good guilt" that changes his selfish behavior.** (Jeff still sighs when he makes pasta. I ignore the sighs and compliment him on the meal. Now he even says, "Ignore my sighing.") **Guilt is a four-letter word when it comes to connecting with men.**

If you meet a Distancer who is extremely giving, be a little suspicious. It might be a technique he's learned to use as manipulation. If he "gives to get," and he doesn't get what he's hoping for, he quickly goes into resentment and reactive distancing. That's another reason you need to set limits. You don't want a Distancer to do too little, or too much.

A Distancer is afraid he'll become dependent and like it too much. You have to ask his permission to help him and nurture him. Don't underestimate the value of asking for his permission. It will help him feel like he is in control. He wants nurturing, but he doesn't want to be hovered over. When Jeff and I were in our early courtship, we sometimes played tennis doubles together on our dates. One time he fell down and hurt his back, and I stopped the point. He got up and asked, "Why did you stop the point?" We were winning, and he felt I overstepped my bounds. When we went back to my place, he lay down on the bed for awhile, and I left him alone because that's what he said he wanted. When I went into the bedroom at the end of the day he asked, "Where have you been all day?" I said, "I thought you wanted to be alone." He explained, "I didn't mean that you had to stay away all day."

Find out if your date wants to be nurtured and how. This is an important part in respecting each other's wishes. If a man knows you will **nurture him as he wants and needs it,** he can relax and feel good about it instead of feeling smothered and fighting it. *Now I nurture the way he wants, not the way I want.*

All the singles that come to see me who can't get past the third date say, "I don't want to get hurt." "I don't want to be rejected." *"I want to be sure."* The search for impossible certainty causes so much anxiety, it paralyzes people. If your childhood wound was rejection or you felt invisible, expect to attract a man into your life that will trigger this wound. Use these opportunities to heal yourself and to help your date heal.

It's also valuable to look at your Oedipal Stage when you're evaluating why you haven't been able to get past the third date. Just like our early development determines what types of men we'll be attracted to, *the Oedipal Stage plays a big part in how much risk we're willing to take and whether we feel good enough about ourselves to move a relationship forward.* I'll never forget when I was five years old there was a boy named Larry who was told by our kindergarten teacher to pick out the prettiest girl in the class. He picked me and Suzie, a classmate with blonde hair. The teacher urged him to narrow his choice to just one of us, and he finally picked Suzie. To this day, I still think blondes are more attractive, and that's probably why I'm a blonde now, instead of a brunette. When I went home crying that day, my father asked me what happened. I was in love with my father (as all girls are at this age), and he told me not to worry, that there would be plenty of boys who would pick me later on because I was very pretty. But that didn't really make me feel better. Because I was in the Oedipal Stage, I wanted my father. Of course I couldn't have him, because he was married to my mother. When I found out I couldn't have Larry either, I didn't feel very good about myself. *As adults, we intellectualize these old memories, but the pain leaves scars that still affect us.*

Getting Past the Third-Date Dramas

One of my Distancer patients, Amanda, is in her thirties, her biological clock is ticking, and she wants to have children. Amanda came to me a few years ago but dropped out of therapy when I insisted she do family of origin work to resolve her childhood issues with her alcoholic father. Now, after a year, she's back and willing to do the necessary work. Her parents come into therapy with her each week to support her in completing the developmental stages that she didn't complete as a little girl, and she's in a successful relationship.

This was a big breakthrough for Amanda because *she's learning to ask for what she wants and needs.* She's developing a close relationship with her overbearing father, which she always wanted, just as she's always wanted a close relationship with a man but wasn't able to have one because she considered closeness dangerous.

Amanda recently got involved in a long-distance relationship with a man from California. She had been deeply affected by the loss of her only serious boyfriend in a boating accident, and every time she started to get close to a man it triggered her abandonment wound. This relationship attracted Amanda because it initially seemed safe. But she realized it was triggering her fears of rejection even more (which is what often happens)!

I told Amanda if she wants to get past the third date, she has to have a dialogue with her potential partner about her fears of rejection and abandonment. "It will encourage connection and allow for disconnection without anger or hurt feelings, so you can have reconnection," I explained. She's never been able to acknowledge her vulnerability. Her pattern was to let men control her—be a good little girl, seek approval, and not make waves. She was afraid to take a risk because of her fear of being rejected. *She had to learn how to make men feel safe about her fears, instead of hiding the fears and then panicking and getting angry when she felt rejected.*

Amanda has accepted that the journey of love comes with fears. If we don't deal with the fears, we have to deal with our own loneliness.

The same advice I gave to Amanda holds true for all relationships, but Distancers who get into one long-distance relationship after another are often avoiding connection, closeness, and intimacy. Part of getting past the third date is telling your date what you want. The following is some model dialogue that you can adapt to whatever it is you want from your date.

Smart Heart Dialogue for Telling Your Date What You Want

"I understand you may not want to have a long-term relationship. I want you to understand that I do. Even if you don't agree with me, walk in my shoes. The most important thing for me is that you consider my feelings."

Smart Heart Dialogue to Validate Your Date and Stand Your Ground

(Here's an example of what Amanda said to Patrick to let him know what she needed and what she was willing to accept.)

Amanda: "I understand you just got out of a destructive, devastating relationship. Perhaps this is not the time for you to be connected to someone consistently. It's okay. I get that."

Patrick: "No, I like you. We have fun."

Amanda: "I think you're terrific and attractive. We have fun and have something special. I'll leave the door open if and when you're ready and if I'm free also so we can see what happens."

Patrick: "No, I want to see you."

Amanda: "Based on my separation anxiety, I need consistency and connections a couple of times a week and seeing each other at least once a month since we are so far apart. If this is not possible, I certainly understand, and I will not be upset with you. I am so sorry that it is not acceptable for me any other way."

Patrick: "I didn't realize others hurt you and left you, like my wife left me. I could live with that formula; in fact it (the structure) would help me. I can be self-absorbed sometimes. I need help in how to handle and treat a woman. It's why I'm divorced I guess. It helps me look in the mirror when I attempt a relationship. Thanks for making me accountable. When you let me off the hook, I didn't respect you or myself. I'll call you three times a week and see you at least once a month so **we don't stop this relationship before it starts.** Call me on it if I slip."

Amanda: "*Thanks. I'll be the Connection Guardian.* Even if nothing comes of this, we've learned how to connect and disconnect so we don't have scars in the next relationship. I'm a Distancer, too, so I'm learning how to connect and ask for what I want."

Amanda was still scared and decided it wouldn't work out. I reassured her, "It's okay to be afraid. Just don't get stuck in it and use it as an excuse. To rise above the fear, think of yourself single and alone!"

Amanda had to tell him what she wanted and share her fears. **She had to be herself and risk losing him in order to have him.** She finally learned, "If I give up control, I have control." She agreed to use attachment skills to thaw her frozen feelings and keep herself from "withholding" or reactive distancing. She said, "Withholding makes me more discon-nected. I will connect. I will not withhold."

Once you share your feelings, you have to let your date make the choice on his own. *Resist the urge to give in or get angry, while at the same time sharing your needs and helping him to be accountable.* You have to make a man reach for you. Don't stop everything to wait for a return call, or if he's vague, confirm the time and the place for a get-together. Don't be wishy-washy and don't wait for him, or you'll wait forever— which is advice straight from the mouth of my Distancer husband! You also have to make your date accountable for his pattern of holding back.

The following is an example of how to let a man know that you are holding him accountable for his own actions. This example is what I shared with Amanda, so she could *gently* teach Patrick that *she* was not responsible for his actions or inactions.

Smart Heart Dialogue to Help Make a Man Accountable

Amanda said: "You may be holding back to protect yourself, so if it ends it won't be so hard. But our relationship has hardly begun. Why stop it before it starts? I learned from Dr. Weil to take the risk. How about taking it with me? It's okay if you don't want to."

You have to go for it and not worry about what he thinks of you. Men are shy and need encouragement, but not too much. *If you need a man to call you, tell him.* He needs to know you have abandonment issues, but he also has to know it's okay if he can't call, and that you don't expect him to "fix" you.

Amanda wanted to write Patrick off because he couldn't make decisions. I said, "You're going to have to write off all the Distancers in the world because they can't make (relationship) decisions either!"

Amanda learned that sharing her fears, needs, and **wounds actually brought her and Patrick closer together.** If you are starting a viable relationship, sharing where you're coming from will help your date to meet you halfway. Use Amanda's examples of Smart Heart Dialogue to plan what you are going to say.

The following list summarizes the Smart Heart Skills that will help you get beyond that third date.

- Get over your fear of coming off as "needy." Take the risk.

- Announce your needs and fears and ask him about his.
- Stand up for yourself and set limits.
- Don't give all the power over to him to please him; take quiet control.
- Stop thinking he can read your mind; tell him what you need and make him accountable so he can change to accommodate you—but don't expect him to be able to fulfill all your needs right away.
- Teach him to entertain thoughts about meeting your needs.
- Don't allow him to be selfish without being accountable.
- Evaluate if he is capable of meeting and handling your needs. (He is if he keeps responding.) If he won't change, you can move on.
- Help men make decisions; don't fault them for not knowing how to make them.
- Deal with his comfort zone.
- Make your partner aware of your developmental wounds, vulnerabilities, human frailty, and feelings. Telling your partner your wounds is as simple as what I said to Jeff when he was going skiing. Or simply say, "I have a fear of being rejected that started in my childhood. I don't expect you to fix it; I just want you to know I'm sensitive in that area." The more you share, the more you can work out together. Sharing your fears and ambivalence enables you to avoid breaking up or sabotaging your relationship.
- Ask questions and fact-find to get answers. Learn to listen to your partner without reacting, so he can learn to open up.

- Help each other to move *slowly* forward, rather than pushing for answers too soon.
- Explain and encourage connection and show how the connection bridge leads to great relationships.
- Help him to shift gears through connection, disconnection, and reconnection, and *teach him to announce his moves.*

Determining If You Have a Viable Relationship

Women often ask me how they can determine if the man they're dating is someone with whom they can have a viable relationship. The following points give you some guidelines on when to keep the relationship going and when to let go.

When to Hang In:
- He makes movement toward you.
- He's somewhat conscious of his needs and is willing to be taught about yours.
- He's willing to look at his (and your) distance and closeness issues.
- He spends more time with you, even if he's saying he doesn't want to get serious.
- He validates your feelings and needs.
- He's connectable by instruction

When to Let Go:
- He treats you as if you are invisible.
- He's not spending time with you and keeps making excuses.
- He puts you last.
- He can't meet any of your needs.

- He calls you demanding.
- He is inconsistent.
- He is dishonest.
- He's not willing to be conscious or aware of your relationship and work on it together.

As my agent remarked when she read this book, **"I didn't know the *natural* state for most men is Distance!"** Once you know this, you don't take it personally anymore. **You get smart and learn how to keep the connection going!**

Reconnect with Less Fear

Many relationships stop before they start because women don't know how to help a man to reconnect after he's disconnected. If *you're* fearful, it's hard to tell if he's afraid or truly disinterested. **You're making it easy for both of you to stay distant. If you're not encouraging him to pursue you, he may see it as disinterest on your part.**

There is absolutely nothing wrong with calling a man who is ambivalent, but you have to do it in a very casual way. Don't even mention that he hasn't called you, just call him up and invite him to do something fun.

Smart Heart Skills to Reconnect with Less Fear

- Slow things down to your comfort level.
- Don't define the relationship or call it anything.
- Enjoy each other and have fun together.
- Don't listen to his words; watch his movements.

Smart Heart Dialogue to Reconnect

If you had a wonderful time on a date and the man doesn't call you within a week, call him.

"Hi, I had a great time when we got together and I have tickets to the baseball game this weekend and wondered if you'd want to go."

If he says he's not available that night, keep it light. Just say, "Oh, I know it's short notice, but I'll call you again if I have anything."

Now, it's his turn to make a move. If you don't hear from him in a few weeks, call him with another invitation, and again *keep it light*. In the meantime, of course, date other men. If he does call back, no matter how long it's been, don't mention it. Just keep the conversation light, talk about fun things and leave the door open for him to invite you out again.

One of the most important things in reconnecting with a man is in showing him that you're not trying to trap him or pressure him. Act as if you don't even notice when he's not **around because Distancers are afraid of becoming the center of your world.** Although they might actually like this, it scares them because they are afraid of losing their own identity.

If he starts to pursue you, pull back a little. You want to show him you're interested—but not too interested. But don't play hard to get, because as much as Distancers fear being engulfed in a relationship, they are also allergic to rejection. **Distancers need positive reinforcement at all times.**

If you don't initiate a reconnection with him, he's not going to get to know you well enough to miss you and before long he will fill his void with another Pursuer. You want to connect, but don't pursue. Again, you are being quietly aggressive.

The other possibility is that in his pursuit of you, he may come on too strong and scare you. **Share your fear, and help him to crystallize his own so you can work together.** When Jeff got scared when we were dating, we held hands and talked about it. I helped him to see that I got scared, too, and that all my patients get scared. He realized it was okay to be scared; it's what you do with the fear that matters.

Here's a typical dialogue after a couple has had three full-day dates, with the third one ending with an "overnight."

"It went so well," he said, "I could really fall for you."

She anxiously awaited the next date. But there *was* no next date until she called *him*—after two weeks of panic.

She asked me, "Should I really call him?"

I said, "Of course. You had a good time with him, didn't you?"

In disbelief, she shrieked, "What does that have to do with it?" I explained that it felt so good, he's running. She mustered up all her courage and called him.

He guiltily said, "Sorry I didn't call you. I've been so busy."

She said, "I'm really not so sure it was because you were busy. I was wondering if maybe those good feelings we had last time scared you the way they scared me. (Never ask a Distancer a question they can answer with "Yes," "No," or "I don't know.")

He said, "It was getting a little too hot and heavy. I'm not sure I want a relationship right now."

She replied, "I respect that and I understand where you're coming from. I wondered if you'd be willing to hang in there and enjoy the moment with me, to continue to have some good times and to commit to seeing where it's going."

He asked, "Does that mean we'll be exclusive?"

She asked, "How do you feel about that?"

He responded, "I'm probably not ready for that."

She reassured him, "No problem. We'll both date other people and just see what happens."

(This couple is now engaged!!)

If the scenario above is the beginning of a viable relationship, it will keep springing back like the rubber band—even as you're both dating other people. The key is for the Pursuer to keep **a nonreactive connection** to the Distancer. You stay connected, but you still date others. **You need to *pull back more* than you connect, but stay connected.** Remember there are lots of other Pursuers out there. Even if you don't want to date anyone else, you should. *It's a lot easier as a Pursuer to pull back when you're dating—than when you're waiting.*

part four

Break Up to Make Up

"Save a place in your heart for me.

Save a place though we are apart.

Save a place in your heart for me.

Save a place where you and I are we."

❧ DENISE TAYLOR
STAR VISIONS

~ 16 ~

Why Break Up?

> *"Once the realization is accepted that even between the closest human beings, infinite distances continue to exist, a wonderful living side by side can grow up if they succeed in loving the distance between them, which makes it possible for each to see the other whole against a wide sky."*
>
> —RAINER MARIA RILKE

When a relationship reaches the point where one or both partners are thinking or saying, "You won't let me in, but you won't let me go," or "You won't let me in, but I can't let you go," it's time for a temporary break-up. Other comments that indicate a need for a temporary break-up are: "I don't know how I feel anymore; I'm numb or frozen; It's too hard; There's no connection; I can't breathe; There's no togetherness."

A break-up is helpful if you or your partner are unsure of your feelings for each other. It can also help a couple decide if they want to get engaged, move in together, get married, stay married, or have a child. If a lot of relationship debris has contaminated a relationship, a temporary break-up can help resolve the issues and revive the relationship.

If a couple has experienced infidelity and the adulterer won't give up the affair, giving him (or her) a brush with death is definitely the thing to do. Infidelity requires breaking up to make up if the adulterer shows no remorse or can't stop cheating. But in 98 percent of the cases I treat, it is possible to repair damage from affairs. After the affair, breaking up to make up creates a stronger union and partnership.

A time-limited break-up creates movement and gives your relationship a healthy shake. Taking this action step before it is forced by a crisis makes reconnecting and making up easier to do. Of course we focus on making up first. But *I have found that in general most relationships need a temporary break-up, or what I call a brush with death.* Breaking up can breathe the life and love back into marriages that have lost their luster, courtships that are not moving in the direction of commitment, and relationships that are about to stop before they start.

Depending on the couple, the break-up can be as short as two days or as long as several months. A temporary break-up stretches your relationship like a rubber band. If you have a viable relationship—and more than 98 percent of you do—the rubber band springs back and pulls you back together. We all want a second chance to beat the odds. Couples want a second chance to create a happy and intimate relationship. **Singles want a second chance to make a first impression so they don't end a relationship before it starts.**

Temporary break-ups and time-limited disconnections give everyone involved a second chance. Couples and singles get a second chance to make their relationships work. You also both get a second chance to go back home and rewrite your old relationship scripts so that he can learn to feel more comfortable with connection and you can learn to feel more relaxed about disconnection.

For example, my patients Paul and Rhonda were both in their late forties. Both had been married and divorced. After four years of dating, Rhonda wanted to get married. Paul, on the other hand, had been so soundly ripped off by his ex-wife that the thought of trying it again was not attractive. In his previous marriage, he had been unfaithful and when his wife found out, she had an affair, too. Paul was extremely wary of marriage—even with Rhonda, whom he professed to love.

They fed each other's fears, rather than sharing their fears and coaching each other through them. Rhonda was terrified at the thought of being rejected or abandoned. Paul has some abandonment issues of his own, but his driving fear was the thought of being suffocated and smothered in a marriage.

Paul needed a brush with death to discover the depth of his love for Rhonda. *But Rhonda couldn't bring herself to take the step and leave him.* Consequently, Paul was never able to experience how he would feel without Rhonda in his life—which was exactly what he needed to make a true commitment. Distancers can't imagine life without their Pursuer partner, because in the words of many of my patients, "She's always here—*how can I miss her?*" **In many cases, we have to be willing to lose love in order to have it.**

Some therapists would counsel couples in Paul and Rhonda's situation to stick together and keep trying to work it out without breaking up to make up. I have found that this approach simply prolongs the problems and *ultimately provides no change or solution.* When a couple is spinning their wheels, they're tearing up the foundation the relationship is built upon—and that foundation is often too thin to begin with! It doesn't work.

My parents experienced two brushes with death—the first one early in their relationship. Shortly after my mother and father began to go steady, Dad decided to go to California to "make his fortune." He thought he could have his cake and eat it, too. My mother decided she wasn't waiting around for him and took off with a sailor. As soon as Dad found out, he made tracks back to New York and asked her to marry him. He didn't want to lose her, and she gave him a needed wake-up call.

If you haven't already experienced an affair, don't wait for one to happen. **If your relationship needs a brush with death, have the courage to give it one.**

A Break-Up Is a New Beginning

A strategic break-up is not the end of a relationship, it's a new beginning. If you want to make it work, and you believe you can, you will. You have to reignite your belief in the power of love. This is something I learned from my parents, and I see the truth of it in my marriage and in the relationships of my patients.

My mom and dad always truly loved each other, as I could see when I was growing up. But they are both Distancers and had trouble connecting, disconnecting, and reconnecting. When Dad was having affairs in my childhood, I had no idea. I just knew that he wasn't around very much in the evenings. I remember my mother being upset during those times, but I didn't know why. I later learned that my mother knew my father was having affairs, but it took her years before she finally felt strong enough to leave him. When my mother realized she could not stop the infidelity, she left him. She still loved him, but she was smart enough to know that if he continued to take her for granted, there would be nothing left of their marriage anyway. She didn't break up with Dad as a "form of manipulation," she left for good because Dad did not value her, and she had learned to value herself. Her therapist supported this, but also said Dad would never change.

When you break up, you're not doing it as a "technique," you're doing it to evoke change and movement because it's the only thing you can do to save the relationship or yourself.

When Dad realized Mom was prepared to walk away forever, he quickly realized how much he loved her—much to my mother's surprise. Meanwhile, Mom realized she didn't need him as much as she thought she did. Their experiences with the break-up brought balance and respect back to their marriage, and Dad never cheated again. They have been married over fifty years now and have reached the tender, heart-melting stage of real and lasting love. They've also learned the Smart Heart Skills and Dialogue I teach my patients, and practice them enthusiastically because they see the value of keeping their love fresh and alive.

The vast majority of my married patients who break up to make up create stronger, more conscious bonds with each other. They make a conscious choice using their hearts and their heads to stay together and shift gears through the many relationship stages.

Break-Ups Are Filled with Gifts and Opportunities

Breaking up can breathe the life and love back into marriages that have lost their luster and courtships that are not moving in the direction of commitment. The length of the break-up will vary, depending on the couple. The key is to follow the right steps to give the relationship the best chance for surviving and improving.

Using the fear of loss strategy is the best way to create lasting change. This critical stage when a relationship can either move forward or end, brings all the cards out on the table so partners can create a winning hand together.

Most of my patients—married and single—discovered that a strategic and temporary break-up made their relationships much stronger and more fulfilling now that they're back together. Breaking up to make up is not a form of game-playing or negative manipulation. It should never be used as a threat, or to hurt the other person. *It should be used as a wake-up call,* so the partner who is afraid of taking the next step in a relationship can discover he (or she) needs you and wants you. **Couples who need a break-up to make up and don't do it will either break up for good or emotionally divorce from each other—even if they remain together.**

Breaking up to make up gives Distancers (most men) a chance to discover they miss and want connection and closeness with you. **They have to lose you to discover they want you.** They have to have a brush with death to be willing to stretch for you and make the relationship a priority. They must learn through the pain of their own emptiness so they can discover their childhood wounds and want to heal them. Unless they experience emptiness, they often don't even know they have old pains and heartaches to heal. **They don't know how to love or see the importance of loving.**

A Distancer wants and needs to be connected, *but he doesn't know it.* He talks himself out of making commitments and runs away when the road gets rough or when he feels his heart beginning to open. Breaking up with him helps him to discover he wants connection and that is one of the most meaningful gifts you can give to him.

Pursuers benefit from the break-up because they discover they **can stand on their own two feet** and they gain a greater level of respect for themselves and a stronger form of independence. They are willing to ask more of their partner in a less demanding or desperate way because they shift from needing him to wanting him. **Without learning this,**

Pursuers can chase mates away. A break-up also helps us realize that we can only *"approach"* unconditional love, because as long as we're human, our love is going to be somewhat conditional.

For example, Alexis (a Distancer) and Nathaniel (a Pursuer) were struggling to put their marriage back together after Alexis had an affair. Nathaniel issued an ultimatum that Alexis stop seeing her former lover. When Alexis refused, Nathaniel left, saying that he still loved her, but he wasn't going to be walked on or taken for granted. He broke up to make up. Only when Nathaniel risked ending their marriage did Alexis realize what they had together. She woke up to how much she respected him and admired his confidence to set limits and fight for her, which helped rekindle her love for him.

Strategic Break-Ups Wake Up Your Love

Most people need a serious jolt to shake them, wake them, and make them willing to learn the skills necessary to stay in love. My patients Kurt and Amelia had been married six years and were having many problems. They were a "polite couple" who had many resentments brewing beneath the surface. The break-up made them want to learn how to resolve power struggles and "fight fair" so they could reconnect and stay together.

Amelia said, "Kurt really set me free when he agreed to fight fairly with me." Kurt reassured Amelia, "If you get pissed off at me, I'm not going to leave you." When the couple avoided discussing their problems, they also diffused the passion in their relationship. Passion comes from the feelings of safety that fair fighting creates.

Amelia said, "I thought if you were sweet and nice, you'd be a good wife. I should know better." Amelia was upset with

Kurt because he had an "emotional affair." Nothing sexual happened between Kurt and his "secret partner," but he connected with her emotionally, which he hadn't done with Amelia in a long while. The "between-the-lines" romance was over, but Kurt and Amelia were both very upset. Kurt was worried **that he might not be able to get his feelings back for Amelia even though he wanted to.** Amelia wasn't sure if she could forgive Kurt for connecting with another woman while he was treating her as if she didn't exist.

Kurt "checked out" during the marriage, and Amelia tried to "sell" him and control him. He was polite, but she became more and more frustrated. I recommended they **break up to make up** because Kurt wasn't sure if he wanted to be married and couldn't get in touch with his deepest feelings. I knew the break-up would create a sense of urgency and help him to decide.

Kurt was worried the relationship might die out if they broke up, even if it was just a temporary separation. *I told Kurt a break-up would accelerate their progress and give them a new beginning.*

He said it would be hard for him not to call Amelia four times a day (as he normally did) and to follow the ground rules for the break-up. But he likes to live on the edge, so the idea of breaking up and having a new beginning—a second chance for love—was enticing to him. But Kurt also had to prepare for the reality that when they got back together his adrenaline rush and magical thinking would eventually end, and he would have to act on his conscious decision to love. "This is where the effort really begins," I warned him.

Kurt was tired of seeing Amelia hurt every day. He knew he was taking Amelia for granted when they were seeing each other every day before the break-up, and he wanted to learn how to appreciate her. To prepare for their reconnection, Kurt was working on not checking out and facing and sharing his feelings. Amelia was working on forgiving Kurt for his emotional affair and taking responsibility for the part she played in it rather than blaming him.

I explained to Amelia, "You forgive in stages and Kurt gets his feelings back in stages. It doesn't happen all at once, it's a dance."

Embracing Emptiness: How Can Something That Sounds So Bad, Be So Good?

Emptiness is quite frankly one of the smartest gifts we can give to our partners and one of the wisest gifts we can give to ourselves. While the word itself carries connotations that frighten us, the experience of going "into our emptiness" **contains the seeds of change that can free us.**

So what do I mean when I use the word "emptiness"? The term as it is used here is made up of many different feelings, including loneliness, confusion, hopelessness, helplessness, sadness, shame, and failure. When we are in our emptiness we experientially get in touch with our early wounds and our yearning for the connection we never had or had and lost.

For Pursuers, experiencing emptiness is an opportunity to discover they can actually meet most of their own needs and are not reliant on a partner to "fill in the gaps" or "complete them." It gives Pursuers a new lease on life and relationships because once they've experienced their emptiness and worked through it, they have more power within themselves and a greater willingness to allow their partners to be in control of certain aspects of the relationship.

For Distancers, experiencing emptiness is a powerful way to discover that their fear of being without the partner they love is actually greater than their fear of being

engulfed in the relationship. There are no words that can simulate this experience. Until Distancers experience the pain of emptiness, they don't value the pleasure of closeness. Some Distancers can't even imagine that closeness is their preference in life until they come face to face with the possibility of losing their partner. *They need to break up to make up.*

In the next chapter you'll learn how to give your relationship a brush with death.

~ 17 ~

How to Give Your Relationship a Brush with Death

"From suffering, I have learned this: that whoever is wounded by love will never be made whole unless she embraces the very same love which wounded her."

—MECHTILD OF MAGDEBURG

It's true that breaking up to make up is terrifying and agonizing, *but you must face your crucible,* or forever stay the same in relationships. The break-up will be for a specified period of time, with permission, *and done with love.* It is a wonderful opportunity for both of you to resolve fears, become stronger, and discover how much you mean to each other. **The disconnection triggers the reconnection** and the fresh start of the relationship. *We have to fear losing someone to raise our anxiety level to a point where we're willing to face our fears and accept the unknown elements of our future together.*

Many couples try to talk through this stage, *but talking rarely works with Distancers.* They don't respond to talking, because

303

they are self-centered and unless they "experience" what we are trying to communicate with words, *they will not respond or take you seriously.* If you try to "talk this out" do not use the threat of a break-up! You don't want to set up a "cry wolf" scenario. **Don't even mention the possibility of a break-up unless you are certain that breaking up is what you need to do.**

If you or your partner are worried about being engulfed in the relationship, that fear must be shared and accommodated. For example, if one of you needs space, you must announce your need to disconnect for awhile. If you are involved with a partner who fears suffocation in a relationship, you must be aware of his needs and watch his movements. You can then take the initiative to suggest some "time apart," *before your partner acts out his fears and disconnects.*

If you're married or living together, discuss your feelings about a time-limited break-up with your partner *before* you announce your departure. Even after you have discussed it, **Distancers are generally taken by surprise when you leave.** They don't take the discussions seriously, and they sometimes are very angry about your "sudden" abandonment—even though there was *nothing sudden about it.*

If you need to break up with your partner, tell him and ask how he feels. You have to let him know he has some control. You may have to break up even if your partner doesn't agree, but announcing your intentions gently helps to ease and cushion feelings of rejection. For example, when I was dating Jeff, a workaholic then, I gave him an ultimatum to take Fridays off (after discussing this for eight months to no avail) so we could spend weekends at my home in the Poconos. When he refused, I left for two days. I didn't tell him where I was going or what I was doing. I simply said without anger, "I need some time to think about things."

Jeff knew I meant business. He thought I was spending time with another guy. I actually spent the two days and nights at my friend Brenda's house. Even though I missed Jeff and was tempted to call him, I didn't. When we saw each other again, he took my request much more seriously. He didn't want to lose me, so he agreed to structure his work week to take Fridays off, which he still does today. He never knew until he read these pages (as I was working on the book) where I was or what I was doing during the time I spent away from him. He never asked and didn't want to know. When he read this he said, "I'd still be working on Fridays if it weren't for your ultimatum. I'm so glad it happened because I love Fantasy Fridays and three-day weekends with you."

Almost all Distancers require ultimatums for change to occur. They are too confident and appreciate you only after you're gone. **So stop talking and start walking!** But remember that when you break up, you must be calm, cool, and collected. *You cannot use guilt, blame, or anger because of his developmental stage triggers.* Show confidence that you feel it will repair, strengthen, and revitalize the relationship.

A temporary break-up must be done as a *conscious* choice, not out of anger or in an attempt to punish your partner. **The less emotional and more loving you are when you initiate the break-up, the better.**

While breaking up can help you to make up, if you don't do it carefully, the relationship can end permanently. Be sure to follow all of the Smart Heart Skills and Guidelines in this chapter. If you have trouble with these skills, enlist the help of a family therapist to give you the support you need.

Getting to Commitment

One woman after another asks me the question, "Why can't men commit?"

For a Distancer to shift gears and move toward commitment he has to overcome his unwillingness to emotionally invest in another person. When he has to move forward, he fears losing control. He figures if he doesn't make a move, he won't get rejected. He may be lonely, but loneliness is the price he's willing to pay for safety. He also experiences physiological discomfort because he equates commitment with danger and flees.

Women are frustrated by men's commitment phobia. Men are overwhelmed because women crave and push for commitment. In general, Distancers avoid commitments and Pursuers press for them. I'm not just talking about a commitment for marriage or a live-in relationship, I'm also talking about small commitments like setting up a date and sticking to it, making promises to take care of things around the house and following through, and calling when he says he'll call.

Men relish being alone—but they don't want to be alone forever. For women, the thought of being alone can be terrifying. Women who are independent, self-sufficient, and successful in other areas of their lives may still tremble at the thought of growing old alone or missing their chance to have children. If you're in a relationship and you don't know if you want to shift gears and take it to the next stage because you're afraid to be hurt or rejected, you're falling into the pit of "wanting to be sure." *You can never be sure.* Everyone who loves has some ambivalence. Everyone who has ever married, had a child, changed jobs, or moved to a new city or neighborhood had at least a little doubt about the wisdom of their choice.

To get to commitment, rely more on movement and less on analysis and words. Gently coax him out of his shell of armor so you can see who he is and be conscious of your own anxieties so you don't sabotage yourself. When I began to notice Jeff's "flaws," I realized I was looking for them because I was scared and trying to talk myself out of the relationship. I had to remind myself what I tell my patients, "Judge someone on their strengths, not on their weaknesses."

I was also judging Jeff for weaknesses that I had in myself. I wanted to blame him for not being able to do things that I couldn't do either. I was lonely, and I was also afraid. Rise above the fear so you can have a relationship. *Loneliness is much more difficult than taking reasonable risks.*

My patient Cathy (a Pursuer) was attracted to men who could not make commitments. She was dating Matthew (a Distancer) and her anxiety went up when he "turned into a pumpkin" every Sunday at 1:00 P.M. and abruptly got up to rush home.

I explained to Cathy that Matthew "turned into a pumpkin" on Sunday afternoons because he was starting to feel the pricking that happens when you get too close for comfort. I shared with Cathy how Jeff and I handled the Sunday "pumpkin syndrome" when we were dating. For many months, Jeff picked up and left abruptly on Sunday.

I explained to Jeff that I felt a sense of loss when he left early on Sunday and asked him how we might be able to deal with it. He was sensitive to my issues and fears and suggested we go to his place on Sunday afternoons. He said, "I can read my mail and get ready for the work week upstairs, you can work on your dissertation downstairs, and we can meet on the second floor and reconnect for dinner or watch a movie together." This worked out great for us. We both were getting our own needs met and meeting each other's.

The Delicate Art of Issuing an Ultimatum

Once you've been dating for about three to six months, it's appropriate to tell your partner you'd like to spend more time with him. Spending time on weekends only or one or two nights a week isn't enough to determine how the two of you will do together in the long run. *You gradually ease into this and a gentle talk or ultimatum is usually needed.*

Most men need you to set limits and give them gentle ultimatums to get to commitment, but at the same time they hate limits and ultimatums. You must do it very gently and with kindness. After my mom and dad went out together every Saturday night for four weeks, my mom gently moved forward for greater commitment. She said they were sitting on the couch after a date and he said, "I really like you."

She asked him, "Am I number three for you?" He said, "No, you're higher on the scale than that." She asked, "Am I number two?" He said, "Keep going." She asked, "Am I number one?" He said yes. She was surprised but she was smart enough not to let the moment slip by. She asked, "Does that mean we're going steady?" He said, "Yes, I guess we are." My mother's not the forward type. In fact, she's a closet Distancer, but she said, "I knew your father was a good catch and I wasn't going to let that opportunity pass me by."

Distancers need to learn to be accountable and they need to learn to move. If they don't learn to invest in the person they're with, they will face loneliness forever. Pursuers need to learn to set limits and create a loose structure for their Distancers. It's a lot easier to do this at the beginning of a relationship, but even couples who have been together for years can turn the tide of their marriage if the Pursuer is willing to take the initiative and be the Connection Guardian.

Being the Connection Guardian means being willing to give ultimatums, gently, nicely, and with love and validation. **Studies show that men who learn to give their partners what they need to feel loved have lasting relationships that are filled with much more happiness. It doesn't come naturally to men, so we have to be willing to teach them if we want them to learn.**

When Jeff and I started dating, we were seeing each other every Wednesday night and every weekend. After three fabulous weeks, he called one night and we talked on the phone for two hours, but he never mentioned the upcoming weekend. I called him the next day to ask about the weekend and he said, "I have things to do." I suspected something was up. He said, "I'm busy this weekend, but let's get together for the Fourth of July weekend," which was one week later.

First I tried to get him to compromise, so that we could spend at least a little time together during the upcoming weekend, but he wouldn't budge. *I was feeling abandoned and made the mistake of not shifting into Smart Heart Dialogue.* I didn't tell him about my abandonment wounds because of his *abrupt disconnection.* He was standing his ground.

On Friday, he called me and we talked on the phone for six hours—something I don't generally advise. It was obvious he wanted to talk to me, so I suggested again that we see each other for at least a few hours on Saturday or Sunday. He said no, and tried to appease me with the Fourth of July invitation. *This time I set my wounds aside and used Smart Heart Dialogue!*

I asked him, "I was wondering if things are getting too hot and heavy for you and if that's why you don't want to see each other this weekend."

He was taken aback by my question. No one had ever asked him why he was slowing a relationship down before. He said, "Maybe that's it. I don't know."

I knew I should take it one step farther so he could get in touch with his ambivalence. I said to him, "In your ad you said you wanted a long-term relationship."

He said, "Did I say that in my ad?"

I reminded him about the line that said, "seeking a caring relationship."

In response, he said, **"Caring isn't commitment.** Why can't we just keep doing what we're doing?"

I said: "You're right. Caring isn't commitment. I want both. You need to decide if you want to go further. I think you're a great guy and I could probably fall for you. You said in your ad that you wanted to have a close relationship and I'd be open to that to see where it will lead. I think we have a great thing going. It's okay if you don't want to have more with me. I can understand that and I'm not mad at you. I really think we have something special and the Fourth of July together would be a tease for me if you don't want to move forward. I hope you understand."

He said, "I'm sorry if I misled you in my ad when I said I wanted a caring relationship. I never said long-term. I'll have to figure out what I want. I have to think about it."

He said he'd call me the following week. *That was the most torturous weekend of my life.* I was miserable. My rejection wounds were sky-high, and I was terribly disappointed. Just when I thought I had found the man for me, he was running scared.

When he called on Monday he asked, "How was your weekend?" I told him it was great! He paused and said, "Mine was terrible. I *really* missed you."

I thought, "That's terrific!" I said, "That's nice to hear and thanks for sharing that with me." I didn't tell him I missed him too. We talked for awhile longer and then he tried to firm up our date for the Fourth of July. I asked him if he had thought about what we discussed and he *said he didn't remember what I was talking about.* I reminded him again that I didn't want to keep seeing him if he wasn't serious about considering and maybe working toward having a long-term relationship with me. **He tried to dodge again, but finally realized I meant it.**

His response was "Alright, we can have a close relationship. Now can we plan next weekend together?"

I wanted to be sure he wasn't just making promises that he didn't intend to keep, so I explored his feelings a little further. "Are you sure? It's okay if you don't want this. I won't be upset with you."

After talking for awhile longer he said, "I really like you and I really do want to have a close relationship like I said in my ad. Let's go for it."

If Jeff hadn't been willing to make that commitment to me, I *would have had to pull back,* skip the Fourth of July weekend with him, and *stay connected by leaving the door open and dating others,* which I told him. **That's one of the hardest things to do when you're falling in love with someone,** so I was relieved that he was willing to move forward.

The following tips will help you keep shifting gears until your reach commitment.

Smart Heart Skills to Reach Commitment

- During the early stages of courtship, Pursuers take the lead and Distancers get used to it and start taking the

Pursuer for granted. To shift gears, you have to pull back a little and make him reach for you.

- Even though there's not much relationship "glue" yet, the incentive for the Distancer to continue in the relationship is a fear of being alone some day. Distancers are fine in their own space, but they don't want to be alone long term. **He has to think there's a chance he could lose you in order for him to make the effort to keep you.**

- At the sign of the first power struggle, hang in to resolve your issues. Work "smarter" and play out the relationship.

- After three dates, when the masks are off and the power struggles are beginning, you both are deciding if you want to move forward. **When a Distancer is faced with a decision, he decides by making no decision.** He may avoid you and the relationship. *This often means he likes you very much.*

- Begin making him accountable by gently asking him if he is distancing because he's afraid or if there's a problem he would like to talk about.

The Marriage Ultimatum

Many more couples would get married if they could experience what life would be like without each other. A temporary break-up gives you both a chance to gain more clarity and certainty about your feelings.

A break-up won't be effective if you do it too early in a relationship. You need to be together long enough for him to know what he'll be missing. Build a history and camaraderie together and have enough good times to create a bond first. **When you do leave, make sure you part with a loving, sweet message that provides him with plenty of validation.**

If you want marriage and your partner doesn't, *risking the strategic break-up is usually your best bet.* It's smarter to take a risk now than to wait until the frustrations and anxiety of your difference of opinion take your relationship to the point *of no return.*

For example, my patient Wendy, whose biological clock was ticking, wanted very much to marry Craig, a man she had been dating for four years. Craig loved Wendy, too, but he didn't take her seriously and took her for granted. She broke up with him **but went back in two days because of her fear of abandonment.** Craig never had the opportunity to experience life without her. He didn't have to face his emptiness and he never missed her because she was always there.

Craig was afraid to become dependent on Wendy because his mother was hospitalized for a nervous breakdown when he was a child, and he was afraid to trust other women or make a commitment. Instead of saying good-bye with love and leaving the door open for Craig to return, Wendy got increasingly more angry and more frustrated. She nagged and screamed at him (as his mother had when he was an abused child), and this made him distance even more. Resentment ate away at their passion and interest and they lost respect for each other.

If Wendy had been courageous enough to wait out the break-up with Craig, he would have reached for her, because he really loved her. The irony is that Wendy's fear of abandonment became a reality because she ran from it, instead of facing it and taking a risk.

When I wanted to get married and Jeff wasn't so sure, I let him know I wasn't waiting forever. As fate would have it, I met a very handsome and successful man who was a periodontist (like Jeff) and was interested in becoming serious. I told Jeff if he didn't want to get married, maybe we should both start dating other people. I issued a marriage ultimatum, lovingly and gently and he felt threatened by the thought of losing me to one of his colleagues. And he also remembered the feelings of emptiness he experienced when I left him for two days earlier in the relationship. Finally he said, "Alright I'll marry you!" It wasn't the most romantic proposal of all time, but it led to a very romantic and fulfilling marriage. It's important to note that Jeff's words *were not reflective of the deeper feelings he had for me at the time.* So don't let words stop you; look at their actions.

My patients Marlene and Geno broke up because she wanted marriage and children and he was afraid to take that step, even though he loved her and they had been dating a year. Geno was so confident in the relationship that he felt he would never lose her and they had plenty of time. Marlene's biological clock was ticking, and Geno would not take her seriously. She broke up with him because she needed to see if he missed her, if he needed her, and what she meant to him.

She did it gently, firmly, and with love, and no anger or blame. First he was in denial, then he turned to someone else out of anger. Marlene realized he was feeling abandoned, so she connected with him and told him, **"I love you enough to let you be free."** She helped him to get in touch with his suffocation wounds and also his feeling of being abandoned by his mother.

Smart Heart Dialogue

Marlene: "You have *as much right not to want to get married or have a child as I have a right to want to.* I'm not mad at you or blaming you for your choice. I want you to have what you want because I love you. I also want to have what I want, and I really want to get married and have children. Maybe you'll decide that's what you want, too, but if not, that's okay. I'm not turning my back on you. **I'll leave the door open and if we have what I think we have together, you'll find your way back to me. I love you enough to let you be free."**

That relieved the pressure on Geno so he could make the decision to marry and even have children.

Boy did he go into his emptiness! He realized what he lost. If he hadn't gone through this, he said he would have wanted to date for at least another two years before he'd even consider marriage. After the break-up, that all changed, and Marlene and Geno are now married.

Let's say you have been dating for three years and he's waffling about marriage. Three years is really too long to wait for a marriage commitment unless he is waiting for a divorce to be final or something similar. **In most cases, it's appropriate to issue this ultimatum after a year to a year and a half of dating. (If your biological clock is ticking, you may want to do it after about six months or a year.)** *The longer you wait, the more comfortable and set in his ways the Distancer becomes.*

First, you set a game plan for yourself and write down your goals for yourself as a reminder of what you are going for. Next, announce it to him lovingly and gently. **Don't expect him to go along with it, and be prepared for resistance.**

Smart Heart Dialogue for Breaking Up

"I understand that our relationship is very good and that you're happy this way. You're entitled to feel that way. I understand and it's okay that you may not agree with what I'm going to say. I would like to move toward marriage within the next six months. *[It's very important to define your time frame.]* It would make me feel secure and rooted. I look forward to a life with you because you're so wonderful. I hope you understand. I know you've tried your best and can't commit at this time. I respect that. I hope you can respect my feelings and walk in my shoes."

Don't get thrown by his facial expression or verbal reaction. Don't feel sorry for him, guilty for your choice, protect him, or defend yourself. *If you do, he won't take you seriously, he will continue to take you for granted, and like a good lawyer, he will smooth things over and talk you out of it by "selling" you his idea of how things should go.* You have just as much right to want to get married as he has not to want to.

"I understand that you want your freedom. You are entitled to that as much as I am to being committed. I think you're a terrific guy. But for now, let's take a chance and find out what we both really want. I'll leave the door open, but I'll be dating others. I hope you find your way back to me because I really think we have something special and that we can make this work for both of us. I'd like to know how you feel."

Make sure you validate him and let him know you understand how he feels. **Remember he isn't "wrong" for wanting his freedom; that's his choice—even if it ultimately means that he will be alone.** Don't judge him. If you blame him, make him feel inadequate, or accuse him of being "screwed up," you might as well slam the door in his face, because that is how he will react if he feels "bad" or "guilty." Don't be whiney, demanding, smothering, or clingy, and don't ask for an answer *now*. Remember he's *correcting the developmental stage, not re-enacting it.*

His response may vary:

"I'm not ready yet."

"I really love you, you know that. We already have a commitment, so why do we have to get married?"

"If we get married it will change things."

"If it's not broken, don't fix it."

"I want to do this in my own time, when I'm ready."

"Next, you'll want to have kids."

"Why can't you think of *me*?"

"I'm not sure how I feel about being together the rest of our lives."

"I don't feel like I want to get married. If I marry you, it would only be to make you happy, and that's not a good enough reason."

"I want to be completely sure first."

"I don't want to marry you because you're giving me an ultimatum."

You respond without arguing. *Instead, you hold your ground and validate his argument.*

"I understand you need to be sure and your desire to have a guarantee that we'll be happy. That makes perfect sense that you want to be sure. Life and love are reasonable risks. It takes courage to love and take a chance. I could help you with this along the way. **I'm scared, too. We have such a special feeling and relationship that I'd like to take a chance with you.**"

When I say you respond without arguing, that means *"no buts."* For example, don't say, "I understand, *but . . .* " That is a form of invalidation.

If he says: "I don't think we need to do this right now. I do care about you and I don't want to lose you."

You say: "I know that. I'm not angry. **I love you enough to let you go.** Maybe you need some time to see what life will be like without me by your side. I'm okay with that. **I have confidence in our relationship that we can weather this.** I love you enough to want you to be happy, even if it's not with me. **I'll leave the door open if you miss me or need me but I hope you'll understand that I can't wait, and if what we**

**have is as good as I think it is, you'll find your way back to
me and I'll help you."**

He says: "Can't we still see each other or still be friends?"
(very typical response).

You say: (First you appeal to *his* needs.) "It might be
really hard on you later. I don't want to complicate things for
you, so you can be completely free. Being friends is more like
a tease of what we can't have. Plus, it will probably be too
complicated for me, too. I'll keep the door open though."

During the Break-Up for a Commitment

**At the first stage of a break-up, you must not call him or
see him, or he will not experience the depth of his feelings
for you.** You must let him know you believe in the relationship,
have confidence in your love for each other and your ability to
stick together through the years and make this work. *You have
to bolster his confidence in the relationship as you let him out
the door. His tendency will be to latch onto another Pursuer to
fill his emptiness;* that's why you're leaving with a reassuring
open-door policy to stay connected without pursuit. That way
he will remember the good in your relationship. If you do it
any other way, he will remember the bad and be less likely to
return. Tell him, "If you get lonely or feel abandoned, let me
know so I can help you."

Once you break up and send the Distancer into his emptiness, *you should go into your own emptiness as well,* so you
can work through your issues and come out of the experience
stronger. This will also shift your focus from him to yourself
and your loved ones. If you do *your* work, you can help him to
do *his.* Dr. Fogarty describes emptiness as "a feeling of being
unloved, unwanted, and not belonging." If you don't feel this,
you haven't pulled back far enough. **If you don't pull back**

far enough, your partner will not miss you and the desire to commit to you will not be sparked. Even if he comes back (under these circumstances), he will not stay, or it will not be how you want it.

You must beware of the temptation of "little pursuits" such as sending cards or an article from the paper, leaving messages on his answering machine, stopping by to pick up your lamp that you can't do without, or connecting with him in any way before he initiates a reconnection. You will be tempted to do these things to ease your own anxiety and try to rationalize it by telling yourself you're doing it for *him*. The only connections you should make with him are those that *occasionally nurture him and let him know that the door is still open.*

One of the problems in the relationship is that you have been avoiding your own emptiness by focusing on your Distancing partner. This puts a burden on him, and while it may temporarily make you feel better, in the long run you are actually stopping the relationship by not giving him the time and space to deal with his own emptiness. It's easy to see why this happens, because a man who is distancing with logic and control provokes your emotionality. **To stay calm during a break-up so you can follow through with your plan, you must use this time to "go back home."**

When you reconnect with your estranged partner, you will be able to avoid asking your partner questions like: "How do you feel? How has this changed things? Are you ready to get married? Did you miss me?" (Dr. Fogarty told me to put Scotch tape on my lips when I talked to Jeff on the phone to remind myself not to talk about wanting to get married—it worked!) Never ask a Distancer how he feels, because he'll say, "I don't know."

The Distancer needs time to realize that in many ways he relies on you for the ups and downs of life. **(Don't make the**

mistake of telling this to him; he will only believe it if he experiences it firsthand.) When you first part, he will probably feel a sense of relief; it won't hit him at first. **It takes about six weeks to two months for the emptiness to set in if you don't pursue him. Don't expect him to call when he's in the "relief" stage.**

In about six to eight weeks, if this is a *viable* relationship and he is connectable by instruction, he'll go into a holding pattern where he will pitifully reach out to you. Don't try to fix things or protect him from the pain. You're not being mean, you're helping him get to the place where he can accept and give love, which only happens when he reaches rock bottom.

When he calls you to say, "I need you," even though you are not seeing him, thank him but don't say, "I miss you" or "I love you." He needs to experience more of the insecurity *he's* feeling. **The emptiness will cause changes for the better.** He will use very tempting triggers that are hard to resist in an attempt to bring back the warm memories of your courtship. He might get tickets to your favorite vacation hideaway or a play he knows you're dying to see. He might offer to wine you and dine you at your favorite romantic restaurant, or use the sentimentality of an upcoming holiday or relationship anniversary to weaken your stance. Do not accept these offers, unless he is proposing marriage or the commitment you want.

Even then, don't make the mistake of jumping immediately. Tell him to think that through and stay apart a little longer. Tell him you have to think things through, too. He'll wonder if you are interested in someone else. That's okay. Don't reassure him that there are no other men, but do validate him. *This is not a form of manipulation, it is a way to prevent him from scaring himself again after you accept his proposal.* He has to really want you and miss you to be sure he wants to marry you. (My husband, Jeff, is grateful that he made the decision to want to marry me by experiencing his own loss and loneliness without pressure from me.)

Remember he doesn't always mean what he says. His proposal might just be a way to get you back and he may not follow through. When he begins to feel desperate, he will probably tell you what he thinks you want to hear—*hoping he can do it, or hoping to buy more time.* You have to be able to decipher which it is because if he's not really serious, you shouldn't see him. Take your time. *Look at the movement, not the words.*

This is the turning point of whether this relationship will move forward into commitment and marriage, or not. Even if you both agree to get married within a certain period of time, once you're dating again, he may forget about his experience in the "empty pit" *and start thinking he can string you along again.* He can go back to his original pattern of dancing around commitment like Paul did to Rhonda. If that happens, you have to *immediately* put on the brakes again, and let him know you mean it by breaking up again if he doesn't take you seriously.

Hopefully the break-up will help him to get in touch with his fears and make him want to learn how to express them and heal them. You also want him to become aware of his difficulty with giving and his pessimistic view that others will not give to him. The break-up will trigger his earliest wounds of when he felt he was let down by the parent he wanted to be close to, or thought he was close to. The deeper he goes into this painful memory, the more likely he will be able to work through these feelings and heal his heart, so he can commit to you. When he reaches out to you to express his feelings, encourage him to do the same with the parent he yearned to be close to, or lost closeness with, so that his change will be a lasting one.

During the break-up, don't see him until he agrees to marry you or gives you the commitment you asked for, and use Smart Heart Dialogue when he reaches out.

Smart Heart Dialogue to Use for Reconnection

He says: "I'm ready to see you again."

You mirror his statement and fact-find: "What I heard you say is that you're ready to see me again. I'm happy to hear that. What exactly does that mean?" (Encourage him to explain without showing any anger or changing your friendly tone.)

He says: "I don't know."

You say: "What I heard you say is you don't know what that means. I need to know if you're calling to get together to see me, or if you decided to take this to the next level and get married?"

He says: "I thought we could see each other and play it by ear."

You say: "I understand why you'd like that. For you it could work and it makes sense from your position. (He is trying to sell you and get you to feel the way he does.) I want to get married, and if that's what you want, too, we can see each other. If not, I respect you and understand your position about keeping things the same. For me, it's much too painful and a tease for us to see each other and not be able to finalize our feelings. I hope you can understand and respect my feelings." (This is respecting where he is, even if it's not where you are.)

He says: "Isn't that kind of controlling to tell me if I don't want to marry you, we can't be together anymore?"

You say: "I understand that you feel controlled by my ultimatum; feeling controlled is a feeling you're having. You have a choice of what you do and how you feel. You're choosing to see me as controlling and I understand that. I'm just expressing what I need. If it's not what you need, I understand that. It's okay. You can have the control back and tell me you don't want marriage and I'd have to respect that. I'm not angry. I'll miss you, and if I really love you I'll let you go so you can be free."

He says: "I want to be able to feel happy and excited about marrying you. Instead I feel depressed because I feel like I'm being forced into it or I'll lose you again."

You say: "I understand that you feel forced and not ecstatic about this decision and it's totally your choice to decide. I truly love you, and I feel we can do this and be happy together. I won't be mad at you no matter what choice you make. We also could go for help to sort this out."

He says: "I'll think about it. Thank you."

If you allow him room and give him encouragement, love, confidence, and patience, he will begin to trust you because you haven't completely turned your back on him. **Remember the "separation and return" wounds he has from childhood. Help him with his second chance to resolve this.** He'll respect you for your strength, courage, belief in him, and for not allowing him to manipulate you. **His deepest fear is that he'll depend on you, which in many ways, he really wants to do.** Through this second "crisis" he knows he can still depend on you. With love, kindness, and no rage, you come through for him and for yourself.

Behind the Scenes of Two Break-Ups

My patient Gina gave her boyfriend Greg a "brush with death" because, "We have no future; we're both stuck in the past and neither of us is enjoying the journey right now. He is so worried about where this is going, he's not even looking forward to the vacation we planned together."

I asked Gina to write a list detailing why she is giving Greg so much power.

- I feel like a little girl who has no control.
- I feel all alone and abandoned.
- I feel like I'm at the end of the road.
- I'm getting older and my biological clock is ticking.
- I feel that no one else will ever love me.

Next, I asked Gina to make a list of how a break-up can help, so she can use her power in a constructive way.

- He needs to be alone to find his direction.
- I'm tired of being a rubber ball and bouncing back and forth.
- I want to learn how to have a balanced relationship.
- I don't want to have to analyze his behavior, which doesn't back up his words.
- I want a commitment without the *kicking and screaming*.
- I want to get on with my life.
- I'm tired of running from the very thing I want.
- I want to develop higher self-esteem by not allowing myself to keep getting shot down.
- I want to learn how to stop blaming myself.
- I will get a chance to work through my emptiness and grieve for the relationship I wanted to have with Greg but never had.
- I will have a chance to disconnect from my parents, so I can reconnect.

Gina decided to set this break-up into motion because she didn't want to be treated this way any more. She has learned to value herself enough to refuse being taken for granted or yanked around. She knew there was a good chance they would not get back together, because although she was willing to learn new skills, he was not. She agreed it was better to break up than to continue on the path they were on, no matter what the outcome would be.

My patient Darla broke up with her boyfriend Steve because they dated for two years and he wouldn't even entertain the possibility of marriage. He also never had closure with his ex-wife. Up until this point, Darla made excuses for Steve and protected him. I told her she had to use an ultimatum, since he had too much of the control in the relationship. "You have to make him accountable and set limits and you have to do it gently and lovingly. Validate him, and remain firm in your stance."

Smart Heart Dialogue

Darla: "We've been together two years and I understand you're still connected to your ex-wife. It's okay. I can't wait. We can either get engaged or you can be free. Either way, it's okay. If we break up, and our relationship is meant to be, we'll spring back and spend the rest of our lives together. I'm letting you go with love. **I'm not angry with you for what you don't know and what you don't know how to do.**"

Darla understood that a conscious choice to commit to each other was needed for the relationship to keep moving. She and Steve had relied on the endorphins in the beginning of their relationship to make their choices for them, but that was no longer working. She agreed to take a reasonable risk to help the relationship along and determine if they really had a future together. Without making this decision, another two years could have dragged on without Steve being willing to be make a move toward marriage. Steve decided to work on making a commitment, saying good-bye to his ex-wife, and getting in touch with his fear about commitment.

Smart Heart Break-Up Skills for Singles

Let him go with love—no anger, blame, or guilt—so he can go into his emptiness and discover what you mean to him. *It's a second chance to finish the early developmental stage of "separation and return" (disconnection and reconnection).*

Tell him he cannot predict the outcome of the break-up. You are taking a risk to give up control, to see where the relationship is going.

Don't judge, attack, or criticize him. Validate and understand.

Ask him to take a step back and not try to fill in his void with another woman too soon, because that will start the vicious cycle over again for him.

If he is going to someone else, tell him that dilutes your relationship, but let him go. Leave the door open but tell him, "I'm not waiting," and "You can't have us both." *Push him to her so he comes to you, but at the same time fight for him by telling him of your love and confidence in him, and how wonderful he is.*

Remember he may need to play out a relationship with someone else before he gets into his emptiness. *Be patient, but don't wait.*

Dating others during the break-up can *help keep you balanced* until you get the commitment you want; you'll feel less needy and will be less likely to pursue. On the other hand, it can also *dilute* your primary relationship (by giving you pseudo-intimacy to hide behind) and prevent a reconnection. It's important to decide which course of action is best for you and your motivation.

Date Others If:

- Your expectations of the man you broke up with are too high. (You need to make him less important; he needs to make you more important.)
- Your investment in your primary relationship is above and beyond a balanced give-and-take.
- There's no definition of the relationship or commitment.
- You want to get change and movement and all else has failed.
- You are being taken for granted.
- He refuses to be exclusive and you'd like to be.

Do Not Date Others If:

- You or he are using it as a way to create a triangle or run from intimacy with your partner.
- You or he are doing it to avoid your own emptiness.
- You can't stand to be alone. (This is something you need to learn how to do.)
- Your partner feels abandoned and it could jeopardize your relationship.

This final point contradicts the advice to date others, but remember there are no hard and fast rules—only guidelines. The reason for this exception is that there are circumstances where one partner feels so abandoned in the temporary break-up that if the other dates, the relationship will surely end. If your partner has severe abandonment wounds you still need to let him go into his emptiness, but you need to stay connected with occasional calls and cards to reassure him that you are there.

How to Break Up with Your Spouse

If you're married and your relationship needs a break-up, issuing an ultimatum to your spouse needs to be done firmly and gently, *and you have to stick to it*. Many of my patients "cry wolf" too many times and their partners don't take them seriously. You must be loving, calm, and certain about your decision to break up to make up. It's best to make this move *before* your relationship deteriorates to the point where anger and resentment are your only bond with each other. **However, even relationships that have begun to crumble can often be revived with a brush with death.**

For example, when Mary Jo called me to schedule a phone therapy appointment, she said she feared her marriage was breaking up and couldn't be fixed, but she thought she should at least try. Ten minutes before her scheduled appointment, she called to cancel. She said, "It's too late. You can't help us. Too much damage has already been done."

I know from my track record with my patients and also from my parents' courage that most marriages can be saved. I encouraged Mary Jo to have the same courage that I had and to trust me and the process. After speaking to her husband, Jimmy, I knew I was right. This was a marriage not meant to break up.

Mary Jo said Jimmy made assumptions. They didn't fact-find and Jimmy wouldn't share his feelings. As it turned out, Jimmy was afraid of abandonment, so he wanted peace at any price. He was using magical thinking—"It will all work out somehow." Instead of talking, they both mind-read.

Mary Jo wanted Jimmy to open up to her, but the few times he did, she criticized him and invalidated what he said. A very polite couple, they didn't create tension in their relationship rubber band by fighting fair, which resulted in very little passion in their marriage. Mary Jo had to learn to fight fairly so they could reconnect with each other through intimacy. They decided to break up to make up because they both wanted to rekindle their feelings and make a conscious commitment to their marriage.

During the break-up, Mary Jo worked on letting go of the grudges. Jimmy worked on building his courage so he could share his feelings with Mary Jo, even if she reacted with anger or criticism. Jimmy and Mary Jo did everything right. They worked through the break-up stage and their reconnection in the make-up stage went beautifully. In fact, they did so well they were willing to appear with me in three segments on the *Today* Show with Katie Couric to demonstrate and share what they had learned to save their marriage and turn it into a loving and passionate relationship. Jimmy—who initially couldn't share his feelings—told Mary Jo on national television, "You light up my life. I'm so happy we're together." Mary Jo said, "Thank you for hanging in. You helped me to learn how to love."

Both partners normally have to agree to the break-up for it to work. That doesn't mean they both have to like the idea—just that they both are willing to try it and commit to working as a team for the good of the relationship. **Breaking up to make up works best if you both agree to the ground rules and know the benefits before you do it.**

For example, my patients Beth and Don broke up because Beth felt extremely abandoned in the marriage and Don was afraid of being smothered. Don also had affairs, which often requires a temporary break-up if the behavior is continued. Beth let Don go with love so he could see what was "out there." She was terrified of losing him, but had to take the chance because Don could not stop womanizing and had a five-year affair that Beth recently found out about. *She never could take a stand, and he was "begging" for her to give him an ultimatum and set limits that he had been unable to set for himself.*

Once Beth left, Don was terrified of being abandoned and wanted her more than he ever had before. He knew she could stand on her own, because she proved it by leaving. He realized she was responsible for herself, and when he saw her independence he knew she wouldn't suffocate him or cling to him. But they were still walking a thin line because at one point Don turned to other women (as Geno did) because he felt abandoned by Beth. I told Don, "You can't have it both ways. Beth let you go as *you* asked. Don't punish or blame her. She is not abandoning you; she is simply giving you what you thought you wanted. You have to choose between being lonely and connecting with Beth with a true commitment."

Don said, *"I abandoned her all those years because I was afraid she'd abandon me."*

Beth said she felt abandoned before she broke up and she survived. She said, "How much more abandoned can I feel?" She knew if she "let him go with love," she would feel less abandoned because *she* would be in control.

The break-up caused a "flip-flop." Beth got in touch with her fears about love and being engulfed, which were partially responsible for her pushing Don toward other women. He became the Pursuer and she became the Distancer. From the fear of loss he experienced, Don got in touch with his feelings of being alone. Beth got more connected to herself and her friends and family.

Don's emptiness triggered his childhood memory of feeling abandoned by his mother when she was ill and hospitalized. He remembered feeling so lost when he needed her so much and couldn't have her. He had sworn to himself he would never allow a woman to have that much power over him again or allow someone to touch his heart so deeply again. He had already let

Beth in, but he did not realize it until she left. These memories helped him understand why he was having such a hard time committing to Beth; *he was afraid to need a woman again.*

Don had to decide if he was going to allow himself to have the love and intimacy he wanted, or if he was going to let her go—as he felt his mother had let him go. **He decided he was ready and willing to pay the price for connection— giving up control and taking a reasonable risk to be hurt, which is always part of love.**

"It hurts more to lose someone you love, than to make a few changes and keep them," said Don. "I needed the break-up so I could get in touch with old feelings for my mother that I never resolved. When Beth broke up with me, it was the catalyst I needed to be willing to love her with an open heart. The break-up gave me courage and insight into my fears. Without the break-up, Beth and I would probably have ended up divorcing." Today Beth and Don are in real life love with each other.

Smart Heart Dialogue for Initiating a Temporary Break-Up with Your Spouse

Here's an example of the dialogue between my patients Linda and Jerry.

Linda (Distancer): "I need some time to myself to sort out my feelings. I'm not sure I love you. I feel so criticized and controlled. I need time to see if I want to be married. I've lost who I am."

Jerry (Pursuer): "I love you enough to let you go. I'll work on not being so controlling and critical. I've felt lonely for years. You probably don't realize this, but the kids always came first for you and I miss you so much. I get critical when I feel abandoned, and of course that makes you abandon me more."

Linda: "I wish I could feel the way I used to feel about you. Give me some time and let's get some help. I can't promise anything."

Smart Heart Break-Up Skills for Married Couples

- Set a time limit for the break-up.
- Break up by permission of both partners and let go with love.
- Do not use anger, blame, guilt, steamrolling, or selling!
- Make reconnections through a therapist or occasional benign interactions to minimize the trauma of disconnection and abandonment, and to foster reconnection later.
- Do not have discussions about where the relationship is going for the time being. When you occasionally reconnect, do not mention the relationship or analyze it.
- "Act as if" you're okay, even if you are angry or feel abandoned. Don't use your feelings to make him feel guilty.
- Get in touch with when you have both felt like this before in your past.
- Stay firm and set limits so he can't have it both ways. Otherwise he won't respect you or himself and you won't have movement.
- Validate. Tell him he has just as much right *not to* want a relationship as you have a right *to want* one.
- Don't put your partner in a no-win situation by first accusing him or her of smothering and then of abandoning. You can't have it both ways.
- If you're a Distancer, move toward the Pursuer for the "right reasons." You should do this only when you are

ready to work at the relationship by learning new skills and leaving the grudges behind. **Resist the temptation to go back if it is based only on your loneliness.**

- Resist the urges to reunite for excuses: birthday, anniversary, kid's soccer game, etc.
- The more you give in now, the less chance of having this marriage forever.
- **Make sure movement and change is occurring; not just promises or words.**

* If you are breaking up to make up because of adultery, see Chapters 21 and 22.

Whether married or single, don't "date" each other during the break-up, but do stay connected. "Dating" during a break-up dilutes the emptiness and doesn't give the relationship a strong enough test. It just puts off the inevitable and prolongs the agony and causes a reverberation.

One of my couples "broke up" but still talked on the phone three nights a week and saw each other once a week. This is not a break-up and they did not receive the results that come from going into emptiness **during a true brush with death.** Consequently, they are still struggling.

It's important to stay connected during the break-up because for Distancers, the saying "out of sight, out of mind" often is the truth. (When I left Jeff, there were four single women for every single man in New York.) Stay connected by sending a card or leaving a short message on his answering machine that is cheerful, encouraging, and positive in nature. **Remember he has an abandonment wound deep down there.**

Smart Heart Skills for During the Break-Up

- Don't predict the outcome, negative or positive—stay in the moment.
- Stay connected through therapy or an occasional card. You can connect on occasion, but don't pursue. *Make him reach for you,* and validate him at the same time.
- If he's furious, let him stew. You may have to repeatedly reassure him by saying: "I love you. Since I love you I'm letting you go with love to find what you need." That's what will bond you—not harsh words or anger, but love, patience, and understanding.
- Let your partner go into his (or her) emptiness; don't try to fix anything.
- **When he's ready to reconnect, don't rush to respond too quickly.** You both need a certain amount of time to go into your hearts and experience your loneliness, or you will go right back to taking each other for granted, and there will be no change. If you give in, he'll learn that he gets what he wants without taking care of *your* needs or appreciating you. Let him be even more sure. Tell him he needs more time, you are patient, and your love can stand the test of time.
- Remember that change often comes only from the fear of loss—the brush with death.
- **Never** ask if he loves or misses you.
- Be firm and make him accountable with loving encouragement and feedback.
- Always leave the door open.

During a break-up I often recommend that couples stay connected *without* having sex, but *there are times* when having sex may be needed for one or both partners to have certainty that the relationship is not completely over. This is particularly true for some married couples, but it can also be advantageous for some single couples, especially if abandonment is an issue.

For example, Marlene and Geno who broke up to make up sometimes slept together so Geno wouldn't feel so abandoned, as he had felt with his own mother. Geno needed to feel the cuddling to know Marlene was not lost or gone. There are not set rules for whether you should occasionally sleep together or not, **however if you do sleep together as a form of reassurance, you must make it clear that your actions do not necessarily mean you will be getting back together. Be careful of him taking you for granted!**

Breaking up to make up brings you to a stage closer to real and lasting love, but only if you do it by using Smart Heart Skills. *Sometimes real life love comes only with a serious jolt, which is what breaking up does.*

How to Help Your Children Through a Temporary Break-Up

If there are children involved, you must tell them what is happening and help to prepare them for it. **You need to take extra care to be sure your children understand that the break-up has nothing to do with them.** Assure them that this is a problem between you and your spouse and apologize to them for putting them through this difficult time.

If the children are about ten years old or older, you can gently explain to them that you are having problems with each other and you think this is the best way to work things out. Let them know you both want to stay together as husband and wife and you are doing everything you can to help that to happen. However, you cannot tell them at this time whether you will reunite, only tell them you will let them know as soon as *you* know. Let them know everyone feels sad about this and it's okay if they feel sad or scared. Ask them to share their emotions with you so you can help them. Do not promise you will reunite since you are not certain a reunion will be the outcome. **Tell your children that no matter what happens between you and your partner, they will not be losing either of you.**

If your children are younger than ten, you can use a toy to help them to understand, as I do with children in my practice. Using this method is called "Family Play Therapy." You center your explanation around one of the child's favorite toys so he or she can understand it on a child's level.

For example, you might take a toy truck or doll that is missing a few parts and tell the child that your marriage is like the toy right now. It is missing a few important parts like the truck and you are trying to find the parts, like in the toys, so you can put the marriage back together and make it work the way it's supposed to work.

Ask your children to tell you how they feel and encourage them to open up and express feelings of fear, stress, or anxiety. If they don't, tell them about yours. Let them know that you are scared, too, and that it's okay to be upset. Assure them again and again that they are not going to lose either one of you. "No matter what happens we will still be your mommy and daddy."

If your children show symptoms of struggling with the break-up, such as behavioral changes, bedwetting, aggression, depression, acting out in school or at home, not sleeping or eating, or being overly accommodating, seek family therapy to get them the help they need. *If they show no symptoms, that is even more serious. Seek help immediately!*

If you handle this wisely, your children can actually benefit from the experience and learn some valuable lessons about relationships. **If you do not handle this with love and care, your children will incur wounds that will affect their intimacy in adult relationships forever.**

Always keep uppermost in your mind that you are breaking up because it is the best way to revive your relationship. Be committed to the process by following the guidelines and learning and using the *Smart Heart Skills*. Remember that 98 percent of couples can save their relationship. Have confidence that you are doing everything you can to make your love stronger and your commitment to each other and your children more secure.

How to Give Your Children Support If You Don't Reunite

Frequently children are the unnecessary recipients of the painful fallout of their parents' troubled relationship. There are some important areas that you should handle sensitively.

Be on the alert for behavioral symptoms that show a problem is going on. Watch for any of the following and take action if you believe your children are in jeopardy:

- Becoming withdrawn or depressed
- Angry episodes and tantrums
- Becoming oppositional or defiant
- Difficulty concentrating
- Disruptions in sleeping or eating patterns
- Bedwetting or toilet accidents
- Problems in school

- Excessive anxiety—clinging or separation anxiety, giving up, or on the extreme end, suicidal thoughts or statements

Decide together how you will tell your children about the change in your relationship—this is especially important if you have decided to dissolve your marriage, but also important if you are *breaking up to make up*. Even a very young child can sense a parent's emotional distress. **Children have astute emotional antennae, and a child's behavior can signal adultery even before the betrayed partner knows about it. Those who lie to their children or hide their problems from them risk raising children who do not trust them.** The children can repeat the legacy if it is repressed or not handled correctly. **Children express what adults suppress.**

~ 18 ~

How to Decide if It's Time to Go Back

"Chains do not hold a marriage together. It is threads, hundreds of tiny threads which sew people together through the years. That is what makes marriage last, more than passion or even sex."

—SIMONE SIGNORET

Deciding when or if you want to get back together is sometimes a very difficult choice. You must be brutally honest with yourself at this point in order to make the wisest choice for yourself and the relationship. *That's not easy when you feel frozen or numb.* If you feel you do want to get back together, the decision of *when* to go back is a *critical* one, and must be treated with extreme care. **While you don't want to wait too long, you also don't want to get back together too soon.**

Many couples tell me what gave them the hope and courage to get back together was a "psychic" connection or invisible bond they had with each other. Vanessa said, "I always felt connected to him, even though we were broken up. I never lost my belief that things could work out for us and that helped him to believe it, too. He told me if I hadn't been so sure, he would have lost hope." *At least one of the partners has to feel this connection to get back together. This is a positive form of magical thinking.*

My mother said the same sort of thing when she left my father. "I could still feel the love we had for each other and I believed that he could still feel it, too. You don't spend twenty-five years loving each other, and then stop having feelings when one of you walks out the door."

If you don't feel this connection, it may be buried under all the relationship debris, fear, and frustration, or you may be numb or frozen. Following the Smart Heart Guidelines will give you the best chance to awaken this connection. It will also give you practice at doing what works and avoiding what doesn't work. Getting to real and lasting love takes time, but if you make it through the break-up, you are one step closer to your ultimate dream!

For example, my patient Robin had been separated for two months when she realized she still had feelings for her husband. "How do I know if the feelings I have for Barry are real love or just need? Barry still cares about me and I think I still love him, even though he cheated." Barry had a three-year affair with the nanny. Robin broke up with Barry in a loving way and left the door open, but she didn't know if she should return.

I reminded Robin that for she and Barry to get back together and make it work, they would both have to change. I asked her to write down her feelings so she could make a decision whether the break-up was permanent or temporary. (I suggest you make the same list.)

Robin's List of Feelings:
- Confusion
- Love?

- Need?
- Illusion?
- Yearning and longing
- A sense that the real person I loved died
- Missing the partnership thing
- Missing his help with chores and the kids
- This "gas-pedal" feeling of "Go" and "Stop," fear and neediness and then love sweep over me.
- Warm feelings of fleeting moments when we were close—when he wasn't guarded and hiding his feelings.

I told Robin if Barry wanted her back, he'd have to pursue her. Robin knew when Barry got too close for comfort, he diluted his relationship with other women. She had to be prepared to face that anxiety and work through it. He had to stop cheating and prove to her that he could be faithful. I told her she should not trust him yet and he had to accept this. **I told Barry he had to give Robin lots of space, and let her "throw darts" at him.**

The following are some insights and advice I shared with Robin:

- If you decide to see him before he changes and shifts gears, that does not mean you are going back or making up. Make that very clear to him, so he has zero expectations (and no hope) and goes into his emptiness. (She shouldn't make him *too* comfortable.) You must set limits and firm boundaries, and keep them.
- When you **think warmly of him, immediately think danger and remember the affair.** This is your way of protecting yourself from falling for him again *until you are sure he can and will change. The painful*

> *memories and your anger are necessary right now to*
> *protect you from going back too soon.*

- Deal with and work through your anger, so you can forgive later—but not forget—if you make up.
- To create the balance—he has to love you more, and you have to love him less.
- He must change and commit to you *before* you should even consider the rebirth of your relationship.
- If you sleep with him, which you may need to do to see how you feel, **explain it's not a signal of reuniting.** It's better to allow yourself to experience this encounter than to be in limbo about how you feel. If you feel abandoned afterward, don't do it again. If you are okay, prepare your partner for *his* possible abandonment.

When to Go Back

Most couples get back together too soon, and that means they'll either have to break up again, or they may break up permanently. Put off immediate gratification for the long-term goal of having a great and enduring relationship. The pain you're experiencing now is worth the pleasure you will receive if you wait until you're both ready to make the conscious commitment to the relationship and to each other. Make sure that you (as the Pursuer) have learned you can live without your mate and are okay by yourself before you get back together. He has to learn he's not so okay without you. It's vital that you make this choice out of love, not out of fear or need.

Some couples wait too long to get back together for stubborn reasons or because they are not willing to *let go of grudges*. They become "reactive distancers" who blame and punish each other. If you do this, you can't build a bridge back. *Unilateral decisions and black and white thinking won't help you to succeed at anything in life—except being alone.* Give up "being right" in favor of being together, being in love, and doing what works for both of you.

If you broke up for a marriage proposal or some form of commitment, you shouldn't get back together **until your partner agrees to move forward with the firm commitment you requested.**

Smart Heart Guidelines for When to Go Back

(At least seven of these points should be met before you go back.)

- When both partners are in excruciating pain, are miserable, and feel helpless or hopeless. (This also happens at the outset of a break-up, so be sure you don't cave in too soon.)
- You can't imagine the relationship really being over. For example, you say that you can't leave or do this to the kids, you feel sorry for your partner, or the sex is too good; but you really mean that you can't imagine life without your partner.
- Movies, plays, music, and food are better with your partner than without.
- You miss him or her when you're alone.
- You go out of your way for your partner—doing little things, even though you are broken up.
- He or she goes out of the way for you.
- He or she brightens your day, even if you are sad.
- You can't wait to share the little things that happen with him or her.
- Your partner is on your side and there for you.

- You feel special, safe, nurtured, and loved by your partner.
- When it feels harder to break up permanently than it is to make up.
- When one partner feels abandoned and will go looking for someone else for all the wrong reasons. Watch out for this because it will dilute the "emptiness" and make it harder to get to the next step. Talk this out, if it's too soon to return.
- If you realize you're meant for each other and you want to commit, or recommit to the relationship.
- When you see that real change (not superficial) has occurred.
- When he moves toward you and the relationship without prompting.
- When he learns to validate you and walk in your shoes.
- When he stops minimizing.
- When he stops "checking out," distancing, or dismissing you.
- When he stops taking you for granted.
- When he recognizes his or her part in leading you to a break-up.
- When you are "visible" again.
- If an affair has occurred, when you or your partner has ended it and shown remorse.
- When you and your partner are able to let go of most of the grudges or are willing to replace them with validation.
- When you are both willing and able to start the process of forgiving each other to make a fresh start, and when you are experiencing each other's renewed connection. (Forgiveness takes too long to

wait for; you may be broken up for good by then. Make up and learn to forgive each other together.)

The more points you can both check off on this list, the more ready you are to make up!

Don't reunite before you are sure it's time and a commitment is agreed upon.

You're not ready to get back together yet, when one or both of you:

- Doesn't feel ready to enter the relationship.
- Still sees yourself as a "victim" or "victimizer."
- Are still punishing each other, holding a grudge, or playing "tit-for-tat."
- Are unwilling to take responsibility for your part in the emptiness in the marriage (or the affair), and are not working toward forgiveness and trust.
- Are so numb, you can't go near each other.
- Provokes fights.

If You Feel You Can't Make Up

Your anger and pain are probably disguising your love for your partner, but the negative feelings will dissipate over time if you allow it. The idea that it will be easier and less painful to give up and quit is an illusion. **A permanent break-up is much more difficult than mending a relationship through breaking up and making up.**

If you feel like you can't make up, ask yourself the following questions to get to the heart of what you're feeling. Rather than mentally answering these questions, take the time to write your responses so you can really help yourself to understand what you're feeling. Many of my patients decide to stay together after answering these questions.

- Did I break off the relationship only because I no longer knew how to deal with the uncertainty of where I stood with my partner, or couldn't stand dealing with it?

- Do I just want it to end because I feel too tired or hurt to continue? (These are the times to work smarter and harder, because you're probably on the verge of shifting gears.)

- Is getting back together appealing because it would feel better right now as immediate gratification, or am I ready to make a conscious commitment to the relationship?

- Am I ending the relationship out of spite, to get revenge, or because I am holding a grudge? (This is one of the most certain ways to hurt yourself and regret your actions.)

- Did I break up with my partner just to take action— any action—instead of the right action? (If this is the case, you are still torn and not ready for a make-up or a break-up.)

- Am I just emotionally exhausted and want to call it quits because it seems easier?

- Has the hurt burned a permanent hole in my heart? (Remember that most wounds can be healed *with an open heart*.)

- Do I have any love left in my heart for my partner?

- Do I want to go out into the singles scene again? Do I dread going to the singles scene again?

- Did I break up because I was stubborn or proud, and this is what's keeping me from making up?

- Am I merely being indecisive? (If so, this is the perfect time to take a stand.)

- Am I refusing to get back together because my partner refuses to get professional help? (If so, remember that you may have to take the lead as the Connection Guardian and get help yourself so you know how to help him or her.)
- Am I treating the break-up as the solution to all my problems? (Getting rid of the person does not get rid of the problem.)
- Have I really been in touch with my emptiness and do I have a conscious awareness of this? (Did I do family of origin work?) Am I going back to avoid my emptiness?
- Did I break up to avoid the pain that I am now going to have to face?
- Do I really understand why the break-up occurred and the part I played?
- What changes am I willing or able to make? What changes do I want or need my partner to make?
- Have I learned enough about myself, my family of origin, and about relationships to do things differently?
- Have I forgiven my partner and myself?
- Do I have the courage to return to the journey that I ran away from, and face my crucible?
- Is numbness covering over my love?
- Are you pessimistic and can't see that the glass is really half full?
- Can you share regretfulness together as you decide to stay or go?
- Do you realize a divorce won't necessarily end a relationship? (If you have children, your relationship will never end.)

If you feel like you can't make up right now, don't despair. Give it a little more time and focus *more of your attention and energy on working with your family.*

For added incentive, remember that numerous studies show that, by and large, married couples are healthier, happier, and wealthier than singles. Your love is worth saving and so is your health. According to a study conducted by Dr. Carl Thoresen, a psychologist at Stanford University, holding on to the anger you feel toward someone can damage your heart. He shows it's also dysfunctional to hold on to grudges, advising, "let bygones, be bygones."

In the meantime, don't underestimate the power of the break-up. A Distancer has to lose you before he shakes up and wakes up. That's what it takes for him to realize he needs you and wants you.

My father, my husband, and many of my Distancer patients needed the "rude awakening" and brush with death to open their eyes and their hearts to the depth of their love. When these men (and some women) have this experience, they become much more motivated to change their ways, learn how to love and be loved, and it sticks. They also end up making some of the best partners. My husband, Jeff—who was initially afraid to marry me—actually said to me the other day, "If I knew how great marriage would be, I would have married you sooner!" Distancers take longer to commit because they take it very seriously.

Don't throw something great away just because you're having problems. Use the problems to make your relationship stronger and better and reap the rewards of making up.

If Divorce Seems Inevitable

If divorce is inevitable you must say good-bye to the old before you can embrace the new. Closure is one of the most important aspects of divorce. Stay open to possibilities when you work through closure because when many of the couples I work with realize it's the end, they change their minds. Closure exercises can help your hearts to open widely enough to give you one last chance together, especially if you are divorcing for the wrong reasons (pride or grudges). While this shouldn't be your *hope* at this point in the process, it is *definitely a possibility*.

Saying good-bye in a way that drives home the permanence of your decision will help you to have closure. I suggest the "Good-Bye Forever" exercise for this purpose. No matter how awkward it may feel at first, this role-playing exercise is certain to move you and help you determine if this is really the end, and if it is, to be able to accept it. (Have plenty of tissues on hand for this exercise.)

Good-Bye Forever

1. Schedule two private appointments with each other—one day apart.
2. The spouse who wants the divorce the least plays dead. Lie down, close your eyes, and remain silent.
3. The other spouse approaches to say the final good-bye. First, tell your "dead" partner what you won't miss—the bitterness, guilt, anger, whatever it is.
4. Next, tell your partner what you will miss—the happy times, the family traditions, the great sex, etc.
5. Express regrets for not growing old together, having grandchildren, or fulfilling wishes, hopes, and dreams.

6. Finally, keeping your eyes closed, kiss your "departed" spouse good-bye, say parting words like "I love you" or "I'm sorry," and *visualize* this person gone forever. (By this time, if there is any hope for reconciliation, the mourner will feel it in his or her heart, and perhaps even cry and want to work it out.)

Wait a day to switch roles so that you each have some time to sort out the emotions this exercise brings up. Often, even if the couple chooses to go forward with the divorce, they both have revived their memories of the good times together enough to proceed with a more amiable break-up. Many times this role-played "death" moves people enough to want to stay together. *They may just need a disconnection from the overwhelming feelings they thought had died. It serves as a good test to see if you can make up instead of break up.*

When Not to Return

On the other hand, there are relationships that are wiser to walk away from. For example, after Melinda broke up with Sam, she believed she really wanted him back even though he was not willing to commit to the relationship or take the necessary steps to learn how to make the relationship work. I asked Melinda, "What are your terms for accepting him back?"

She was so depressed and upset after a few weeks of being broken up that she was about to get back into the no-win situation they had before the break-up and take him back no matter what. I reminded Melinda that if her goal is to get married and have children, she can't keep wasting time with men who are not willing or able to move forward with her.

Together we came up with the terms under which she would accept Sam back and she agreed to stand her ground.

I will take him back if:
- He shows that he is taking action on his promises.
- He stops treating me like I am invisible.
- He appreciates me.
- He is willing to work out his fears.
- He is willing to help me work out my fears.
- He is willing to accept help from therapy sessions.
- He is willing to work on his past and reconnect with his family of origin.
- He is willing to close the door to the past (to his ex-girlfriend) so he can open the door to the future.

As it turned out, Sam was not willing or able to meet any of Melinda's requirements. She was very sad, but she learned some extremely valuable lessons. She also altered her attraction pattern and no longer zeroed in on men who were extreme Distancers. She learned how to have closure on the old relationships by connecting with past boyfriends so she could say good-bye to the old and say hello to the new.

Most relationships can be saved and are worth saving, but there are circumstances where you shouldn't get back together (at least not yet) after a break-up.

Don't return after a break-up when your partner:
- Is too narcissistic to notice you left.
- Can't see his part in the problem—or won't.
- Won't go for professional help.
- Is critical and puts you down.

- Promises, but doesn't deliver; has no intention of changing, makes "superficial changes," or "says what you want to hear."
- Is unfaithful and won't stop.
- Doesn't consider your needs, emotionally or physically, or is abusive.
- Doesn't compliment, appreciate, or notice you.
- Withdraws and plays tit-for-tat.
- Holds grudges and has bitter buckets filled to the brims.
- Takes you for granted and/or treats you like you're invisible.
- Shows no passion.
- Will not practice fair fighting.
- Does not make you feel safe.
- Disconnects without announcing to punish you and *refuses reconnection*.
- Will not compromise or negotiate with you.
- Lies to you.
- Does not walk in your shoes.
- Acts passive-aggressive or still seeks peace at any price.
- Sabotages or provokes you.
- Exhibits compulsive and self-destructive behavior that is harmful to himself as well as other family members, and is unwilling to get help.

My patient Tara had to make the difficult choice of not going back to her boyfriend because he was too selfish and did not miss her during the break-up. He was also extremely pessimistic and never believed the relationship could work. Tara had never been married and had a pattern of attracting Vanishing Men. Tara decided not to go back because she was the only one in the relationship. He was *out* before he was *in*.

She left because he:
- Was too selfish.
- Had no belief in the relationship.
- Put forth no effort.
- Was not willing to change.
- Could not shift gears.
- Was not over his last relationship.
- Would not consider therapy (because he didn't want to make it work).

Tara learned that it is better to let go of relationships that are not viable. *While her self-esteem dropped in previous break-ups, this time by making a conscious choice and understanding her reasons, she actually felt better about herself.* Of course she was still sad for awhile, but Tara is learning what's truly important to her in a relationship and now feels confident that she can—with time and skills—get the love she wants.

If you're breaking up, try to see that it is a new beginning as well as an ending. I remind my patients who opt for a permanent break-up or divorce of the advice of Richard Carlson, author of *Don't Sweat the Small Stuff*. **"Your problems are your potential teachers. See problems as a source of reawakening to practice patience, to grow to learn."**

It takes courage to break up or divorce, but if this is truly your best option, then it is essential to have closure on this relationship so that you can be emotionally free to seek love again. After allowing yourself to grieve, refer back to Chapter 11 and reread the segment on putting ghosts to rest so that you can move forward in your life with freedom and confidence. *Remember, you can't open the door to a new relationship until you've closed the door on the previous ones.*

~ 19 ~

Repairing the Damage

"Real love begins only when one person comes to know another for who he or she really is as a human being, and begins to like and care for that human being. . . . To be capable of real love means becoming mature, with realistic expectations of the other person. It means accepting responsibility for our own happiness or unhappiness, and neither expecting the other person to make us happy, nor blaming that person for our bad moods and frustrations."

—JOHN A. SANFORD

Couples who break up to make up have a second chance for love. To succeed, they have to handle the break-up wisely and be willing to do what it takes *to make the reconnection a success.* Getting back together after a break-up isn't only a second chance for love, **it's also a second chance to make a first impression**—a fresh start. Couples who make it through the break-up and make-up stages *develop very strong and bonded relationships.*

When you make up after the break-up, you're saying, "I'm going to love you the way you want to be loved, not the

354

way I want to love you." During the make-up stage you *do need* to have some "positive" magical thinking. Be optimistic and believe you can work it out. You also need to continue with your family of origin work to get through this stage successfully. Couples who are committed to take the journey together, "in good times and in bad," discover the joys of real and lasting love. They grow old together and their love stays alive and fresh because they nurture each other and the relationship. They make the relationship and each other a high priority and they coach each other and support each other through difficulties, rather than blaming and attacking each other.

There's no doubt that breaking up to make up is one of the most powerful ways to save a relationship, **but the challenge isn't over when you get back together.** In fact, in many ways the challenge is just beginning. The make-up stage is a critical period because both partners are scared. They are both learning how to modify and change their behavior, learning how to accept and appreciate the changes their partner is making, and sometimes struggling with denial. They're both walking on thin ice, and they have to make it safe for each other so it will be safer for themselves.

It's a critical juncture because of all the fears and because both partners have to "change positions" or roles. The Distancer has to be more of a Pursuer and the Pursuer has to be more of a Distancer. On top of all that, they have to learn how to dance together in their "modified" positions. You must enter the make-up stage *with a firm commitment* to stay together and make permanent changes despite fears and regressions. You may even want to write up a simple "love contract" together to put your intentions in writing.

Change Gears Instead of Partners

Couples who do the best in the make-up stage did some family of origin work (during the break-up) and discovered they are ready and willing to change. Couples who get back together before they do family of origin work or before they are really ready to make a conscious commitment to the relationship run the risk of ending the relationship permanently. *This happens because they have not stayed apart long enough to reap the full benefits of the break-up, and they have not experienced the link between their current behavior with their partner and their behavior with their parents.*

In most cases it's the Pursuer (usually a woman) in a relationship who is anxious to make the reconnection; **they usually want to go back too soon—often at the first moment the Distancer "becomes a Pursuer" and appears desperate and helpless.** While there are no rules for who should initiate making up, my experience shows **that the reconnection is much more effective if the Pursuer can wait for the Distancer to reach out to her.** In rare instances, Pursuers need to connect so the Distancer doesn't bail out. But in most cases, wait until you see a *real* change, not just a situational change caused by his discomfort.

Reconnect with Love

If you do not enter the make-up stage with the *intent* for heartfelt forgiveness and a new sense of trust it won't work. These feelings must come from your heart and your mind. Seeing each other as wounded children will help your hearts melt and make it easier to lower your expectations of each other. It will also give you more courage to set limits and keep each other accountable with coaching because you'll understand your issues and how they dovetail with your partner's.

The formula for lifelong love:

Trust + Forgiveness + Courage = Connection
Connection + Courage = Change = Real and Lasting Love

When the time period for the break-up is over, or when you decide it's time to get back together, **announce your intention to reconnect with each other.** Since connecting, disconnecting, and reconnecting are integral parts of a relationship, and each movement brings its own pains and pleasures, partners must announce their intention to make a move to increase security and safety, decrease pain, and minimize misunderstandings.

Smart Heart Skills for Reconnection

- Announce the reconnection and ask your partner how he or she feels about it.
- Shift gears instead of staying stuck.
- Face and share your fears together; the relationship is easier than the fear of the relationship.
- Coach each other with attachment skills. Do not blame, criticize, or belittle each other.
- Do not throw up old relationship debris or use the threat of breaking up again.
- Make sure your partner feels visible and heard.
- Hang in for real and lasting love. Don't give up. Be positive and act confident.

When my patients Beth and Don made up after breaking up, they did beautifully, but they still both had a lot of fear. Both Beth and Don were afraid he would cheat again. This is a natural feeling for couples who break up to give their marriage a second chance after an affair. I told Beth and Don to take turns being the "team captain." They switch roles every other week. The team captain's role is to make sure they are both following their game plan and to gently and lovingly coach their partner if and when they stray off course.

Team Captain's Responsibilities:
- Be kind. Remember that respect breeds love.
- Don't "check out," shut out, or shut down if you're upset. Check in daily to share, and make it safe.
- Announce connections, disconnections, and recon-nections.
- Check in to see how your partner is doing.
- Don't mind-read, assume, "prick," or offer advice unless your partner asks for it or you have permission.
- Respect your differences. Don't be right; be a winner instead.
- Give up some freedom and control for connection.
- Give up some closeness for connection.

When to Distance:
Separate or disconnect to connect. If your partner is verbally abusive, say in a calm, non-emotional voice, "I will not be treated this way," and distance without anger.

Clearing Relationship Debris

When couples reunite after a break-up, they still have problems from the past to resolve. They also have debris to clean up from the break-up. These are the guidelines I gave to Larry and Marlene to prepare them for rekindling romance and passion.

Fight Fair and use attachment skills to reconnect before, during, and after a fight. Disconnect with an announcement when your partner goes into "crazy-making" behavior. For example, if your partner pushes you away when he feels smothered, and then punishes you for going away, **that's crazy-making behavior.** If he does this you have to disconnect for an hour, or maybe even a day, to awaken his fear of losing you.

Smart Heart Dialogue

When Marlene started crazy-making behavior, Larry would say: "I love you, I'm not abandoning you, but I'm going out right now because you're not making it safe for me to speak. You're asking me to open up and getting angry at what I'm saying. I hope you can calm down and make it safe."

That was perfect, but when he came back, he rejected Marlene's attempts to reconnect. He held grudges for days because he still felt physiologically sick from the fight they'd had. When she tried to reconnect, he'd punish her. So now *he* was doing the crazy-making behavior.

I told Larry when he returned after a disconnection, he had to do so with an open mind. "Marlene is not the same person when you come back as she was when you left. **When you disconnect, her fear of loss reminds her that she appreciates you and she looks forward to welcoming you back.**" Use attachment skills and touch to reverse your "sick" feelings from the conflict. Act counter-intuitive, and use these "touch skills" during crazy-making behavior and after.

See the relationship as a Jack-in-the-Box. I told Larry, "You are keeping the box from staying open by getting angry when she gets upset. You slam the box shut with your behavior, then you wonder why it suddenly pops up again later. You can't react to Marlene's anger with more anger. You have to validate her, keep the box open, and not suppress her so she can have her say. Then the box won't pop up and surprise you with such force all the time."

When your partner is not "consolable," set aside your own despair so you can help her to move out of her despair. During a phone therapy session, I told Larry to connect with Marlene only if she fights fairly to get validation by using Smart Heart Dialogue. She had to learn a new pattern. Larry had to keep from getting angry, and Marlene had to reach out for Larry when she was ready. They both agreed to the guidelines.

If your partner has trouble with mini-disconnections, disconnect with love, so you can reconnect. Use love, not judgment, when your partner confronts you or is mean. It will help him to feel calm when he or she returns.

Use self-discipline, set limits, and keep it safe. The guideline is: "If I reveal something to you, you can't get hurt by it." (Make your vest or bubble tighter to help you do this.)

When I shared these guidelines with Larry and Marlene, Larry said, "I hold back validation for myself and sympathy for myself and when you, Marlene, get hurt by what I said after you've asked me."

It's a Catch-22 that's very common for couples who have broken up to make up. That's one of the big reasons they have to break up. Larry used to clam up and withdraw, and then feel sorry for himself. **It's hard for Larry to give Marlene attachment skills because he needs them himself. But he knows if he coddles her when she really needs it, he will get it back from her.**

If your partner puts you in a no-win situation, you have to stand your ground, put on your emotional vest, and say, "I'm not going to communicate because it's not safe. I will not answer that unless you agree *not to* put me down or get upset by my response."

Marlene finally realized she has a "script in her head" and there's no way Larry could know what she wanted him to do or say. If he doesn't say the "right thing," he gets punished. **I asked Marlene to tell Larry her script so there was no miscommunication.** She could get her needs met as she wanted and Larry could feel good about getting it right. That gave him confidence to keep wanting to please her. *It's much easier for your partner if they know the formula!*

Smart Heart Savvy

Don't ask a question if you know the answer.
Don't ask a question if you don't want to hear the answer.

Hold Hands, Not Grudges

I remind my patients of the wise words from the sixteenth-century English poet and pastor George Herbert, "He who cannot forgive others destroys the bridge over which, he himself must pass." In other words, *forgiveness is a gift you give yourself.*

People use grudges to protect themselves from being hurt again. But holding grudges doesn't allow you to get close enough to each other to change or move. **They create paralysis and perpetuate frozen feelings. To thaw your feelings and let go of grudges, you have to reverse the flow of your**

emotions. You do this by going counter-intuitive and doing the opposite of what you feel. When you make up after a break-up, you have to agree not to use grudges as a wedge in your relationship.

An enormous amount of energy is used to hold on to a grudge. It's like walking around with a heavy chip on your shoulder. It throws you out of balance and keeps your hurt or anger alive.

People who opt for "peace at any price" eventually develop grudges and they also don't give their partners a chance to dissolve grudges. Sooner or later, one or both partners will want to "walk" because they're being steamrolled, sold, or ignored instead of being heard. They know they are not being taken seriously and they often leave without warning. Their partners (usually Pursuers) are left wondering what happened. Many times they had no idea their spouse had been unhappy, and they don't have a clue how they contributed to the break-up.

Leading Reasons for Holding Grudges

- You have delayed reactions.
- Partner minimizes your problem and doesn't take you seriously.
- Partner refuses to validate your feelings, is critical, or shows no remorse.
- A grudge is being held as an excuse for not getting to the bottom of the real problem (often your own fear of confrontation, being vulnerable, or getting hurt.)
- Partner is fusing with you and you're pricking each other.
- You're being controlled, but it's easier to say nothing and you've given up trying.

- Grudge-holders say yes when he (or she) means no and is now holding a grudge.

Instead of holding grudges, *go distant, without anger.* Your partner will respond because his fear of losing you as his "attachment figure" will be triggered, and he will take you more seriously. If your partner minimizes your needs or concerns, dismisses you, or doesn't take you seriously, going distant will encourage him to miss you, take more responsibility, be more accountable, hear you, and reach out to you. This will reduce grudge-holding and saying yes when you mean no. Remember that those who have delayed reactions (many Distancers) are more prone to grudge-holding and revenge, so "coach" each other to avoid this.

Distancers build walls to:
- Protect themselves from the vulnerability of closeness. The message to Pursuers is "don't expect; don't come close. I'm in control."
- Remind Pursuers that there are still problems and the pursuer still needs to change. They're basically saying, "you're not off the hook yet."

Both of these behaviors are self-sabotaging. You don't need the wall. You've had it your whole life and that's why you're so often lonely, even when you're with people you enjoy. Use the "bubble" and "bullet-proof" vest instead.

If your partner is building walls instead of bridges, it might be a sign that he may never be able to completely commit to the relationship. **Grudges that go unnoticed, or are ignored, can lead to affairs, break-ups, and other forms of triangling.** When someone refuses to let go of a grudge, they are putting the brakes on the relationship going any farther.

We hold grudges because they guard us from the complicated mix of emotions we experience when the anger falls away and we are making up. We use them to prevent the painful work of forgiveness and emptiness. **We also hold them to try to keep our partner in line.** Learn to move through your anxieties instead of away from them.

If you're holding a grudge, you're taking the role of "the victim" instead of the "victor." **Whatever you are holding over your partner's head, you are also holding over your own.** You lose strength, optimism, and zest for life. When you try to hurt your partner in this way, you are hurting yourself just as much. Trade in your victim role for one of power. Be proactive and change the climate of the relationship by changing the way you *feel* about your partner.

If you don't know how you feel, cushion it and announce this to your partner with vests, bubbles, and gloves on! **Don't avoid him** and make him wonder what he "did wrong this time." Go counter-intuitive and move toward your partner, instead of away from him. This is particularly important for sexual healing to occur during the make-up stage. **Grudges will come out in sex,** which stifles rebuilding sexual and emotional intimacy and can cause break-ups.

If you're holding a grudge, you probably *didn't get the consoling* you needed as a child, and you're still not allowing yourself to be consoled or comforted, which is clearly a form of self-punishment. You're pushing your partner away, then accusing him of "not being there for you," as Marlene did to Larry.

Instead of building up anger and resentment that eventually turns into a grudge, **take care of it right away.** The following are skills you can use to express your thoughts and feelings *before* they turn into a grudge.

Smart Heart Skills to Avoid Grudge-Holding

- Tell your partner what is "important" to you.

Say, **"This is important,"** to give your message emphasis and let your partner know he *has* to listen.

- If that doesn't work, **announce your bottom line or non-negotiable stand.**

Hold this line no matter what your partner does or says. Stay firm and do not give in. If he gives you excuses for his behavior, threatens you, or tries to sway you, block it out. Use a firm voice, but no anger.

- If all else fails, pull back *without anger.*

Stay distant until he misses you, takes responsibility, stops minimizing, and is ready to take you seriously.

- When your partner is ready to listen, tell him again.

When he asks you what's wrong, you now have his attention. Use Smart Heart Dialogue and reiterate your bottom line. **Your power is in getting "heard," not getting mad.** It won't help if you get mad at your partner for taking so long to be able to hear you.

In order to prevent a grudge from developing, you and your partner must reach a resolution to have your needs met together. If either of you gives in because of "pressure" instead of for the "good of the cause," you will have a delayed reaction and resent it later, or feel suffocated. If you give in when you really need your partner to compromise with you, you will eventually explode and/or become passive-aggressive. "I won't ever do what you ask me to do again. I will disappoint you because I silently resent you (and myself) for going along with what you wanted the last time." The build-up of these delayed reactions creates silence and grudge-holding.

When one or both of you are holding a grudge, part of the reason is because you didn't and still don't feel *safe enough* to tell your partner what you need and stand your ground. In order to be able to do this, you need to restore safety to the relationship. The following ground rules should be closely adhered to so that you both feel safe enough to begin dissolving the grudges.

Smart Heart Ground Rules to Increase Safety for Dissolving Grudges

- Stop beating yourself up; forgive yourself.
- Stop beating up your partner; forgive him or her.
- See each other as wounded children.
- Take and give space without guilt or manipulation.
- Disconnect and reconnect with announcement, preparation, and tenderness.
- Don't punish or shame.
- Check the temperature of the relationship frequently, daily, at first (see Chapter 20).
- Remember that it will take a while to get your feelings back; that doesn't mean the love is gone.
- When you're dealing with your partner's hurt, you are healing your own as well.
- Use attachment skills and have sex even if you don't "feel like it." Doing it will make you feel like it and help you to knock down barriers the grudges have built.
- Check in daily to see how your partner is doing and how you can help.

Once safety is restored in the relationship—or is on its way to being restored—it's time to begin dissolving the grudges. Take on only one grudge at a time. **If you are both holding grudges, take turns,** so that you can both feel good about the progress that is being made. It's important to work as a team on each grudge, no matter who's holding it, or for what reason.

The following exercise will help you to begin the process of dissolving the grudge.

Smart Heart Grudge-Dissolving Exercise

1. Write a letter to your partner detailing why you're angry and don't want to let go of the grudge. This is for your eyes only to help you clarify your thoughts and feelings. Get to the pain to get to the change.

2. Write a letter to yourself detailing the part *you played* in whatever you are angry about, and the part you play in keeping the anger alive by holding the grudge. Look in your family tree. How are grudges handled, who holds them and for what? **Discuss with other grudge-holders in the family and sort it out.**

3. Write the letter you'd like to receive from your partner saying what you need to hear to be able to let go of the grudge. This is part of your "script." Share this letter with your partner and give him a chance to tell you his "script" too. He may be doing what he would want *you* to do under the same circumstances and be frustrated that it isn't working.

The decision to let go of, or hold on to, grudges is one of the most important crossroads in making up after a break-up or adultery. This is the cause of most break-ups!

Grudges hold you back, but the grudge-holders often are resentful because they feel it is unfair for them to have to do so much work to dissolve the anger when their partner "did the hurting." (Particularly when your partner has had an affair.)

Your partner has to work harder and smarter, too. *He has to allow you to get angry and get it all out without getting upset with you or punishing you.* This is a big stretch for both of you, and a giant step for the relationship if you do it! **(One of the reasons Alexis hasn't let go of her grudge is because Nathaniel has never stopped getting angry at her for being angry!** The underlying problem is *that he has not forgiven himself* for what he did. Each time Alexis gets upset about it, **he feels guilty and turns his anger on her.)**

Determine what it will take for you to dissolve the grudges so your feelings can thaw out. Without taking these steps, you will remain stuck and forever be the "Ice Queen" or "King."

After working with me on this, Alexis agreed to lift her grudge if Nathaniel:

- Assumed responsibility for his actions, changed, and showed remorse.
- Stopped turning on her when *he* feels guilty.
- Stopped treating her as if she were invisible and letting his "work" come before their marriage. (Nathaniel was a workaholic and was "having an affair" with his job. He was not emotionally available to Alexis and did not want to take responsibility to learn how to connect with her.)
- Agree to learn and use Smart Heart Skills and Dialogue and to "coach" and "be coached."
- Stop getting angry at her anger.

If you don't learn to let go of grudges and forgive, you will inevitably end up alone—either divorced or in an emotional divorce. **Anger and guilt destroy love.** The following dialogue shows you how to ask your partner to help you, instead of pitting yourselves against each other. Many divorces occur because of guilt, not because of lack of love.

Smart Heart Dialogue

"I know this is going to get better if I talk to you. You're terrific and I know you can help me."

Acknowledge him for his strengths and tell him you don't expect him to "fix" you, just to help you to help yourself.

"I need to know you feel remorse so we can work through this. I want to give you a chance to express everything you still feel guilty about, so we can both work on getting over it and I can stop being angry."

He must give you ten minutes of remorse. The first five minutes are based on *his* script, and the next five minutes must be based on *your* script that you shared with him in the letter you wrote. (*Get over the idea that "it doesn't mean as much" if you have to tell him what you want.* Sharing your scripts with each other allows you to create the magic that will make you both feel loved and connected.) **The more he expresses his remorse, the less you will remind him of his guilt.** He will feel relieved and be more loving when he gets over the guilt.

To reassure you that he will not return to his old ways when you drop the grudge, he must offer you a pledge:

"*I love you. I will not act out. I will share my remorse. I will not take you for granted or make the same mistake again.*"

When you get stuck or one of you feels frustrated or wants to attack or check out, go counter-intuitive. Sit facing each other, hold hands, and gaze into each other's eyes until you feel your hearts starting to open again. This will help you remember that you're on the same team and release some "cuddle hormones," which will assist in smoothing the road ahead.

Remember that your partner's grudges are just as valid and important as yours. *The more supportive you are in helping him to dissolve his grudges, the sooner your relationship will be back on track.* If your partner is holding a grudge, you can't minimize it. Don't get into childlike magical thinking by brushing it under the rug and telling yourself wishfully but unrealistically, "It will all work out," or "He'll get over it in time."

If your partner is holding a grudge, offer to help him by saying something like the following.

Smart Heart Dialogue

Ask your partner, "What do you need me to do to show you that I love you or that I'm truly sorry?"

Encourage him to share "his script" for what he believes has to happen before he can let go of the grudge, and then make sure you do it! **Don't criticize your partner for holding the grudge.** Instead, help him through it by gently coaching him through the steps he can take with your help and support.

Smart Heart Skills for Helping Your Partner Dissolve a Grudge

- Make your partner feel safe to express his (or her) grudge with you.
- Encourage your partner to use Fair Fighting to air the grievance and work on solutions. Please listen and take it seriously.

- Do not minimize what your partner is saying; validate instead.
- Keep in mind that grudge-holders are afraid to let go of their anger **because they think it is their only way to maintain some control.** They're also afraid to show their anger *because they don't want to hurt you or create more conflict.* They want peace at any price and think you "should know."

Holding grudges adds a great deal of negative energy to a relationship and you have to balance that with positive actions so that you both continue to enjoy the relationship—outside of the grudge. The following is a list of actions to help balance and reverse your negative feelings.

Smart Heart Actions to Reverse Your Negative Emotions

Set up "Play Dates." At least once a week go out and play together. Pick sports or action-oriented activities that make your hearts race. Go all out to relieve stress, release endorphins, and let your light-hearted side come out. **No problems, grudges, "attitudes," or negativity are permitted during Play Dates—only fun, laughter, camaraderie, and bonding!**

See your partner as a wounded child. When you relate to the "wounded child" within your partner, it is easier to feel tenderhearted, melt, and forgive.

Announce your intentions. **If you are holding the grudge, tell your partner that letting it go does not mean the work is done, and it does not mean you are staying together, or ready for love.** It *does* mean you are going to give it everything you have, and take one small step at a time together.

Share your fear. It's okay for the Distancer to remind the Pursuer that you're afraid the problems will come back if you let go of the grudge. This is why **most Distancers hold on to the grudge, as a way of maintaining control and making sure the Pursuer's changes stick. It keeps the Pursuer's hopes from going up, but it keeps the Distancer from the positive form of magical thinking that says "it can work out."**

Don't use grudges to avoid making decisions. Distancers often fear they'll make the wrong decisions, so they hold on to a grudge and make no decisions.

Bridge the cut-offs with those you are most angry with, including your family of origin. **The grudges that are hardest to let go of are those that come from the unmet expectations in your childhood.** You're still angry and trying to prove that "you're right" for feeling that way. Blaming your partner or parents is an attempt to avoid pain, but it brings more. **Revenge is a protest for the consoling you didn't get as a child.**

You must take care of the anger as soon as it comes up, so it doesn't turn into a grudge. Once it becomes a grudge, it's harder to bridge the distance back to each other. **Instead of letting the hurt feelings push you apart, use them to pull you together. Don't fall into the tit-for-tat game "I'll get you. I'll spite me," a form of revenge that boomerangs back to you.**

How to Get Your Feelings Back

Remember when you first met and you both dropped everything to make it happen with each other? It's time to do that again. The make-up "honey*moan*" hormones will get you started, but it's up to you to do the rest. Begin by making the relationship and your partner your highest priority. *Don't "fit* *them in" like you did before the break-up; fit in other things around them.* Handle this second chance with kid gloves. It's a golden but *fragile* opportunity that can shatter if it isn't treated with tender loving care.

It's not unusual for it to take a while for frozen feelings to thaw out. Don't get discouraged if the passion is missing or you don't feel head over heels in love with each other again right away. *Whatever you do and practice the most, you become.* When you "act as if" and use attachment skills, you rekindle romantic feelings. Even if you don't feel romantic, you have to *be* romantic. *This will trick your feelings.* You can't wait until you "feel in the mood" before you cuddle and make love with your partner. **Take the action steps and the feelings will follow.**

When my patients Vernon and Joy made up after breaking up, Joy was afraid to face him in the bedroom again. She was still hurt by the way he had taken her for granted and treated her as if she were invisible before the break-up. When they entered into the make-up stage, Vernon pledged to put Joy and their relationship first—instead of fitting them in around work, golf, and watching sports. He was keeping his word, but Joy didn't trust him. She was terrified of having sex with him because *she didn't want to face her own feelings of vulnerability.*

I explained to Joy that she could get past her terror of feeling vulnerable only by facing it and having sex with Vernon. I instructed Vernon to make arrangements for the children to sleep at their grandmother's, and invite Joy out for a romantic evening. I suggested he take her to one of the romantic restaurants they enjoyed when they began dating and out to a theater performance, as this was something they both loved but had stopped doing together years ago.

I told Joy when Vernon asked her out, **she was to accept and begin reliving their first dates together in her mind to help bring back her feelings.** I also told her to prepare for the date by pampering and soothing herself. She scheduled a massage, manicure, and haircut and spent the day relaxing.

When date night came, Vernon surprised Joy by sneaking outside and ringing the doorbell. When she opened the door, dressed for the date, he was standing there to "pick her up" with a beautiful bouquet of flowers and a bottle of wine.

The night went fabulously and by the time they arrived home, Joy was willing to face her fear and make love with Vernon again. She still "*wasn't in the mood*," but she agrees that after following this routine for a few weeks, her feelings began to return.

In the next chapter you will learn how to restore the magic.

～ 20 ～
Restoring the Magic

> *"Perhaps love is the process of my leading you gently back to yourself."*
> —ANTOINE DE SAINT-EXUPÉRY

Making up after breaking up is very powerful because it re-enacts the honeymoon of your courtship. The feel-good hormones and adrenaline are flowing freely and you are in a perfect place to make a conscious decision to stay in love—no matter what.

Enjoy your second honeymoon and use it to build your confidence in the future of the relationship. Don't allow it to make you complacent or go back into the negative form of magical thinking. The second honeymoon won't last long because the hormones will subside again, just as they did after the first honeymoon. **Use Smart Heart Skills and Dialogue, including fair fighting, *to replace* the feelings of safety the hormones created.** It's especially important to use attachment skills (touching each other's face, gazing into each other's eyes, stroking each other's hair, etc.). Announce your connections, disconnections, and reconnections, and prepare each other for the moves you're going to make.

Paul Pearsall, Ph.D. and author of *Making Miracles*, says **"Ritual is one of the best means of maintaining** connection. . . . **Rituals make and reaffirm memories that can energize, protect and heal us."** Smart Heart Skills and Dialogue will help you to make stronger connections and provide you with a structure to create your own meaningful rituals—whether that means gazing into each other's eyes and saying I love you each time you disconnect, or setting aside a special day each week just to have fun together and love each other.

Restore the Sizzle

Restoring the sizzle is one of the best parts of making up, but it's also one of the biggest challenges. **You have to be proactive and patient at the same time.** Learn to get pleasure out of watching your partner have a good time. *When you both put each other first, everyone wins.*

This part of making up—or rekindling romance in any relationship—**is all about tricking yourself into thinking you are in the Euphoria Stage of love again.** Remember that you are each other's "attachment figures" now, meaning that you will want to rely on your partner as much as you did on your parents when you were a child—and even more if you didn't feel you could rely on your parents! *Because each of you will want to be "nurtured" first, couples have a tendency to hold out and wait for their partner to make the first move.* Don't wait. The more you can nurture and be nurtured, the more you can trust each other, and the more the flames of passion will soar!

Many women, including my patient Linda, have a difficult time warming up to sex when they reunite after a break-up. But once these women reframe their way of thinking by understanding that sex is a form of *connection and nurturing,* they are more willing to "act as if" and give it try.

Making love is one of the best ways to nurture and connect with each other.

When Linda and Jerry reunited after their temporary break-up, Linda worried that she didn't feel attracted to Jerry anymore or see him as sexy. I said, "Because you're looking at the flaws and all the negatives. You can only be attracted to Jerry if you don't feel threatened. You have to feel safe."

Making up after a break-up, as Linda and Jerry did, is like delicate surgery. You have to follow the steps and ground rules to get it right. Meanwhile, this intricate heart surgery is being done *without anesthesia* while you're wide awake. It can be frightening and it can hurt, but it's temporary. If you need surgery to save your life, you're willing to go through the pain of the operation and the recovery process. **Be willing to do the same for your love, because without love, life can be meaningless.**

Linda and Jerry had to use more attachment skills with each other and be present with each other's feelings. *When you don't have the hormones working for you, you have to create the image to turn your mind on.* Go out and dance cheek to cheek together like you did when you were falling in love the first time. You have to see each other with new faces to restore the sizzle and explore each other as new people. I told Linda, "Take a step back and pretend Jerry is not your husband. Try to get him again. Give yourself a challenge to get the hormones going."

Meanwhile, Jerry had to tell Linda he was afraid to be rejected and **announce it when he wanted more physical closeness.** Linda was avoiding closeness because Jerry was "patronizing, critical, and overbearing." She felt intimidated by his put-downs, so she clammed up and held on to her resentments. Jerry had a pattern of trying to brush his behavior under the rug by apologizing. Linda stood her ground, **"I'm sorry doesn't cut it. I don't want words, I want action."**

Jerry and Linda both had to stretch more. They needed to do the opposite of what their old hurt feelings were telling them to do. She had to open up more, and he had to make her feel safe so she could. I told Jerry and Linda they can't wait for things to "happen," **they have to make them happen.** This isn't a game of chance. *You* are in control of the outcome.

Use action to get what you want instead of shutting down or shutting off your partner. Unless you change, you stay in a vicious cycle. Changing takes trust in yourself and in your partner, but it's worth it, because otherwise the relationship will end and you will go through the same cycle with your next partner. Should we all say it together? **Getting rid of the person doesn't get rid of the problem.**

Restoring Sizzle: 12 Creative Ways to Please Your Lover

1. Simplify Your Life
   Let go of the things that are weighing you down so you can devote more energy to your relationship.

2. Take a Trip Back in Time to Childhood
   Watch each other's home movies, or share childhood photo albums and scrap books. Even if you've done this before, you'll be surprised how much insight this will give you into each other.

3. Be Adventurous
   Try something that neither of you have ever done before. Challenge yourself and channel your adrenaline rush into your romance.

4. Let Music Soothe Your Souls
   Go to a concert, symphony, jazz club, or musical together. Music has wonderful healing powers and

allows you to get back in sync with each other. (Paul Pearsall says, "Music makes the heart sing.")

5. Schedule "No Complaints or Abruptness" Days
   Label two bowls (your name on one and your partner's on the other). Each time one of you complains, cops an attitude, or uses a "tone," you have to put a dollar in your partner's bowl.

6. Make Something Together
   Focusing your energy to create something positive together brings you closer.

7. Plant a Seedling
   Plant a tree seedling and watch it grow as you nurture it. This is a great way to remind both of you to nourish your love. When the seedling is big enough, transplant it outside. It will become a friend and remain a wonderful reminder of your relationship.

8. Learn Something Together
   Take music lessons or attend a course or lecture on a topic you're both interested in.

9. Play Fantasy Fridays
   Take turns planning "fantasy evenings." Every other week, one of you gets to pick your fantasy and the other one plays along. Your fantasy Friday could be as innocent as going to a hockey game together. On the other hand, it could be a more risqué fantasy. One of my patients' fantasies was to be "picked up" by her mate. They arrived at a night club separately and he had to win her over to bring her home. They both loved this one!

10. Schedule a Day of Silence
    Spend an entire day with your partner, without speaking. If there's something you must say, write a note. Distancers often realize at the end of the day

that they missed talking and hearing the Pursuer talk. Pursuers realize they don't have to talk so much to get their point across and learn to read their partner's actions, so they don't have to rely so much on his or her words.

11. Trip the Light Fantastic
Go dancing. Holding each other cheek-to-cheek warms your heart and stirs your passion.

12. Go Out of Your Way
Go out of your way to do something thoughtful for your partner. It can be as simple as making an extra stop on your way home from work to pick up the dry cleaning, or as elaborate as planning a special date that you know your mate will love.

Smart Heart Dialogue Is Your Relationship Maintenance Warranty

Smart Heart Dialogue smoothes the road so you can restore the magic in your relationship. Think of it as your "Maintenance Warranty." Loving each other doesn't mean saying whatever you want without considering how it will affect your partner. Practice thinking about your words before you say them, and cushioning them just as you would if you were talking to a customer or a client. You can be honest and kind at the same time, and you must.

Set limits if your partner punishes you. Say "enough," and "help me move to forgiveness." You have to make a conscious decision to move toward forgiveness, even if you're not ready.

Look for your partner's "script" and your own. Everyone has a different script—meaning varying opinions, thoughts, needs, and desires. Get to know your partner's script and know your own. Part of *your* script is the script you have *of your partner;* how you see or perceive him or her and what you expect based on previous behavior or things he or she has said. (Countless fights start because you expect your partner to respond by your script, and he doesn't have a clue what it is!)

Use the dialogue process for forgiveness. Reframe your partner's negative statement in a positive way and send it back to him or her. Thank your partner for the gift of the insight, instead of taking it as criticism and feeling hurt. This will help you to both grow and feel closer.

Keep the negatives to yourself. Negativity can create a heavy dark feeling in your relationship; it's like a storm cloud hanging overhead that could burst at any time. Each time you have a negative thought or start to be critical, replace it with a positive thought or say something complimentary to reverse the flow of feelings.

Shower each other with compliments. Twice a day for thirty seconds, tell your partner all the positive things, big and small, that you admire and like about him or her. Be lavish— but sincere—with your praise and intimate in the details.

Taking the Relationship's Temperature

During the make-up stage, take the relationship's temperature frequently so you can stay in touch with whatever is happening. You do this by looking at how much fun and play you have together and "checking in" with yourself to see if your needs and your partner's are being met. (This is a concept from PAIRS.)

To take the relationship's temperature, ask:
- Are you being loved the way you want to be loved?
- Are you loving your partner the way he or she wants to be loved?

- Are you using coaching as a gift to help you shift gears and reach the next stage of love?
- Are you acknowledging your partner every day?
  (Jeff starts and ends each day by telling me something he loves about me. He instinctively felt it in his heart to do this because he wants to make sure I always know how much he loves me and appreciates me.)
- Are you spending enough time together? Time means: quiet time sitting and not talking, and picking out things you both enjoy or want to learn and doing them together. This keeps new and novel energy flowing through your relationship. Fights often break out when you're *not* spending enough time together.
- Are you helping each other to reconnect?
- Are you fighting fair?
- Are you disconnecting in the morning and reconnecting at night in a loving manner?
- Are you sharing meals together (without the television on) and talking?
- Are you going to bed at the same time so you can share, cuddle, or make love before you go to sleep? (Even if one of you needs to get back up to do paperwork or complete something, spend some time together in bed first.)
- How much are you talking and communicating?
  (It should be at least ten to twenty minutes each day. However, one study says couples talk only ten minutes a week!)

When your relationship thermometer doesn't read "hot enough," you know you have some work to do. *Don't feel sorry for yourself or get discouraged at this point, get to work!* Remember that couples who make up after a break-up, like my parents and 98 percent of the couples I counsel, stay together and reap the blissful years of real and lasting love together. These relationship are stronger, safer, more exciting, and more fulfilling than those that have not stretched the rubber band and grown from their troubles.

Jump-Starts as Preventive Medicine

One of the most invigorating ways to keep your love alive and your passion burning is to rev up your relationship with a jump-start. Just like jump-starting a car can bring it back to life, jump-starting your relationship will give it new energy and power, and it may prevent unnecessary break-ups.

Couples who play together, stay together. One of the reasons so many couples have affairs, split up, and divorce is that they forget the importance of playing together and having fun. Jump-start your relationship by trying new things together, changing your routine, leaving the work at the office, the troubles on the doorstep, and your heart in each other's hands. The couples who call me because their relationships have stalled out admit they don't fight fairly and they don't make time to have fun together. **Relationships stall out either because they have too much connection or not enough.**

When you don't have the courage to jump-start your relationship, you stay stuck in the same place, spinning your wheels and digging yourself deeper into the same rut. *Relationship stalemate is often mistaken as an end, when it's really just a chance to catch your breath,* assess your relationship, and decide which action steps and skills to use to get things moving again. A stalemate may be the end of a chess game, but in relationships it can be the doorway to greater respect, commitment, romance, and love.

You jump-start your relationship and your romance by being proactive and nurturing it with Smart Heart Skills and Dialogue. Jump-starts are action steps, taken in love, to create new energy and novel experiences for you and your partner. **Jump-starting a relationship, just like jump-starting a car, is about connecting, disconnecting, and reconnecting—and timing is everything.** If you jump-start your relationship before it stalls out, you may never have to break up to make up. Jump-starts are excellent preventive medicine.

Begin by seeing your partner with a "new face." Pretend that every time you see your partner, it's the first time. It will keep your mind open and allow you to notice the subtle changes that are taking place. It will also help you to be more present so you can tune into him again, the way you did when you first met.

It's also important to apply the positive side of "magical thinking." This is the feeling or intuition inside you that "knows" everything will work out. It was this type of magical thinking that helped me to keep my heart open to Jeff after he went out with another woman, just after I moved in with him. *I could feel a thread between us—a beam of love that was still connecting our hearts.*

Once you've committed yourselves to jump-starting your relationship, you must also agree to some important ground rules.

Jump-Start Ground Rules

One of the reasons couples experience so many problems is because they've never taken the **time to set ground rules for**

their relationship. This is where the negative side of magical thinking comes in that says, "relationships develop naturally."

Let's look at this myth. Imagine you just started a new company. You and your business partner are excited and have high hopes for the success of your venture. Rather than setting ground rules for how your business will operate, you decide your company should develop naturally and with no networking. *You toast to Abra Cadabra* and before you know it you're singing the blues. No business would make it with that type of foundation, and yet love is somehow supposed to prosper under those same conditions. *Relationships stop before they start* because they're so often built on shaky foundations. *Put the ground rules in place. Practice them, and I guarantee you will see results within a week!*

Twenty Ground Rules for Smart Heart Jump-Starts

1. *Make a conscious decision, emotionally and physically, to fall in love all over again.* The more you "act as if" you are in love, the more you will "feel" like you are in love again. Your heart will eventually thaw and melt and your love will be stronger than ever before.

2. *Treat your partner like you did at the beginning of your relationship.* Make a list of all the things you enjoyed doing together when your love was still a seedling. Also list some new fantasies to fulfill! Now, make them your top priority by planning them and doing them. No excuses are allowed.

3. *Use Smart Heart Dialogue to validate your partner and create safety.* Help your partner to feel more secure so he or she can feel safe enough to open up

to you and express their thoughts as well as their love without being attacked or shamed.

4. *Don't make unilateral decisions.* You're a team. Check in and make decisions together and be willing to compromise.

5. *Be present.* When you're with your partner, really be with him or her. Train your mind to stay in the moment.

6. *Pay attention to your physical appearance.* Take the time to stay in shape and go out of your way to look good for your partner, even when you're at home. It's not shallow for your partner to be turned off or distant if you gain weight. Remember you were "Imagos" when you were thinner. That's who he's still in love with. **The concept of "Take me and love me as I am," is not realistic and it doesn't work.**

7. *Put your relationship first.* Plain and simple. Let nothing and no one come before each other or between the two of you.

8. *Increase your compatibility.* Couples who are having difficulties focus on all the things that are "different" about them, whereas new couples look for similarities and think their differences are cute. Build compatibility by taking turns planning activities to do together. If you don't like the choice your partner makes, you're not allowed to complain.

9. *Use the weather to stay together.* When you are choosing vacation destinations, go south! **Sixty-two percent of men feel more amorous in hot climates.** Sunlight stimulates the hormones, which is why I suggest the Caribbean for your first holiday together. Of course, cuddling by the fire with the

snow coming down outside can be incredibly romantic too!

10. *Replace blame and criticism with solutions, attachment skills, and tenderness.* Problem-solve together while you hold hands. Hug, sit close together, cuddle, look into each other's eyes, compliment each other, touch each other's face and hair. At least once a day, share a thirty-second kiss, a bonding tip Katie Couric shared with me and viewers during a three-day segment on Staying in Love that I did on the *Today* show.

11. *When your partner makes you angry, see him or her as a wounded child.* Be grateful for the second chance you both have to heal childhood wounds.

12. *Don't relax, coast, or bow to your moods.* Make time for each other every day. Eat together, share your thoughts, and discuss the day's events. Remember that having a bad day doesn't give you the right to dump on or lash out at your mate. What happens outside the bedroom, ends up inside the bedroom!

13. *Make sex a top priority.* Create the mood. Plan a sexy date at least weekly with your partner and enjoy it. Sexual healing, safety, and excitement takes a while to get back and it won't happen naturally. *Trick yourself into the feelings* even if you feel frozen, and your heart can catch up. It can take six months to a year or so to relax and heat up the passion again. Couples like Beth and Don—who broke up to make up—have a better, more passionate sex life than they ever had before.

14. *Connect when your partner disconnects.* **This ground rule can make or break a relationship.** When your partner disconnects, don't take it personally or allow

it to hurt your feelings. That will make you go distant, too. Instead, give him or her some time and then you reconnect with love.

15. *Help each other heal old heartaches.* Coach, support, and be emotionally available to each other so you can both become stronger and more complete by healing your wounds together.

16. *Fight fair and by appointment only.* There are very few things in life that can't wait. Love is one of them, but arguments are not. When you have an issue with your partner, schedule a time-limited appointment with permission and keep your issues and surrounding emotions confined in this arena. It's easier for you both to relax and feel safe during dinners and dates out when you know that nothing heavy or negative is going to spoil the serenity or the fun!

17. *Check in—don't check out (especially after announcing connections, disconnections, and reconnections).* If you do check out—emotionally or physically— announce it and check back in as soon as possible (announce that, too). Remember that the ultimate check-out is divorce. Check in and stay in love.

18. *Prepare for check-outs.* Everyone checks out from time to time, so expect it and prepare for it. Give your partner time and distance to avoid fusion. We need to know we can have some time alone when we need it without being punished or made to feel guilty. If you don't give each other enough time and space, you will end up pricking like the porcupines and risk an emotional or physical divorce.

19. *Fact-find; don't mind-read or assume.* Fact-finding is one of the first Smart Heart Skills you learned, and it remains one of the most important things you can do.

Even if you've known each other fifty years and you think you "know" or can "assume," you can't.

20. *Remember that touch is magic.* Touch daily, use pet names, giggle, wrestle, and allow your playfulness and love to come out. Touch reverses the hormones of physiological discomfort for men.

In addition to following the ground rules for jump-starts, ask yourselves these Smart Heart questions every day

- What can I do to show and tell my partner I love him or her today?
- What can I do to make my partner happy today?
- How can I love my partner the way he or she wants and needs to be loved?

Relationship expert John Gottman's research backs up what I see work with my own patients. "Men who express admiration and fondness for their wives stay married," said Gottman. "When a man is willing to do this, he has freed himself from the childhood chains that bound him."

The reason marriages fail today is that people quit too soon. Connection, commitment, and compromise are the keys. When your relationship needs a jump-start to restore the magic, do it, and have fun with it!

part five

Relationships at Risk
Shake Up to Wake Up

"We all yearn for love and long to be in close relationships with others. Yet it is extraordinarily difficult to achieve this. Whilst our relationships can be a source of great fulfillment for us, they are also often the cause of our greatest pain and sorrow."

↳ EILEEN CAMPBELL

⸰ 21 ⸰

Understanding Adultery

"Love is an act of endless forgiveness."
—PETER USTINOV

Infidelity—the unforgivable sin (as many people call it)—*is forgivable.* **It is possible to repair the damage from an affair and create an even stronger and more loving relationship with each other.** You can also prevent adultery by anticipating the developmental wound of your partner and thus have a second chance for your marriage and "rewiring" the stage where he's stuck. An affair is an attempt to complete the developmental stage with the lover instead of with the partner who is further wounding him—unbeknownst to her.

My professional experience and my parents' experience have convinced me that most marriages can survive and even prosper after this betrayal, if the couple is willing to do what's needed—possibly even *break up* to make up. **Remember, second marriages are higher in divorce and adultery than first marriages, so it's worth trying to work it out before you walk away.**

My theory for adultery is very different from the mainstream way of thinking, but I have seen it proven in my family therapy practice so many times now that I know it has great merit. *Ninety-eight percent of the couples in my practice who experience adultery make up and stay together with Smart Heart Skills.* If they can do it, you can do it, too!

First of all, I believe that adultery is most often the result of an inherited emotional behavior pattern, rather than a desire to be unfaithful. *The adulterer is trying desperately to finish his childhood and heal his wounds.* Sometimes these wounds occur because of adultery or some form of betrayal in the family of origin that has been passed down from generation to generation. The adulterer is trying to finish his (or her) developmental stage through the affair, instead of with his partner. You can help prevent adultery by knowing the stage your partner is stuck in, and helping him to heal those wounds and rewire his circuits so he doesn't look elsewhere. Taking this preventive measure gives you both a second chance to make your marriage better. Taking this step after adultery has occurred gives you a second chance to rewrite your relationship scripts and move on together.

Second, **many men commit adultery because of physiological distress that comes from confrontation or conflict in their relationship.** Men flee from this discomfort to attempt to relieve, self-medicate, and soothe the physiological effects that conflict produces in them. (Refer back to Chapter 10, "Fighting Fair," for a deeper understanding of these physiological responses.)

There is a correlation between the many men who engage in extramarital affairs and the level of stress in their household. I remember my own father often leaving the room during stressful discussions with my mother. He didn't understand why my mother was so upset by his leaving before they reached a solution, because he was trying to deal with his own emotions and soothe his physical responses.

Third, I have recently developed a biological theory that helps explain why some *adulterers cannot stop cheating, even when they want to stop.* I have witnessed that people who have experienced severe stress, loss, or separation from one or both of their parents at an early age often suffer an impact on their hormones that affects adult relationships. **This hormonal change results in a biochemical craving for connection vis à vis an affair.** The wounded one is impelled to recreate stressful situations because they are familiar and help to re-establish a certain equilibrium physically. *That's why so many adulterers thrive on danger and stress.*

That may be why President Clinton risked his presidency and his marriage. I believe he *was trying to fulfill a biochemical craving for connection (self-medicating).* Men who have a need to satiate this craving say they feel like they have very little control over their own actions. One of my patients said, "I knew I shouldn't do it. Part of me didn't even want to do it. I felt like I couldn't stop myself; it was like I was an addict who needed a fix."

When I discuss infidelity I am talking about any breach of trust between two people who are committed to one another. *Any activity or relationship that drains too much time and energy from life with your partner is a form of unfaithfulness.*

Contrary to its salacious image, adultery is rarely about sex. In fact, sometimes the sex adulterers have in their marriage is more fulfilling. The reasons for seeking the new person are usually emotional, not physical. Rather than simply seeking sex, *the betrayer is living out an emotional compulsion to heal the past by repeating it.* Some of the most devastating affairs are those "affairs of the heart" where no sex is involved, but one partner's intense emotional connection with a third person creates a cavernous rift in the relationship that bears the same feelings of betrayal and abandonment that follow a sexual affair. Many of these types of affairs *are rampant on the Internet today* and may never be acted out sexually.

The 2 percent of my patients who have not been helped by therapy alone are those with *the deadly combination of both the biochemical craving and emotional emptiness.* We can no longer view adultery as having just an emotional inheritance. Just as with the alcoholic's physical craving for alcohol—it's time we treated adultery as *a disease.*

The Three-Part Theory

- Part I: Adultery's emotional inheritance—the childhood wound being the adulterer's parent's infidelity or other betrayal.
- Part II: Extramarital sex as an attempt to physiologically soothe and relieve actual physical distress from conflict (to "self-medicate").
- Part III: Extramarital sex *as a reaction to a biochemical craving for connection to self-medicate.*

In addition to my three-part theory, I have observed a number of points that help to make adultery easier to understand and therefore to forgive.

- An affair is a cry for help. **It shakes you to wake you,** reverberating throughout the system. Only people who are in some kind of emotional pain commit adultery. (Sometimes the pain is because they were not in love when they married, and still are not.)
- The affair **is not the predominant problem** in the relationship, but rather a symptom of mutual disconnection, emptiness, and a lack of intimacy in the relationship that the affair is masking.
- An affair **is a triangle to avoid or deny problems** in the relationship that must be faced and resolved. *Two*

people in a relationship unconsciously collude to have an affair.

- An affair is **not therapeutic in the long run.** While some may believe that taking a lover will resolve or improve their problems with their spouse, you cannot fix what's wrong in a relationship by adding another complication. It only gives you another problem.

- The goal of healing comes from both the betrayed and the betrayer accepting and taking responsibility for the affair. They should envision an "equal sign" between them, both seeing their part.

- For many couples, adultery is the necessary obstacle they must overcome in order for them to *stop being polite* and start fighting so they can have passion and learn to communicate, to be intimate, and to connect and bond.

Affairs are also the result of one of the partners' "checking out." For example, my patient Hope had an affair to "check out." Checking out is purposefully avoiding making a connection and working on the goals of the relationship with your partner—it is not the same as not knowing how to connect, but rather choosing not to connect.

Emmet said Hope checked out intentionally. He said, "Hope punished me for not knowing how to connect, thinking I'm checking out, but at least those are things I can learn. This is really her projection onto me."

Hope was actually the one who kept checking out and shutting down. She had to decide whether to do the work in her own relationship, which meant being patient with Emmet as he learned connection skills. As long as she continued to put the blame on Emmet for not knowing how to connect, and kept seeking affairs as a way to avoid connection (which was heart-breaking to Emmet), they would not have the intimacy Hope claimed she wanted with her husband. *It's senseless to punish someone for something they don't know—especially if they're willing to learn.*

Some adulterous women marry for other reasons than love, such as ticking biological clocks, prestige, money, or pressure from family members. They feel cheated, so they cheat, knowing that men are not forgiving. It is an "escape hatch" that alleviates the guilt of leaving her family in any other way.

Those who betray through infidelity:

- Are unable or afraid to directly communicate their emptiness, dissatisfaction, and pain to their partner or don't know what it is, so they run to another.
- Are often unable to tolerate genuine intimacy, and so attempt to create a kind of pseudo-intimacy with a lover.
- Are often minimizing the problems in the relationship, and instead of talking them out, are "acting out" by having an affair.
- Are trying to punish their partner—whether consciously or not— trying to "betray back" an adulterous parent or an emotionally betraying, "checking-out" partner.
- Are using a drastic measure to be seen and heard.

The information presented in this chapter and in Chapter 22 is the same that I share with my adulterous patients and their partners, so you will have immediate access to the help you so desperately need. For a more extensive discussion of the subject (including exercises and "How Tos"), I encourage you to seek out my book, *Adultery, The Forgivable Sin.*

Whether you have been betrayed or have betrayed your partner and want to save your relationship, **you are not alone.** The road to healing may seem long and arduous, but there is definitely light at the end of the tunnel. Just as many of my patients have undertaken the journey toward healing from the devastation of an affair—you, too, can put this crisis behind you and move forward with your mate to have a better relationship than you've ever had before.

If you are tempted to stray, **do whatever it takes to avoid making this mistake.** Adultery has lasting repercussions, and it is much less painful to resolve your problems with your partner than to add new problems on top of the old. Say something like the following to elicit your partner's support.

Smart Heart Dialogue

"I am lonely and I don't want to stray. I need love, nurturing, and attention. I want you, not someone else. Please help me to stay faithful."

In the next chapter, you will learn what to do if you suspect adultery has been committed, or if you have committed it yourself. **Remember, the best affair is the one you can have with your own partner!**

◦ 22 ◦

What to Do if You Suspect Adultery

"The worst thing in your life may contain seeds of the best. When you can see crisis as an opportunity, your life becomes not easier, but more satisfying."
—JOE KOGEL

Adultery truly is a forgivable sin and the couples who make it over this hurdle develop the strongest relationships imaginable.

My parents, whose fifty-year marriage is crowned by twenty-five years of fidelity and intimacy, *have showed me that love truly does conquer all.* The happiness they share today was made possible because twenty-five years ago my mother had the insight and courage to say, "Enough!" What my dad values most about that time in his life is my mother's love and courage. He said, "Your mother woke me up. I realized she was the one woman I loved and I didn't want to lose her. She gave me the confidence to say "no" to all the other pretty faces because she loved me and believed I was worth keeping. I learned the hard way that you need to have the willpower to say no, as if pretty girls were drugs."

The reason only 35 percent of couples who experience adultery stay together is because the other 65 percent don't know how, not because it can't be done! Use the Smart Heart guidelines in this chapter and confess your affair or confront your partner if you suspect (or know) he is straying.

How to Confess an Affair

To prepare yourself for this talk, keep uppermost in your mind that adultery is a symptom of an existing problem in your relationship, not the problem itself. You have to get to the real underlying problem, rather than focusing solely on the affair. This is where most couples go wrong. Don't get stuck in a no-win blame game!

Smart Heart Approach to Confessing an Affair

- Your motive for confessing should be a genuine desire to improve your relationship, not to ease your own guilt, vent anger, or get back at your partner.
- Be sensitive to timing. Consider your mate's energy level, mood, schedule, and events or crises she is already dealing with. If you're afraid to tell or keep putting it off, consider meeting with a therapist.
- Reassure your partner of your love. Recall special times together with him or her and as a family.
- Use the fair fighting techniques discussed in Chapter 10, including making appointments for time-limited fights, and the bullet-proof vests and invisible bubble to keep you from fusing.

- Keep talking and listening, no matter how long it takes. Be open to your partner's reactions—especially listening to and validating any feelings of abandonment and betrayal without anger or blame. An inclination to speed through this talk or minimize its significance could jettison your relationship.
- Tell the truth about whether or not you plan to end the affair. *If you want to make your marriage last, you must end it.*
- Be willing to answer any questions about your lover— but **don't give too many details.** If you don't answer these questions, your partner will dwell on them, imagine the worst, and become obsessed. The less you tell, the more they dwell.

Things to share with your partner:
- If you still love him or her
- If you love your lover or ex-lover
- If you want to stay together
- Who your lover was/is
- How long this has been going on, when, and where
- Who else knows about the affair
- **Do not defend your lover.** Make it safe for your partner to express anger, and *don't get angry back.*
- **Do not expect immediate forgiveness, no matter how much you apologize or show remorse.** Your partner may be in shock or overcome with pain, and it's normal to expect tears, rage, and recriminations.
- **If you have confessed an affair, or are about to, congratulations! This is a major step in repairing your relationship.** In many ways, the confession is the easiest part, even though it may feel incredibly difficult. Once you have confessed,

follow these guidelines to help smooth the road for better relations:

- See the lover for what he or she really is, flaws and all.
- Make time for your partner to express his or her feelings about the affair daily. Don't attempt to deny, minimize, or avoid this. Expect the verbal darts to be thrown.

How to Confront an Affair

If you know, or strongly suspect that your partner is having an affair, the sooner you confront him or her, the better. Angry or hurt as you are, *the way you handle the confrontation carries a great deal of importance in whether you will be able to work through this obstacle and repair your relationship.*

Smart Heart Approach to Confronting an Affair

Be direct, but not critical. Don't ask, "Did you have an affair?" (That leaves more chance for denial.)

Smart Heart Dialogue

- First, validate him: "I know you've been lonely. I haven't been there for you, and I know there's someone else."
- If he admits it, ask: "Can we talk about it?" and "Can you leave her?"
- If he doesn't admit it, say: "I don't want to get into a power struggle over whether you are or aren't. I just know there's too much distance between us, so there might as well be someone else. We need to get help

and bring back the intimacy in our relationship. I want to work this out with you."

- Nine times out of ten, if you make him feel safe and don't judge him or get angry, he will admit the affair. He's feeling guilty and wants to be relieved of that burden; that's why so many adulterers leave clues (to be stopped). He really doesn't want to live two lives. Be encouraging and loving and show him why it's in his best interest to tell you the truth. Once he does, don't throw it up to him, or it will end the marriage.

- Make it safe for him to admit it. Say, "Let's work it out." Then allow your partner to speak and force yourself to remain calm and listen. If you get angry, start crying, or attack him, you won't find out what you need to know.

- Anticipate that your partner might lash out at you, accuse you of betraying him, or throw up other nonrelated issues. Keep bringing the focus back!

- Express your suspicions despite your fear of abandonment. Avoiding the issue condones the affair and increases the chances of a break-up.

- Be compassionate. If your partner is cheating, he or she is probably in a lot of pain, too—feeling guilty, angry, afraid, and ashamed. The more you can set your partner at ease and reduce his or her guilt, the more likely your discussion will be productive and you'll find out the truth.

- Do not threaten divorce or call a lawyer.

- Insist that the affair end, otherwise there is no hope of repairing your relationship.

- Don't try to forgive prematurely. You will need time to grapple with your anger, hurt, pain, and remorse.

- Reach out—reconnect with parents, siblings, friends. If you are a Pursuer, you are likely to feel isolated and it is crucial for you to take your loneliness back to the family you grew up in and deal with the betrayal.

Working Through the Rage

First of all, if you haven't ended the affair—end it now and show remorse. Second, in some cases you must be willing to break up with your partner to make up, using the Smart Heart approaches explained in Chapter 15. This is necessary if the adulterer shows no remorse, the affair continues, or you are being taken for granted or minimized. After you break up, you need to work together to repair the marriage and start anew.

Just like a brush with death that brings a will to live and a new outlook on life, a couple who breaks up to make up *can create renewed commitment* to one another and a strong will to work at the marriage. Couples who learn effective dialogue skills come away with greater camaraderie and improved ability to compromise, communicate, problem-solve, and negotiate due to the motivation this brush with death brings.

You must both be willing to validate the other's anger and understand the necessary verbal "dart throwing" that the betrayed spouse must do in order to discharge his or her rage in a healthy way (i.e., *fighting fair, daily at first, if necessary,* keeping it time-limited and by appointment only) to reach forgiveness. Paying penance may be necessary, like changing the diapers for two months, or taking on some other responsibility to ease your partner's load.

The adulterer must be careful not to express anger toward the betrayed partner while he or she is in the midst of obsessing over the injustice of the affair, since this will

short-circuit the process. This is a real challenge for most adulterers, and it is even harder for men because they experience physiological discomfort from this obsessional bombardment. *If you are the adulterer, the more you listen now, the less you will have to listen later.* If you don't validate and console, your betrayed partner's rage will escalate. This ranting and raving is a necessary step toward working through the pain and anguish.

This formal obsessing, which I call "Lashing the Lover," should be done for ten minutes each day, by appointment only. Let the adulterer say when he's had enough! Lashing the Lover helps the betrayed partner to review his or her life around the time of the affair and its discovery, and to emotionally reconstruct the past to make sense of the crisis. It is my experience, with thousands of patients, that only *when the betrayed spouse is validated by the adulterous partner for obsessing, and only when the adulterer takes responsibility for what he or she has done, feels remorseful, and stops the affair, that the betrayed can see the part he or she played in the rift and take responsibility for it.*

Validation Heals

Nothing will help the betrayed partner forgive or regain connection in a relationship more than for the adulterous partner to validate her pain and rage daily. *Without validation there can be no forgiveness, and without forgiveness continuation of the relationship is nearly impossible.* If the adulterer can't validate his partner's pain, and the betrayed is unwilling to give her partner a chance or acknowledge his changes, you have a tragic combination. One of you has to take the lead and do what works so the other one can follow.

If you don't learn to validate, you will get stuck in a power struggle like my patients William and Donna. Just weeks after Donna gave birth to the couple's second child,

William was having an affair with his best friend's wife (who was also Donna's best friend). Although William initially denied the infidelity, when Donna threatened divorce he admitted to and discontinued the affair. The core of their struggle was William's inability to validate Donna's emotions. Validating Donna made him feel controlled. He felt he could never validate enough or say the right things to please Donna. Whenever he felt they made progress, his expectations went up. She would regress, and he would get angry and say, "Get over it!"

Donna was enraged that William wouldn't validate her sense of rejection and pain, so she refused to validate him. She was also afraid he would go back to being the "old selfish William," and she held on to her grudges to keep William in line. She was masking her own need to work on forgiveness by pointing a finger at whatever William couldn't do. I insisted she validate him and be patient with his inability to validate since he was just learning. She had to take the lead if she wanted to save their marriage.

I told her, *"You are keeping the affair alive long after it's been over. William ended the affair eight months ago, but you're still having it!"*

"Yes, Dr. Weil," William said. "Just when I think we're doing okay—POW—out of nowhere she starts bombarding me about the affair again! I ended the affair, why can't she?" He had reached his physiological threshold and was feeling sick on a daily basis. He faced his discomfort with Donna's anger as best he could, but he didn't think he could handle much more.

Donna agreed to contain her "obsessing" to five- or ten-minute dialogues, which was all William could handle. He was allowed to ask for time-outs, but initially she did not respect his requests, which made dialogue and validation nearly impossible. This was her way of unconsciously sabotaging his efforts toward changing.

Beware of this common tactic: Donna punished him with dialogue and used his revelations against him as a way to avoid her own difficult work of forgiving the betrayer. She eventually accepted that her unwillingness to validate his experience made him feel more shame and guilt for what he had done. Neither could move. I explained that more adulterers leave out of guilt than out of a loss of love for their partner. "You say you want him to stay, but you're doing everything you can to push him out the door. He needs your support."

Donna knew she was pushing William away, as she had felt pushed away before and during his affair. She told William, "My mother smothered me when I didn't need love and rejected me when I did need her and I feel that way with you, too. Maybe the affair was my way of keeping you close, but not too close."

William said, "I love you and I hope you can find it in your heart to someday forgive me so we can work this out."

Donna said, "I may never forget, but I forgive you, and I do love you and want you to stay." Now, eighteen months later, although they are still working through their pain, Donna's loving feelings for William have finally returned.

William's Smart Heart Game Plan

- Recognize his handicap (being stuck in the developmental stage of suffocation from his mother, having a fear of being controlled, rebelliousness to listening to women).
- Tell Donna when he's feeling controlled, mention the link to his mother, and accept coaching.
- Work hard at validating—not seeing it as control, but as a way to move toward forgiveness.

- Be more open to hearing Donna express feelings without reacting defensively. Don't get angry when feeling helpless or controlled.
- Express frustration in a gentler way.
- Lower your expectations, and when things are improving, expect that Donna may regress again. Don't get mad at her; *help her.*
- Share your script with Donna.

Donna's Smart Heart Game Plan

- Take responsibility for her part in their conflict.
- Let it be okay that William can't completely empathize with the way she felt, and let William have his own script.
- Understand that the affair was necessary in this marriage so you could both learn communication skills, increase your intimacy, and learn to connect and bond.
- Keep "lashing the lover" to ten-minute segments each day so that William doesn't get overloaded.
- Stop punishing William for having trouble validating and for having the affair; coach him and tell him your script. *Don't expect him to know it.*
- Close the exit to breaking up; don't threaten, it gets you the opposite of what you want.

Helping the Adulterer Grieve the Affair

Those of you who have been betrayed are not going to like this, but one of the most important steps to healing adultery is for the betrayed to help the betrayer to grieve his affair. We always talk about the grief of the betrayed, but the adulterer's grief is just as intense, if not more. He is still "in love" or "in like" with his mistress and is grieving the Euphoria and Magical Thinking Stages of that relationship.

Remember that the affair was his attempt to finish his childhood. He is not grieving for the woman. He is grieving for the honeymoon stage where all his needs were met, and for what the woman represents. He doesn't really know her. He has only his fantasy of who or what she symbolized.

You're not "competing" with the lover; you're competing with his fantasy and his emptiness. He strayed because he felt something was missing in himself and between the two of you. Now it's time to help him find it. His feelings of emptiness began long before he met you, and your relationship opened his old wounds. His lover appealed to the developmental stage in which he was arrested, so he connected to her.

It's incredibly difficult for the betrayed to console her spouse under these gut-wrenching conditions, but she must do it. It's a two-way street. He has to help you to "lash the lover" every day and you have to help him grieve. One of the biggest reasons men go back to their lovers is because they feel guilt!

Grieving sessions must be scheduled by appointment and should be no more than ten minutes long. If the betrayed partner needs a time-out, she announces it and asks permission first. This is a chance for the adulterer to grieve his emptiness; for her, you, himself, his childhood, whatever comes up. Your role is to be the Connection Guardian and encourage him to get it all out. The more he expresses and heals, the more chance of him leaving her!

Smart Heart Skills for Helping the Adulterer Grieve

• The betrayed puts on her bullet-proof vest and bubble. Your role is to help your partner with his unresolved childhood wounds instead of thinking about how bad you feel about what he says about her.

Remember the equal sign; you both played a part in causing the affair.

- The betrayer puts on his "cotton boxing gloves" to remind himself that he must be honest, but he must also cushion his words. *When your partner has made it safe for you,* grieve to her for what you miss and tell her how she can fill that void. Tell her when you felt the same in your childhood.

- The betrayed partner listens and validates. Let him tell you if he loves her. **Most times, with your help, he will realize he doesn't love her, but only the idea of her.** Stay calm and loving. He's letting you into his most vulnerable areas. Ask him to make you a list of what changes *you* can make to help him fill the void he's feeling.

- **Tell him it's okay if he misses her, but be firm that you will not tolerate contact.** (If he needs to see her one last time to have closure and grieve, he should. But he must promise you that he will not sleep with her.) Remember that he is grieving and longing for the parts of himself that are empty or missing, not for her.

- **If the betrayed breaks the safety zone by getting reactive, angry, or judging, stop immediately and take a time-out.**

Smart Heart Guidelines for the Grieving Betrayer

- Every day announce to your partner that you are not seeing or having contact with your lover.
- If your former lover contacts you, announce that, too.

- If you are grieving, announce it so your partner knows why you are distant or withdrawn. (If you forget to announce, your partner should coach you and ask, "Are you grieving? I'm here if you need me.")

By committing to using the types of dialogue offered in Chapter 10, "Fighting Fair," as well as the other skills discussed throughout this book, you can both accept responsibility and put an end to the vicious cycle of blame, obsession, avoidance, and attack. In addition, the **adulterer can heal his emotional wounds and begin the process of reconnection with his spouse, and the betrayed can move from the horrible confrontation of finding out about the infidelity, through the recovery, rebuilding, and sexual healing, so she can reach forgiveness.**

Remember the bullet-proof vests, bubbles, and cotton boxing gloves from Chapter 10? I want you both to imagine having all of these invisible reminders on—all the time—at least for the first few months after the affair has been brought to light. Don't expect instant results. *It will sometimes feel like you're taking one step forward, then two steps back.* You also may feel that you're "damned if you do and damned if you don't." That's okay— as long as you're still moving forward. **Use the guidelines for fighting fair for all of your talks, including Lashing the Lover and Helping the Betrayer Grieve.**

Remember that only 5 to 10 percent of affairs turn into long-term relationships. **Divorce is not the answer in most cases.** Hold off the dissolution of the marriage and move toward the goal of repair. Use this situation to your benefit— to learn a healthy way to fight, problem-solve, and attain intimacy. Then you can clearly evaluate whether to stay together or not.

Conclusion
I Did It, So Can You!

> *"To love means never to be afraid of the windstorms of life: should you shield the canyons from the windstorms, you would never see the true beauty of their carvings."*
> —ELISABETH KUBLER-ROSS

Love grows like a flower. It needs a firm and rich foundation. It needs sunshine, and it needs a little rain. It needs calm clear days so it can reach for the sky and windy tempests to keep it flexible and make it strong. Real life love—the kind that lasts forever—is the most magical, heart-melting gift life has to offer. Love is so amazing and awe inspiring because the more you each give, the more you both have. Your bond with each other becomes an eternal flame that endures even beyond death.

My husband Jeff and I exchanged flowers as symbols of our love at our wedding ceremony because they are beautiful, complex, fragile and can't be taken for granted, must be nurtured, given care to grow and maintained—just like our love. We frequently give each other flowers, often calla lilies, because that was our wedding flower, to show our love. The gift of flowers is a wonderful way to keep your love alive. Not only will your partner love receiving them, but they will be extra special because they were sent from your heart. Studies have proven that fresh flowers help to create a sense of serenity and promotes mental and physical healing.

Jeff also referred to me in our wedding vows as the "Guardian of the Relationship." Women who reach real life love honor this role and their husbands appreciate them more for it. For example, when I was growing up, dinner time was an opportunity for sharing. Mom wouldn't let us watch television so we could all catch up on each other's lives. Many of the couples who have trouble eat while they watch television and miss this daily opportunity to talk to each other, connect, and share. It's up to the Guardian of the Relationship to create some loose structure and limits to promote connection.

The only time I allow the television on during dinner is on Super Bowl Sunday. Even though Jeff came from a family that always watched television during dinner, he sees the value of keeping meals separate from television. When our dinner time coincides with a televised sporting event or a program one of us really wants to watch, we tape it and watch it later—often together. I love to snuggle up with Jeff and watch football and baseball and he loves keeping me up to date on the game and the different players. In turn, Jeff likes going with me when I shop for clothes, especially for special events like television appearances. He thinks it's fun to watch the "fashion show" and helps me decide what looks best. Sharing in each other's favorites is an excellent way to connect.

Gabriel Marcel says, "presence and availability," are the essence of love. Make a vow to your mate that you will do whatever it takes to hang in and keep your love alive, through good times and through bad.

Smart Heart Vow:
"I will connect with you,
detach myself from my own thoughts
and emotions so I can hear you and walk in your shoes."

Real life love—or what I sometimes call "Smart Heart Love" is the ultimate stage in a relationship. It stems from a conscious decision to connect. This type of love is mature and knows how to endure and triumph moment after moment, day after day, and year after year. Real life love doesn't "just happen," you and your partner have to *make it happen!* It takes time, focus, attention, presence and a deep desire to master the intricacies of connecting, disconnecting, and reconnecting on a daily basis.

To stay in real life love and keep it growing, you must be willing to do whatever it takes. Sometimes that means making a sacrifice in other areas of your life, *but your love should never have to take a back seat to anything else.* When you make your partner number one and put your relationship first, it blossoms into everything you've ever dreamed love can be.

The couples who reach real life love, like my parents, have made it through the power struggles with flying colors! They have also mastered the art of loving each other as they each need to be loved.

My parents are a fabulous example of this type of love. They have triumphed through difficulties, traversed the bumpy roads, shifted gears through all the relationship stages, and broke up to make up *twice.* But through the fifty-one years of pains and pleasures, they both **agree that real life love was worth the effort and the wait!** To watch them together is such a wonderful gift for me. They are so tender-hearted toward each other and they are best friends as well as lovers. Many people think the Euphoria Stage of a relationship is the way real love is supposed to be—easy, conflict free, romantic, exciting, and fun. But real life love is much more fulfilling, magical, and meaningful than the illusions created by the flood of endorphins that are the foundation on which the "honeymoan" of a courtship and marriage are built.

When you reach the real life love stage, you've risen above the pain, you're no longer struggling over *power*, you've successfully traversed the winding road and shifted gears through all the relationship stages. You value yourself and each other and you don't take one another for granted. You recognize the importance of romance and you *stoke the fire* and keep the love light burning. You accept each other's negative traits as part of the whole package and you use these traits to help each other to continue growing, both individually and as a couple.

Remember that the path of least resistance rarely, if ever, leads to real life love. I hit my share of potholes and made lots of mistakes before I connected with my husband Jeff, who *truly* is a prince among men. He's not the fairy tale type of prince who fills our childhood story books and gallops through our adult romance novels. He's a real life prince who is willing to stick by me each day as we find our way together toward greater and lasting love.

The Smart Heart Skills I used prior to meeting Jeff and the skills we use together are the same ones I teach my patients and have mapped out for you in *Make Up, Don't Break Up*. You *deserve* real and lasting love and you *can* create it! All you have to do is begin learning and growing, and refuse to give up until you succeed.

Never underestimate the power of love and never take it for granted. **Think of your relationship as a beautiful garden that you planted together and now have the opportunity to harvest, providing you nurture it and take care of it.** The adage that you reap what you sow is an important one for all areas of life, but it is paramount in a relationship. Plant flowers in your relationship garden every day so the weeds don't have a chance to spread and take over. When weeds pop up, as they inevitably do in all relationships, pluck them out *together* by problem solving and fighting fairly.

Real life love makes life worth living. It brings out your joyfulness because you accept each other as you are, and also coach one another to become better, more satisfied, and more fulfilled. As Gottman's research shows and my personal and professional experience attests to, "The happiest couples are those that accept that partners, relationships and marriages have their limitations."

Real love supports and comforts you when you need it, and provides an encouraging push when you're stuck and need to shift gears. You are secure, protected, sheltered and also free to grow and progress on your own. You plan, anticipate, and savor those "Kodak Moments" so your story of love continues to unfold. You make time for the things you love and do them together. You'd rather be together than apart, and carve out space for your relationship. In essence, you keep exploring, rediscovering, and recreating yourself and your relationship.

Real life love is worth working smarter and harder to get to; not only because of the *magic* it brings into your life, but because it truly is an *eternal and everlasting love.*

I stand firm in my belief that anyone who wants to have a loving relationship or marriage can have one. If you haven't had much success yet, it's not because there's something wrong with you, and it isn't because you're not deserving or unlovable. You just haven't had the *skills and dialogue* you need to connect with someone, get past the third date, and rewrite your relationship script so you can move on to commitment. I didn't have them either when I first started dating again after my divorce. **But I have them now, and so do you!**

It was Smart Heart Skills and Dialogue that helped hundreds of my patients and Jeff and I to become a couple. The skills you have learned in this book are the same ones that have seen us through the good times and the power struggles so we could create the marriage we have today. It hasn't always been easy and we've hit our share of potholes on our road to love too, but each one has made our love, commitment, and intimacy *stronger and deeper.* Don't let yourself run away at the first sign that it's not "perfect." Jeff and I could have both run away so many times in our courtship that we stopped counting. If we had made hasty judgments, we would have never made it past the *first* date!

We hit if off on our phone call before our first date and the "Imago" attraction began the moment Jeff lifted his pen to write the personal ad I responded to. I was anxious to meet him for the first time in person, and hoped I would be as attracted to him physically as I was mentally and emotionally.

My first surprise was that Jeff had a beard. My grandpa had a beard and I loved it when he would tickle me with it when I was a little girl. Grandpa would tell me he had a secret and when I got close to hear it, he'd cuddle me, tickle me, and "gobble me up." I would laugh and protest, but I loved it and still love cuddling today. I liked Grandpa's beard, but I had never dated a man or kissed a man who had a beard. Seeing Jeff with a beard triggered my Imago—which was largely influenced by my grandpa. It was a positive perception, but I wondered how I would feel when I kissed him, beard and all. These are the kinds of questions that send you running too far forward, or too quickly away. Try to reserve judgment, as I did, and just get to know each other. In addition to Jeff's beard, he didn't have the type of build that I'd associated with my Imago. He was thinner and built more like a runner than the big, burly bears I'd been attracted to in the past. Actually, as I looked at him, I realized, he's not built like Grandpa, he's built like Dad. (Just like Dr. Fogarty reminded me would happen.)

Jeff won me over on our first date because he was so adorable, smart, fun, sensitive, and flexible. We spent the entire day at my country home but I wouldn't let him into the bathroom because of the "naked spread eagle" episode I shared in the Potholes Chapter. Jeff could have put me down or been perturbed for not allowing him inside, but he didn't. He was very sensitive and understood why I was hesitant and he went along with it with no complaints. He, did, however "christen" a lot of trees that day! Be willing to bend with the winds and be flexible like flowers so you can get past each other's fears and into each other's hearts.

In your quest for real and lasting love, expect the potholes and patch them up together, instead of running away, which single people and couples are always tempted to do when the going gets rough. Remember that the problems and challenges in your relationship are gifts to bring you closer together. Each time you jump another hurdle together, *you create more relationship glue*—the kind that keeps couples together through thick and thin!

Nothing in life that is worth having comes easily, but relationships are not as daunting as they may seem once you learn the skills you need to succeed. **Remember—it's tools, not rules—that will help you to traverse the road and take the journey to real life love.** Believe in yourself, believe in the power of love, and believe that you can have the love you want.

Fairy tales *may not* come true, but the magic of true connection outshines even the *best* of fantasies. Don't let love pass you by. Go out and make it happen. You deserve to have the best life has to offer, so reach for the stars, keep your face to the sunshine, and remember that without the rain and wind, there would be no flowers.

*I did it, so can *you!*

From my heart to yours,
Dr. Bonnie Eaker Weil

Dr. Bonnie Eaker Weil

Bibliography

Bennetts, Leslie. "Cheating." *Ladies Home Journal,* September 1996.

Brody, Jane E. "Controlling Anger is Good Medicine for the Heart." *New York Times Health,* 20 May, 1996.

Campbell, Eileen, Ed. *A Lively Flame.* London: The Aquarian Press, an Imprint of Harper Collins, 1992.

Carlson, Richard, Ph.D. *Don't Sweat the Small Stuff.* New York: Hyperion, 1997.

Fogarty, Thomas F., Ph.D. "The Distancer and the Pursuer." *Compendium I and II, The Best of the Family.* New Rochelle, N.Y.: The Center for Family Learning, 1973–1983.

Gottman, John, Ph.D. *The Family Therapy Networker,* Vol. 18, No. 3, May/June 1994, p. 40.

Gray, John, Ph.D. *Men Are from Mars, Women Are from Venus.* New York: Harper Collins, 1992.

Hendrix, Harville. *Getting the Love You Want: A Guide for Couples.* New York: Henry Holt, 1988.

_____. *Keeping the Love You Find: A Guide for Singles.* New York: Pocket Books, 1992.

Pearsall, Paul, Ph.D. *Making Miracles.* New York: Avon Books, 1991.

Taylor, Denise. "Save a Place in Your Heart," Star Visions, 1999. Starvisions@mindspring.com.

Weil, Bonnie Eaker, Ph.D. *"Validation as a Facilitater of Forgiveness for Adultery."* In Healing in the Relational Paradigm, ed. Wade Luquet, MSW, and Mo Therese Hannal, Ph.D. Washington, D.C.: Taylor and Francis Group, Brunner/Mozel, 1998, p. 241

Weil, Bonnie Eaker, Ph.D. *Adultery, The Forgivable Sin.* New York: Hastings House, 1993.

Weil, Bonnie Eaker, Ph.D. "Unlocking the Family Secrets in Family Play Therapy," *Child and Adolescent Work.,* Vol. 3, No. 4, Human Sciences Press, Winter 1986.

Index

Dr. Bonnie Eaker Weil

Dr. Bonnie Eaker Weil, author of *Make Up, Don't Break Up*, is internationally acclaimed and one of America's best-known relationship experts; named by *New York Magazine* as one of the city's top therapists. She was featured in a three-day series on the Today Show, and a four-day series on *Current Affair*, (Fox). She appears frequently on ABC, Fox News, CBS, and NBC. She has been a guest on The View, appeared on Oprah five times, and has appeared on nearly all of the top talk shows.

Her cutting edge skills have been featured in the *New York Times*, *New York Magazine*, *USA Today*, *Time*, *Cosmopolitan*, *Ladies Home Journal*, *Good Housekeeping*, *New York Post*, *Toronto Sun*, and *People*, just to name a few.

Her first book, *Adultery, The Forgivable Sin* has sold over 50,000 copies, been translated into five languages and was made into a movie *Silence of Adultery,* starring Kate Jackson.

Dr. Weil has a thriving private practice in New York City, consults by phone all over the world, and is a distinguished lecturer and consultant.

She is currently teaching the following seminars at The 92nd Street Y in New York: "Meeting Through The Personals," "Why You Pick The Person Who Gives You The Most Trouble," and "Getting Past The Third Date." At the New York City Seminar Center, she presents "How to Get Men to Commit," and "Great New Ways to Meet People," and "Make Up, Don't Break Up." In addition, she facilitates workshops on these topics and Male Dilemma of Intimacy at the exclusive Canyon Ranch Resort in Arizona.

"Dr. Bonnie" is also a favorite on the iVillage.com message board for "Adultery, the Forgivable Sin," and chats on this topic with singles and couples from around the globe who are trying to put the pieces of their relationships back together. She resides with her husband in New York City and the Pocono Mountains.

A Note to Readers from Dr. Bonnie

Thousands of singles and couples have benefited from the safety of "Smart Heart" Skills, Tools and Dialogue they've learned from me in seminars, consultations and therapy sessions, both face to face and by phone. I welcome you to share this wisdom and experience with me.

I can be reached at 212-606-3787 for more information regarding singles and couples, personal appearances, therapy sessions, lectures and seminars.

You can also reach me through my websites:

www.doctorbonnie.com;
    e-mail: info@doctorbonnie.com
www. makeupdontbreakup.com;
    e-mail:info@makeupdontbreakup.com
www.smarthearttherapy.com;
    e-mail: info@smarthearttherapy.com